VISIONS OF TRANSFORMATION

AARON AUGSBURGER

VISIONS OF TRANSFORMATION

Hegemony, Plurinationality, and Revolution in Bolivia

THE UNIVERSITY OF
ARIZONA PRESS

TUCSON

The University of Arizona Press
www.uapress.arizona.edu

We respectfully acknowledge the University of Arizona is on the land and territories of Indigenous peoples. Today, Arizona is home to twenty-two federally recognized tribes, with Tucson being home to the O'odham and the Yaqui. Committed to diversity and inclusion, the University strives to build sustainable relationships with sovereign Native Nations and Indigenous communities through education offerings, partnerships, and community service.

ISBN-13: 978-0-8165-5520-8 (hardcover)
ISBN-13: 978-0-8165-5278-8 (paperback)
ISBN-13: 978-0-8165-5279-5 (ebook)

Cover design by Leigh McDonald
Cover art *Comunidad* by Walter Solón, courtesy of Fundación Solón
Typeset by Leigh McDonald in Warnock Pro 10.5/14 and Bufalino (display)

Publication of this book is made possible in part by funding from University of South Florida College of Arts and Sciences Office of Research and Scholarship.

Library of Congress Cataloging-in-Publication Data
Names: Augsburger, Aaron, 1981– author.
Title: Visions of transformation : hegemony, plurinationality, and revolution in Bolivia / Aaron Augsburger.
Description: Tucson : University of Arizona Press, 2025. | Includes bibliographical references and index.
Identifiers: LCCN 2024025381 (print) | LCCN 2024025382 (ebook) | ISBN 9780816555208 (hardcover) | ISBN 9780816552788 (paperback) | ISBN 9780816552795 (ebook)
Subjects: LCSH: Indians of South America—Bolivia—Government relations. | Bolivia—Social conditions—21st century. | Bolivia—Politics and government—2006– | Bolivia—Economic conditions—21st century.
Classification: LCC F3327 .A95 2025 (print) | LCC F3327 (ebook) | DDC 984.05/42—dc23/eng/20241228
LC record available at https://lccn.loc.gov/2024025381
LC ebook record available at https://lccn.loc.gov/2024025382

Printed in the United States of America
♾ This paper meets the requirements of ANSI/NISO Z39.48-1992 (Permanence of Paper).

CONTENTS

ACKNOWLEDGMENTS

This book originally began as a dissertation at the University of California, Santa Cruz (UCSC). I therefore begin by thanking the advisers and mentors who guided me through my studies and provided invaluable feedback on the initial ideas of this project. I had the good fortune of meeting Guillermo Delgado-P. when I started at UCSC. During our regular meetings over coffee and croissants at Lulu's Cafe, Guillermo helped me refine my own ideas while also always pushing me to think them from other perspectives. Those conversations played an important role in my thinking about Bolivia and are embedded in the pages of this book. Guillermo also introduced me to a number of contacts in Bolivia as I began fieldwork, and I learned more about La Paz strolling around with him one afternoon in 2015 than I had in the previous six months of living there. Ben Read has been a great source of encouragement and an intellectual guide for immersive, qualitative fieldwork in political science. Megan Thomas provided critical feedback on the dissertation and invaluable professional advice. Fernando Leiva always offered probing questions that sharpened my thinking. My deepest appreciation to all.

Special thanks go to Paul Haber, who introduced me to the study of Latin America when I was an undergraduate at the University of Montana. Paul changed the way I understand the world and remains a mentor, colleague, and dear friend. Indeed, I was lucky enough to carry out a short period of the fieldwork for this book with Paul.

In Santa Cruz at UCSC, my thanks go to Andrew Wood, Logan Puck, Jan Kotowski, Don Kingsbury, Sarah Romano, Michael Wilson Becerril, Samantha Cook, Alicia Calle and Jorge Duque, Juan Diego Prieto, Jeff Sherman, Scott Newsome, Alena Wolflink, Omid Mohammadi, Steven Araujo, Martín Ordoñez, Emilia Valenzuela, Robert Cavooris, Delio Vasquez, Trey Highton, Chelsea Pearson, Alejandro Artiga-Purcell, Chris Lang, and Isaac Blacksin. Additional thanks to Sylvanna Falcón, Eleonora Pasotti, Roger Schoenman, Dan Wirls, Mike Urban, Jonathan Fox, Gabriela Arredondo, Maria Elena Diaz, Madeleine Fairbairn, and Matt O'Hara. A particular note of appreciation to Stacy Philpott and Peter Bichier.

I have been fortunate to join a department at the University of South Florida (USF) full of kind, interesting, and supportive colleagues. In the School of Interdisciplinary Global Studies, I would like to thank Peter Funke, Holly Dunn, Nick Thompson, Scott Solomon, Cheryl Hall, Manu Samnotra, David Ponton, Tatsiana Kulakevich, Arturo Jimenez-Bacardi, Felipe Mantilla, Kellan Anfinson, Ed Kissi, Alex Ponomareff, Golfo Alexopoulos, Steve Tauber, Harry Vanden, Bernd Reiter, Jaime Stiffler, and Jamie Lane. Thanks also to my colleagues at USF's Institute for the Study of Latin America and the Caribbean, especially Beatriz Padilla and Barbara Cruz for their collegiality and support. Additional thanks to Kevin Yelvington, Elizabeth Hordge-Freeman, Adriana Novoa, Renato Cavani, Nicole Ruiz, Gabo Harris, Natalia Patiño González, Zachary Kuntz, and Naomi Gutterman.

My gratitude to a number of other friends, colleagues, and teachers whose thoughts, feedback, and general companionship have been most welcome over the years: Jaime Wandling, Kohl Thacker, Bob Stumvoll, the late Dan Rogenes, Karen Adams, Christopher Muste, Ramona Grey, Dan Spencer, Jody Pavilack, Rebecca Pettit, Thad Honaker, Hudson Blair, Jeff David, Bill Novak, Tamila Meladze, Dylan Laslovich, Jess Lawson, Nicholas Feeney, Justin Musa, and Matt Cleary. At the University of Arizona Press, Allyson Carter supported this project from our first conversation and pushed me to complete it with both enthusiasm and patience. I also appreciate the assistance from Alana Cecilia Enriquez, Leigh McDonald, Jessica Hinds-Bond, and Amanda Krause, who helped get the manuscript over the finish line. Three anonymous reviewers provided insightful comments and much-needed critique, which improved the book and my own thinking.

Institutional support and funding for this work have been provided by the UCSC Politics Department, the UCSC Chicano Latino Research Center, the Humanities Institute at UCSC, the USF Humanities Institute, the USF Institute for the Study of Latin America and the Caribbean, and a USF College of Arts and Sciences Humanities Project Completion grant.

My most gracious thanks go to those in Bolivia who patiently gave their time and their thoughts to yet another researcher asking questions. Many remain anonymous in these pages but have my greatest appreciation. Thanks especially to the communities of Charagua, Jesús de Machaca, and Totora Marka, and to the many individuals at the Consejo Nacional de Ayllus y Markas del Qullasuyu (CONAMAQ), Confederación Sindical Única de Trabajadores Campesinos de Bolivia (CSUTCB), and Centro de Investigación y Promoción del Campesinado (CIPCA) from whom I have learned so much. Individual thanks to Teddy Zeballos, Linda Farthing, Luis Tapia, the late Xavier Albó, Jorge Casso Echart, Diego Murillo Bernardis, Fredy Villagomez, Magali Gutierrez, René Antonio Mayorga, Esteban Ticona, Oscar Vega Camacho, Silvia Rivera Cusicanqui, Moira Zuazo, Wilfredo Plata, Félix Muruchi, Jose Luis Saavedra, Rafael Bautista, Loyola Guzmán, Marxa Chávez, Roger Cortez Hurtado, Katherine Salamanca, Renata Albuquerque, Radek Buben, Jorge Derpic, Ben Dangl, and Claudia Fuentes. My gratitude to both Fernando Mayorga at the Centro de Estudios Superiores Universitarios, Universidad Mayor de San Simón, in Cochabamba and René Pereira Morató at the Instituto de Investigaciones Sociológicas, Universidad Mayor de San Andrés, in La Paz for hosting me as a visiting researcher during fieldwork. Lola Paredes at the Centro de Investigación y Promoción del Campesinado library and Carla at the Biblioteca del Vicepresidencia del Estado Plurinacional went out of their way to help with books, articles, and other archival material. Extra special thanks to Derren Patterson and Sarakinlan Murrillo (and now Timo, too), for their friendship and welcoming home in La Paz.

Final thanks go to my family, who never let me take myself too seriously. I am grateful to Susan and Mickey, Eric, Josh, Gretchen and Ben, Andrew, Henry, Nolan, Ruby, Ellis, and Augie for their love, levity, and encouragement. I would not be who I am today without the care and support of Jack and Char, Steve and Jan, Sharon, Sandy and Joe, Pat,

Kevin, Terry, Karen, Lisa, Ellis and Myrna, Doug, Cindy, and all of their families. *Gracias también a* Guillermo, Lorena, Manuel Antonio, Mama Lucha, Marta, *y toda la familia en* México. To Estelí and our daughter, Emiliana, both of you make me a better person and I am deeply grateful for the life we are building together.

This book is dedicated to my mother, Susan Forster, whose limitless encouragement, love, and support I am unable to adequately acknowledge here.

VISIONS OF TRANSFORMATION

INTRODUCTION

Visions of Transformation in Bolivia's *Proceso de Cambio*

The sky is still black when we leave the house in the early morning hours of June 21, the winter solstice in the southern hemisphere. It is cold, below freezing, as a friend and I hail a taxi to El Alto. We are not sure exactly where we need to go, but, with a quick phone call, our cab driver helps us find the corner where we can catch a minibus at this early hour to Jesús de Machaca for the ritual celebration of Willkakuti, the Aymara New Year. Officially named a national holiday in 2009, the celebration is a ritual inviting Tata Inti, the sun god, to provide a bountiful harvest in the coming year through offerings of coca, alcohol, and a sacrificial llama. Critics have charged the Movimiento al Socialismo (MAS, Movement Toward Socialism) government with mobilizing indigenous symbols and practices such as Willkakuti for political gain, which is certainly true, but it is also possible to read these ritual celebrations as expressions of the power, vitality, and continuing relevance of indigeneity in Bolivian society.

We arrive to the area just outside Jesús de Machaca, near the ruins of Qunqhu Wankani, about an hour before sunrise, to a crowd of people surrounding a large fire in celebration of Willkakuti 5523. Not nearly as popular as the celebration at the pre-Incan ruins of Tiwanaku, where thousands gather for Willkakuti, this gathering is one of the less prominent across the highlands and attendees number in the hundreds. As bottles of the local Bolivian spirit Singani and bags of coca are shared, we shiver and wait for the first rays of sunlight to creep over the horizon, bringing both a reprieve from the cold and a new year. Hands raise to the sky as the sun begins to appear, and cheers ring out while offerings are made to Tata Inti, to Pachamama (Mother Earth), to health, to land, to Qullasuyu, to Bolivia, even to *hermano* Evo. More than just a celestial ritual of rejuvenation, the celebration and its accompanying symbols are thoroughly embedded in and representative of the ongoing processes of political, social, and economic transformation. With these thoughts in mind, I ask those around me how Willkakuti relates to the ongoing changes under the government of Evo Morales and his MAS party. A few people express to me their ongoing hope that the attention Morales has brought to the country can bring more tourists to the half-buried ruins, whose weatherworn structures might both provide economic benefits and foster appreciation of precolonial indigenous history. "While these cultural ruins are buried, they are still present," one man tells me. "We are different now, nowadays we live in different ways, but what you see in the dirt here gives us life. It is a history with knowledge, one that offers guidance."

Additionally, as part of the day's celebration, community members choose their leaders for the upcoming subnational elections. Demonstrating a particular vision of democratic responsibility and accountability, community members line up behind their chosen candidates in an open grass field for all to see. After the electoral proceedings, the party really gets underway, with music, dancing, drinking, and general merriment to usher in the Aymara *machaq mara* (new year), at the midpoint of the Gregorian calendar year.

Willkakuti is organized through indigenous symbols and ritual practice that point to a continuous indigenous history in what is today called Bolivia. Yet, despite this traditional underpinning, Willkakuti is interlaced and overlaid with any number of other, so-called modern symbols and practices. In its current form, the solstice celebration emerged in the late 1970s as part of a larger indigenous cultural revival, and its official recognition in 2009 symbolizes the continuation of that movement in a new phase. The ritual, at least at the local level, expresses the salience of a plurinational project that emerged around the same time as the current version of Willkakuti. At a larger national or international level, the ritual celebration also provides legitimacy for the MAS project of nation-state hegemony as one composed of indigenous worldviews and indigenous bodies. This ritual offers a contrasting set of social symbols and practices and, therefore, serves as a good representation for much of what I analyze and argue in this book. The juxtaposition of "tradition" and "modernity" in the particular ritual of Willkakuti, I believe, offers insight into Bolivia as a social and political formation, while also helping us interpret contemporary processes of change that have been underway since the beginning of the twenty-first century. With both the national tricolor Bolivian flag and the indigenous multicolored *wiphala* flying over the festivities, local modes of democratic practice and official electoral contests operating alongside one another, and temporalities based on indigenous and Western calendars occurring concurrently—this scene offers a vision of Bolivian society as a mosaic of contrasting yet overlapping political, social, and cultural forms that exist side by side yet express distinct historical trajectories and alternative visions of a future Bolivia. Yet, more than just symbolizing Bolivian society, the solstice celebration offers a theoretical and empirical point of entry for making sense of the ambiguous and contradictory process of social change in Bolivia during the era of Evo Morales.

ORGANIC CRISIS, EVO MORALES, AND THE PLURINATIONAL STATE

Nineteen eighty-five was a watershed year in that it clearly and decisively marked the termination of the Bolivian state founded by the 1952 National Revolution. It was the year that Bolivian political and economic elites initiated the neoliberal policies of the Washington Consensus, maintaining macroeconomic stability through austerity, disciplining labor, privatizing state-owned enterprises, and opening the country up to foreign capital.[1] After the initial neoliberal policy reforms failed to realize the promise of economic growth and stability, a second round of reforms were implemented in the 1990s, focusing on what was labeled "good governance." A program of decentralization, ostensibly seeking to make government more accountable and enhance democracy at the local level, further shrunk state involvement in the economy, while multicultural reforms sought to contain growing social resistance by incorporating previously excluded sectors into the neoliberal project through piece-meal recognition. Underlying these economic and political reforms was neoliberalism's social design, which sought to increasingly marketize society while promoting the vision of human beings as self-sufficient, profit-maximizing individuals rather than social beings embedded in a given society with accompanying rights and responsibilities.[2] The year 1985 was important not only because it brought neoliberalism, but also because it appeared to symbolize the demise of popular power, specifi-cally the power of unionized mine workers. Miners, historically the heart of the Bolivian labor movement, had brought the "State of '52" into being, and they forced governments, both civilian and military, to maintain it, at least to a certain extent, until the mid-1980s. Mine workers protested neoliberal restructuring by calling for a general strike in August 1985, but to no avail. They were instead laid off in droves, a move that decimated the political power of organized labor and in effect exterminated a social subject through the liquidation of its material foundations for reproduc-ing itself.[3] Politically and economically ascendant, neoliberalism thus appeared hegemonic in late twentieth-century Bolivia.

By the early twenty-first century, however, the neoliberal project had reached a tipping point and entered into crisis. Pace Antonio Gramsci, this period could be viewed as an organic crisis. More than just mere con-junctural disequilibrium, an organic crisis is one where the economic and political contradictions of an era combine to undermine the very bases of social consensus and control and open up opportunities for trans-formation.[4] The economic contradictions of Bolivia's neoliberal exper-iment exposed its class foundations and amplified the economic and social divisions in society. After the initial inversion of finances from the selling off of state properties and the privatization of state enterprises, neoliberalism was unable to maintain fiscal solvency. Contrary to the promises of the "New Economic Policy," the neoliberal reorganization of the state increasingly relied on a combination of austerity measures and external debt to sustain itself, resulting in rising prices for energy and basic staples, growing unemployment and the informalization of labor, and increased inequality. The changes in global capitalism of the era were expressed in Bolivia through the collapse of the tin mining indus-try, which precipitated the neoliberal reforms, representing, as James

Dunkerley notes, a "reversal of 'normal' historical evolution . . . throwing 'modern' wage workers back into social circuits associated with other historical epochs."[5] Economic restructuring threw many miners out of work and made much other labor "flexible," which not only affected the power and organization of labor but also compelled many into relations of production, exchange, and consumption with so-called traditional logics. These economic shifts were important to the growing revitalization of indigenous and popular forms of social organization and reproduction, as I will discuss. "Stabilization plans" throughout the 1990s only further entrenched the neoliberal economic model, compounding its effects and leading to growing protest and social unrest.

Related to the economic crisis, a general crisis of political legitimacy revealed the political system's lack of representation. The political system was viewed as an enclave of clientelism and elite corruption, while the party system comprised political parties more or less aligned with the neoliberal project and lacking legitimate linkages to society.[6] The economic policies of neoliberalism threatened the corporatist party-society linkages that had developed out of the 1952 Revolution and defined the political system in the following decades.[7] The pacted democracy of the 1980s and 1990s only achieved a semblance of political stability by preventing the majority of the population from having any significant influence, what Willem Assies has labeled the "representation deficit."[8] The rise of antisystem parties such as the MAS and Felipe Quispe's Movimiento Indígena Pachakuti (MIP), the increasing political influence of popular and indigenous movements, and the social convulsions of the early 2000s (which ousted sitting presidents in 2003 and 2005) were all indicative of the political system's lack of legitimacy. Traditional parties' inability to represent, incorporate, and/or co-opt antisystem forces drove formally democratic governments to increasingly rely on coercion to implement policy, only further delegitimizing the Bolivian political system in the process.

Perhaps the most important aspect of the Bolivian crisis of the early twenty-first century was what Luis Tapia refers to as a "crisis of correspondence" between social composition and state form.[9] While the intertwined economic and political crises were direct products of neoliberalism, the crisis of correspondence had deeper historical roots, borne of the colonial encounter between indigenous and nonindigenous worlds. In Bolivia, there was historically a lack of correlation between the country's mononational state form and a multicultural and plurinational social formation. That is, Bolivia's formal structure of political authority has tended to represent the will and interests of a small ethnic and social class, at the expense of the country's majority popular and indigenous population. Ranajit Guha has labeled this colonial form of state-society relation as "dominance without hegemony," a state form that was sustained more by outright coercion than by persuasion and consent.[10] This structural split between elite and subaltern political forms in Bolivia unfolded not only during the colonial era proper, but also during the postcolonial republican era through techniques of internal colonialism. The elite have failed to integrate vast areas of the life and consciousness of the indigenous majority into a legitimate structure of governance, while the indigenous majority has largely been unable to constitute itself as a coherent bloc with the power to express its political project. For René Zavaleta Mercado, Bolivia's political form has been "a State in a situation of perpetual war with its own [indigenous] population," "a State constituted against its society." "It was, above all," he argues, "a State that could not exist outside of its own incapacity. Its weak form guaranteed its own precarious existence and was, in sum, a *rosca* [a screw, a coil], that is to say, a vicious cycle."[11]

The crisis of correspondence operated on two distinct levels: a clear absence of individuals from the country's indigenous and popular majority positioned within the institutional apparatus of state power (executives, ministers, members of the legislature, judges, ambassadors, etc.), and a lack of correspondence between the actual institutional structure of the state and the diversity of cultural and political forms throughout Bolivia. The MAS was able to remedy the former situation to an extent beyond any previous government, but Morales and the MAS were ultimately unable or unwilling to amend the latter.

The lack of correspondence between state and society has been challenged at various moments in Bolivian history, perhaps most forcefully during the indigenous rebellion led by Pablo Zárate Willka during the 1899 Federal War, the revolts of the caciques in Jesús de Machaca in 1921 and Chayanta in 1927, the 1952 National Revolution, the Katarista movement of the late 1970s (which helped reestablish democracy), and, most relevant for the purposes of this book, the revolutionary upheavals of

2000–2005, which brought Evo Morales and the MAS to power.[12] While the incongruity between political and social form has been a historical axis of conflict, it has also played a key articulatory function for the country's indigenous and popular social forces to coalesce during moments of crisis and rebellion.

Recognizing the Bolivian crisis at the turn of the century as a combination of both conjunctural and historical conditions is important for understanding the construction of contemporary Bolivia in general, but more specifically for interpreting the accomplishments, failures, contradictions, and ambiguities of the ensuing Morales years. The failures of neoliberalism provided the grist for shorter-term grievances against the economic model, political parties, and governing class, while the lack of correspondence between the Bolivian mononational state and plurinational society framed the demands for the structural refoundation of Bolivia over the longer term. The *proceso de cambio* (process of change) of the Morales years, to a significant degree, overcame the conjunctural economic and political crises of the neoliberal era through a strategy of hegemony. Yet, aligning a newly hegemonic MAS state with the country's motley, plurinational society proved much more difficult, creating a number of contradictions and conflicts between the government and its erstwhile supporters, conflicts that were increasingly interpreted through collective memories of colonial domination and rebellion.

The resurfacing of indigenous nations in the 1970s played an essential if not exclusive role in the early twenty-first-century revolutionary era in Bolivia and was the driving force behind the demand for plurinationality. Proposing that indigenous identity sit at the core of a new vision for society, the resurgent indigenous movements articulated a rupture with the recent past while expressing themselves in terms that drew on traditional forms. They symbolized the reemergence of something that had supposedly been eliminated with the forward march of historical progress, an efflorescence of ancestral worldviews and practices that had been previously spurned and marginalized. Yet, indigenous nations in contemporary Bolivia are not communities outside the flow of history; they are communal associational forms that have been constructed through processes of political, economic, and cultural imagination and creativity in contexts of unequal power. This ostensible return of the traditional, rather than the allure of its colonial opposite, modernity, is an important element of what distinguishes Bolivia as a fascinating model of contemporary revolution.

LATIN AMERICA, BOLIVIA, AND SOCIAL CHANGE

During the rise of the so-called Pink Tide in Latin America, much scholarly debate centered on how (or, indeed, whether) this political swing to the left actually led to fundamental social transformations throughout the region.[13] Within this general discussion, Bolivia received significant attention and, along with Ecuador and Venezuela, was often typologized as one of the more radical or revolutionary Pink Tide governments.[14] However, the general consensus is that there has been at least as much continuity with the old order under Morales and the MAS as there has been fundamental change. This is certainly not to dismiss the many important reforms since Morales came to power in 2006, including increased attention to societal racism, increased participation in decision-making by the popular majority, a rewritten constitution, alleviation of poverty, increased access to health care, and infrastructure development. Despite these changes, a number of structural continuities remain, such as the reliance on an extractivist mode of production, the centralization of political power, political patronage and clientelism, and social and economic inequality. All these general characteristics point toward the uneven and contradictory nature of social transformation in contemporary Bolivia.

Scholarly positions on how to best understand Bolivia's *proceso de cambio* within the larger historical study of revolutionary social transformation can be categorized into four analytic and interpretive approaches. The first underscores that a revolution indeed took place, although Evo Morales and the MAS were the products of the revolution rather than its producers. That is, the revolution, defined as "the direct interference of the masses in historic events," actually occurred during the 2000–2005 upheavals that ultimately brought Morales and the MAS to state power.[15] The second view agrees that the historical conditions for a revolutionary rupture were in place but holds that the transformative potential of revolutionary groups has been appropriated and demobilized by the Morales government.[16] As Pablo Mamani Ramírez argues, the MAS's "new technology of power has been to make the Indian-popular [*lo indio-popular*] more visible, but with the end of maintaining a neocolonial project of Western civilization that was almost overcome."[17] Morales and the MAS lacked the political will to fully break with the colonial past and therefore ended up reproducing colonial relations of power under the guise of indigenous liberation. From this perspective, the MAS version of a plurinational revolution has been nothing more than "a historical scam."[18] Despite their differences, these first two approaches complement each other. If Morales and the MAS were in fact the products of the revolution—that is, if the direct intervention of the masses created the opportunity for Morales to become Bolivia's first indigenous president— then the assumption of power was almost preordained to be a deflating experience. It then becomes easy to claim a lack of revolutionary transformation for Morales, for his failing to uphold the radical potential of the insurgency and reestablishing the conditions for capital accumulation.

A third view acknowledges that there was a revolutionary situation in the early years of the twenty-first century but claims that radical transformation was inhibited by a number of structural constraints, both material and ideological. Focusing on the political economy of extraction, Bret Gustafson argues that the country's continued reliance on and struggle over hydrocarbons both radically transformed Bolivia and, at the same time, reproduced historical structures and relations of power.[19] The continued dependence on gas and mineral extraction distorted political incentives, intensified inequality, and weakened democratic processes. Gas and mineral extraction, according to Gustafson, "had a numbing effect on Bolivian politics, contributing to feverish struggles over rents and the gas assemblage, and dislocating and distorting other political projects and visions."[20] Gustafson ably demonstrates how the structure of the global fossil fuel economy, and Bolivia's place within it, essentially set limits on what was possible for Morales and the MAS to think and do. The commitment to gas extraction to fuel development derailed, or put off into the distant future, more revolutionary political goals. Yet, this is not to simply lay blame on the shoulders of Morales and the MAS, although they made certain choices; it is to emphasize the structural bind of extractivist global capital. "The underlying point," Gustafson notes, "is that nationalist, revolutionary, and Indigenous paradigms of struggle have also been 'spent' during the age of gas."[21] Regardless of who was in power and whatever ideology was guiding them, structural confines limited what was possible in a political economy structured by fossil fuel extraction. In the end, the Morales years were not so much about securing the hegemony of the MAS, but rather about securing the hegemony of fossil fuel capital. The struggle to decolonize Bolivia, "as long as it depends on gas work," Gustafson claims, "will be something less utopian than a world otherwise."[22]

Luis Tapia, too, adheres to this third view, but he homes in on the epistemology of modernity as a structural constraint on radical social transformation, one that has proved insurmountable during the *proceso de cambio*.[23] While there are indeed alternative modes of being that represent a challenge to the dominant form of contemporary capitalist life, Tapia claims that when they are translated into the grammar of modernity they tend to lose their radical potentiality—for instance, when the demand to refound Bolivia was redirected toward the writing of a new constitution, or when the indigenous concept of plurinationalism was ultimately proposed as a plurinational state. For Tapia, the potential of these nonmodern social forms was subsumed by the epistemology of modernity when they were (re)presented in the political organizational logic of modernity. Thus, it is not so much that Morales and the MAS have neutralized the potential of social transformation but that there are certain limits to what can be legibly expressed or indeed thought within the structural parameters of modernity.

The final approach highlights the conflicting views within the revolutionary process that have produced a fragmentary and ambiguous social transformation. Mark Goodale, for instance, argues that Bolivia's "democratic and cultural revolution" has been constituted through a series of crystallizations, "historical, ideological, and institutional fragments that were often in tension with one another."[24] Goodale convincingly and quite rightly highlights how the contradictory ideological formation of the MAS corresponded to the equivocal transformations under the Morales government. The fragmentary nature of the revolution, he argues, has resulted in a "polyvalent vision of transformation," an ideologically ambiguous process that, nevertheless, was largely directed through the instrumentalities of state bureaucracy. For Goodale, the instantiation of the revolution through the governmentality of the state opened the possibility for a number of important changes in the context of Morales and the MAS's electoral route to power but also ultimately limited what was possible. "The legalization of the process of change in Bolivia demonstrated yet again that the law is a superb mechanism through which to create, legitimate, and historically embed 'key categories,'" Goodale notes. Yet in practice, "the juridification of politics in Bolivia was the mechanism for much more limited, exclusionary, and ambiguous shifts."[25]

In the earlier years of the Morales government, Nancy Postero persuasively analyzed the multiple and often conflicting ideological currents that make up the MAS as a political movement that endeavored to form an indigenous popular hegemony.[26] In her more recent *The Indigenous State* (2017), Postero explores the dynamics of indigenous politics and the formation of the plurinational state, arguing that indigeneity has been transformed from a struggle for emancipatory decolonization into one of liberal nation-state building.[27] Drawing inspiration from Jacques Rancière, Postero distinguishes between *politics* and *policing* to make sense of the contentious and promising nature of the Morales era. While policing refers to the maintenance of the existing social order and distribution of roles and identities within society, politics involves calling attention to this distribution and taking action that challenges and reconfigures the existing order. Postero argues that the indigenous struggles to decolonize Bolivia under Morales can be seen as an emancipatory form of politics while also acting as a form of policing. Indigenous movements, engaging in the politics of performative action that made themselves visible, sought to draw attention to the continued exclusion of indigenous peoples from the nation. Yet, under Morales the MAS state has "utilize[d] the ideas and rhetoric of decolonization to legitimate its own power, turning decolonization from a call for alternative epistemologies into a state-sponsored form of multicultural recognition."[28]

Combining certain elements from all the perspectives outlined above, *Visions of Transformation* develops a distinction between the theory of hegemony and the theory of plurinationality to interpret and make sense of the many tensions, contradictions, and ambiguities in Bolivia's *proceso de cambio*. I argue that these theories represent two distinct visions of transformation, two contrasting *political logics* confronting each other on an ideological plane, sometimes overlapping but most often remaining incommensurable, that produce and are visible in moments of concrete, material social conflict. While Morales and the MAS may have indeed lacked the political will to push forward a truly plurinational revolution, I take the ideas of Morales, his vice president Álvaro García Linera, and other MAS intellectuals seriously as a legitimate and sincere theoretical practice of revolutionary change. I argue that the social conflicts that exposed the principal contradictions of the *proceso de cambio* are borne of the confrontation between two completely separate logics of politics or worldviews that envision two distinct horizons of social possibility.

VISIONS OF TRANSFORMATION: HEGEMONY AND PLURINATIONALITY

The central argument of the book is that the theories of hegemony and plurinationality represent contrasting, often conflicting, visions of power, organization, identity, and governance within culturally diverse societies, and that this theoretical divergence helps us interpret the central conflicts and contradictions of Bolivia's *proceso de cambio* during the era of Evo Morales and the MAS.

Hegemony and plurinationality are theoretical worldviews that each assemble various, sometimes disparate, political claims, desires, assumptions, and techniques that, when combined, coalesce into a more general logic of politics, with each part supporting and reinforcing the others. We can think about the relation between hegemony and plurinationality as an ideological struggle between contrasting worldviews, a contest for how Bolivia should be conceptualized and organized socially, culturally, politically, and economically. The theory of hegemony is inherently linked to the nation-state form, which is, as I envision it here, a combination of territorial political authority, economic organization, and intersubjective identity formation. These three elements have combined in such a way over the past 250 years to produce the nation-state form. Plurinationality, on the other hand, suggests a different form of political authority, economic organization, and intersubjective identity. While the contours of this form are still not clearly defined—indeed, part of my project is to help with this process of collective definition—it contrasts radically with the nation-state form. In the course of this book I analyze how these contending logics have shaped the ideological and material struggles of Bolivia's *proceso de cambio*.

As in all social struggles, the contending forces—in this case, theoretically informed strategies and practices—do not always confront each other directly and straightforwardly. At times they may overlap and complement each other, while at others their relation is unequivocally one of antagonism and conflict. Additionally, just because these two theories are presented as coherent, integrated, whole logics does not mean that they are always internally consistent. Like all ideological abstractions, hegemony and plurinationality are pieced together in contradictory and ambiguous ways as they attempt to make sense of a complex and contingent social reality. Thus, while I present these two theories as if they are coherent and consistent, I do so to provide an abstract, interpretive lens through which to make sense of the very real contradictions, conflicts, and antagonisms of Bolivia's contemporary era.

At the most general level, hegemony, as conceptualized by Gramsci, highlights the ability of a dominant group to establish and maintain its economic and cultural-ideological dominance over subordinate classes. It emphasizes the ways that a particular worldview, a common sense, that prioritizes the interests and perspectives of a dominant group is produced and perpetuated by suppressing and marginalizing the identities, aspirations, and views of subordinate groups. In the context of Bolivia, hegemony sheds light on how a particular culture has exercised its political, economic, and cultural domination over a variety of other cultures, which have been lumped together under the term *indigenous* since the colonial era. In large part, the practice of hegemony is mediated through the nation-state form: culturally and ideologically through the various tropes surrounding Bolivian nationalism and citizenship; economically through the ongoing construction of an internal, domestic capitalist market; and politically through the institutional governing apparatuses of the state. While analytically distinct, these various spheres operate together to form and enforce a "universal" hegemonic project. Within the theory of hegemony, the nation-state form is where hegemony is actually constructed, consolidated, and legitimized. It is the sociopolitical terrain over which a ruling class seeks domination by shaping beliefs and values, structuring political possibilities, and enforcing a particular economic logic, all through mechanisms of coercion and consent.

While hegemony seeks to establish a dominant ideological and material framework that subordinates secondary groups, plurinationality proposes a model of cultural, economic, and political coexistence of various forms, respecting and dignifying the multiple cultural nations within the territory of a given state. Plurinationality does not just imply the existence of different classes, ethnicities, or races, but also entails multiple rationalities, value systems, cosmologies, modes of production and consumption, and nature-culture relations—that is, different *cultures* in the most general sense of the term. Rather than one culture dominating others, plurinationality seeks to build cultural relations, systems of economic organization, and forms of political governance that foster dialogue, cooperation when possible, dignity, autonomy and self-determination, and shared decision-making among cultural units. That is, it entails a mode of social coexistence that may, indeed will, generate tensions and contradictions, but also one in which these conflicts are managed and processed in a nondominant and noncoercive fashion. Plurinationalism is a method, a political logic, founded on cultural, ethnic, linguistic, social, political, and economic multiplicity, and, as such, it seeks to provide the necessary conditions for the ideological and material reproduction of that heterogeneity. In Bolivia, the demand for plurinationality emanating from the country's indigenous peoples puts into question the cultural singularity and social totality of the nation-state form and its hegemonic mode of political governance.

While the distinction that I make between hegemony and plurinationality might easily map onto an ethnic dichotomy of nonindigenous and indigenous, this is not the argument I am making. The political logics of hegemony and plurinationality do not adhere to ethnic identities with assumed interests and essentialized traits. Rather, these contrasting theories should be interpreted as distinct modes of cultural creativity and understanding situated within changing historical conditions, similar to the different forms of cultural invention laid out by Roy Wagner in *The Invention of Culture*. For Wagner, all cultures evolve over time through processes of what he terms *invention* and *convention*, which operate dialectically. Invention refers to the creative process through which individuals and communities generate new symbols, practices, and meanings, whereas convention refers to the established patterns, rules, norms, and shared understandings of a given social formation. Convention provides a general framework for social interaction that is continually invented and reinvented through novel cultural expressions that arise in relation to changing circumstances. For Wagner, cultural invention is obviated by convention and vice versa. Through processes of cultural invention, cultural convention becomes apparent, while it is only in conventionalized contexts that invention is possible.[29]

According to Wagner, there are generally two ways in which the dialectical relation of invention and convention are maintained, each of which corresponds to a particular cultural mode and conception of self, society, and the world. "Either the dialectic can be used consciously to mediate the conventional forms," he says, "or the articulation of conventionalized contexts into a conscious unity can be used to mediate the dialectic."[30] These two different forms of culture are what he calls *differentiating* and *collectivizing*. Differentiating forms accentuate particularity against a background of similarity, while collectivizing approaches emphasize integration and similarity against a background of differences:

> Cultures that mediate the conventional dialectically make differentiation (including qualities of paradox, contradiction, and reciprocal interaction) the basis of thought and action. They play out the dialectical and motivational contradictions consciously in their management of roles, rituals, and situations, and thus continually reconstitute the conventional. Cultures that mediate the dialectic through the conventional, on the other hand, pattern their thought and action on a model of consistent, rational, and systematic articulation, stressing the avoidance of paradox and contradiction.[31]

Drawing on Wagner's typology, I understand the theory of plurinationality to be imbued with a *differentiating* logic, while the underlying logic of hegemony is a *collectivizing* one. As a form of social relation, plurinationalism mediates convention through the dialectic; that is, the dialectical interaction of principles as such brings the world together. Under the logic of hegemony, on the other hand, dialectical relations are mediated through conventionalized contexts; that is, society invents itself through the syncretic fusion of the dialectic into a singular principle. Hegemony masks the continued dialectical relations of society, however temporarily, through what Wagner refers to as collectivizing action. In other words, as a collectivizing cultural mechanism, hegemony creates the illusion of overcoming the dialectic, if conditionally and only for a time, through the appearance of a universalized particular. Plurinationalism, as a mode of cultural differentiation, embraces and embodies the dialectic; it necessitates not integrative synthesis but continued particularity and liminality. These are alternative notions of what society is, how it is organized and reproduces itself, and what is socially possible and desirable. Grasping these distinct logics is key to understanding not only the differences between hegemony and plurinationality but also the existence of contrasting modes of cultural configuration in Bolivia. It is these distinctive cultural forms that I argue are expressed ideologically through the theories of hegemony and plurinationality, and by understanding them we can most fully interpret and understand the tensions and contradictions of the *proceso de cambio*.

A NOTE ON METHOD

Academic research is often presented as a search for truth, whatever that truth may be. This is undoubtedly a fine ambition, yet research is also a process of exploration, critique, and creation. Wagner highlights this by describing ethnographic research as a process of cultural invention.[32] It is a means through which we try to understand a given social phenomenon and, in the process, also make sense of our own position in and relation to the world around us. Research permits us to see, on an individual level, how our perception and understanding of the world are deeply cultural in the sense of what we lend our attention to and choose to interrogate—that is, value—at an epistemological and ontological level. The essence, and importance, of immersive qualitative fieldwork is that it can, and often does, bring us into contact with value systems and ways of being that are fundamentally different from our own. In this sense, my quest to investigate and understand Bolivia's *proceso de cambio* has been as much a discovery of self, an exploration and evaluation of my own culture (which, like all others, involves seeing the world in certain and particular ways), as it is a cultural analysis of a different world for a particular society at a specific historical conjuncture.

The twenty-one months of fieldwork for this project were carried out between 2013 and 2022 (two months in 2013, thirteen months in 2015–16, three months in 2017, one month in 2018, and two months in 2022). In an attempt to grasp the ongoing processes of change in Bolivia, my time was split between various areas of the country. Much of my research took place in and around La Paz and El Alto, where I conducted many of my formal, semistructured interviews, a lot of informal immersion, and a bit of archival work, and where the participant observation work for chapter 4 occurred. I also spent time in the cities and surroundings areas of Cochabamba, Santa Cruz, Cobija, Potosí, and Sucre for specific interviews, gatherings, and events, but more so in an effort to grasp the different rhythms, perspectives, and circumstances of the *proceso de cambio* across space. Additionally, I carried out months of ethnographic work on indigenous autonomy for chapter 5 in the communities of Charagua, Jesús de Machaca, and Totora Marka.[33] In sum, the book utilizes various qualitative and interpretive methodological tools to investigate events at multiple analytic levels. Throughout my research I talked with just about anybody that I could: politicians, bureaucrats, taxi drivers, social movement actors, miners, academics, journalists, indigenous community members, neighborhood shop owners, random bar patrons, indigenous healers, university students, striking workers, and others. Some of those folks' words are quoted herein, and, unless they are well-known figures, I use pseudonyms to identify them, following common practice.

Methodologically, this book combines the interpretive approach of ethnography with the theoretical focus of comparative political theory.[34] Whereas comparative political theory looks beyond Western theoretical ideas and traditions toward non-Western thinking as an equivalent and necessary component of political thought, ethnography opens the possibility of engaging alternative cultural worlds. Therefore, in this book I ethnographically interpret concrete moments of political, economic, and cultural conflict in order to flesh out the theoretical logics that both help produce and are recursively produced by those events. In my ethnographic fieldwork, I sacrifice the depth of settling in a single location for the breadth of "hanging out deeply," as Renato Rosaldo once put it, in numerous locales.[35] This freedom of range allows me to trace thematic resonances across space and connect them into more general, abstract concepts and theories that serve as an interpretive guide for Bolivian politics, society, culture, and economy in the twenty-first century. Although he did not express it in a purely methodological sense, I take inspiration from René Zavaleta Mercado's claim that "conoce mas el que se mueve mas" (one who moves around knows/learns more).[36] That is, those who move about in a social sense, experiencing and interacting with different cultures, classes, regions, ethnicities, worldviews, and so forth, are in a better position to understand and know the composition and complexity of a place. But what makes the study of the social world so interesting and complex is the fact that the object of investigation and the tools used to do the investigating are inescapably intertwined. As Paul Rabinow and William M. Sullivan note, interpretation begins from the postulate that the web of meaning constitutes human existence to such an extent that it cannot ever be meaningfully reduced to constitutively prior or predefined elements.[37] I am, therefore, interpreting others' interpretations of specific situations and historical moments through observational and participatory fieldwork, interviews, and the evaluation of secondary sources. The symbolic interpretation of Clifford Geertz this is not, but it is interpretation nonetheless, and it is interpretation all the way down. As interpretation, my project invents a conceptual and theoretical apparatus, although not out of whole cloth (again, going back to Wagner), to make sense of Bolivia's *proceso de cambio* proper, the era beginning right before the election of Evo Morales up to the overthrow of his government in 2019.

Through both disciplinary training and professional association I am a card-carrying political scientist. But I was lucky enough to do my graduate work at an institution that specializes in and values qualitative and interpretive research on politics. Epistemologically, therefore, my training directed me toward the study of politics broadly, not necessarily political science. I have been equally fortunate to join a department as a faculty member that recognizes and respects the same. With this book, then, I am making the case for the importance and utility of combining abstract political theorization with immersive, ethnographic research for the study of politics, for the discipline of political science.[38] Too often, interpretive and ethnographic research in political science is regarded and justified, even by some of its practitioners, as the means to another end, as merely providing the base material, the raw data for larger-N causal analyses. While this may in fact be one of the many uses of qualitative interpretive work, this view empties interpretive work of its capacity to challenge the practices of knowing and knowledge production within the discipline of political science. Interpretive political ethnography is more than just an exercise in generating hypotheses or producing base data to be used in more "scientific" ways by others. Interpretive ethnographic research in political science pushes us to rethink what "data" actually is, how we know it when we see it, how it might differ across time and space, and how it is thought of, understood, and put to use by actual people. These are critical epistemological and ontological questions, and they are just as important for the discipline as the gathering of local data in service to more quantitative and positivist causal inference. So, although my project and method are thoroughly interdisciplinary, I am at least partially directing a specific methodological argument toward the discipline of political science, to which I am most closely aligned.

STRUCTURE OF THE BOOK

The next chapter analyzes the theory of hegemony largely through the work of Antonio Gramsci, René Zavaleta Mercado, and Álvaro García Linera. Gramsci's thought has significantly affected the strategies and practices of revolutionary change around the world, nowhere more than in Latin America. I examine how Gramsci's ideas around hegemony influenced the work of Zavaleta Mercado, one of Bolivia's most important twentieth-century thinkers, which, in turn, affected the thought of former MAS vice president García Linera, who is generally recognized as the MAS's most prominent intellectual strategist. The theory of hegemony and its attendant ontological view of politics, I argue, guided the MAS on its rise to power and shaped its governing practice. While successful in theoretically grounding the MAS's seizure of state power, the political practices of hegemony faltered when indigenous and popular social movements sought to push the process of change toward a more radical break with the territorial structure and social form of the contemporary nation-state. As one of the contending theories of revolutionary change in twenty-first-century Bolivia, hegemony has provided the ideological foundations on which the MAS sought to radically reform the country from a position of political, economic, social, and cultural domination. In other words, through this theoretical perspective, the MAS as the hegemonic subject represented the universal will of all oppressed Bolivians in their struggle for emancipation.

Chapter 2, "Articulating Plurinationality," outlines an alternative ideological schema to hegemony and explains how plurinationality functions as a theoretical apparatus for envisioning a political horizon beyond the nation-state form. First arising in Bolivia out of the indigenous and peasant struggles of the 1980s, plurinationality is still a concept in development. It has been used to articulate a multitude of subnational sociocultural formations (indigenous communities, rural peasant unions, neighborhood organizations, feminist movements, among others) in their attempts to transform the Bolivian state and society. A central element of the concept is its theoretical centering of social, economic, and cultural diversity and political contingency. Whereas hegemony envisions a more or less cohesive social formation with a determined universal historical subject under the control of a unified state apparatus (although allowing for conflict and contradiction), plurinationalism challenges the theoretical need to overcome particularism through a dominant universality. Plurinationality is theorized as a utopian political logic of nondomination and, as such, seeks to deconstruct the material and ideological bases of domination embedded in the territorial nation-state form.

Chapters 3, 4, and 5 form the empirical core of the text and demonstrate how the theoretico-ideological conceptualizations of hegemony and plurinationality have come into conflict and played out in material terms. Each chapter examines a specific conjunctural moment at analytically distinct economic, social, and political levels to highlight the differences between the logics of hegemony and plurinationalism. Embedded in these chapters are concrete struggles between attempts to reconstruct hegemony around the nation-state form and the articulation of an alternative plurinational form. Chapter 3 analyzes the attempted construction of a highway through the Territorio Indígena y Parque Nacional Isiboro Sécure (TIPNIS, Isoboro Sécure Indigenous Territory and National Park), a national forest preserve and indigenous territory in the center of the country, in order to highlight the relationship between processes of extraction and development with hegemonic control of the nation-state. Indigenous groups opposed to the highway sought to challenge this infrastructural development through recourse to the internationally recognized right of free and informed prior consultation to development projects that might affect indigenous territories. This chapter shows how various notions of "development" operate at distinct social, economic, and cultural levels, both promoting and challenging political projects of hegemony.

Chapter 4 examines an internal power struggle over control of one of the most influential indigenous movement organizations in Bolivia, the Consejo Nacional de Ayllus y Markas del Qullasuyu (CONAMAQ, National Council of Ayllus and Markas of Qullasuyu), in 2013–14. An early supporter that helped bring Evo Morales and the MAS to state power, CONAMAQ increasingly came into conflict with the government and officially went into opposition after the TIPNIS crisis analyzed in chapter 3. Contention within the organization surfaced during leadership elections in 2013 over whether to continue in opposition to the government or realign with Morales. The MAS intervened on the side of the progovernment faction, helping it seize control of the organization and its headquarters. Through discussions of indigeneity, representation, and populism, I argue that this episode sheds light on hegemony as a particular strategy and logic of political action that requires social categories to be unified, homogenous, and total. Alternatively, a plurinational politics as espoused by the opposition faction provides the space for a variety of contrasting and, at times, conflicting indigenous identities to (co)exist.

Chapter 5 analyzes an attempt to radically transform the institutional structure of the state through the construction of indigenous autonomy. Based on the long-standing demand for indigenous self-governance, the 2009 constitution, which founded Bolivia as a plurinational state, outlined a formal process for the creation of indigenous community autonomy. Drawing on ethnographic research in the community of Charagua, the first indigenous municipality to officially become autonomous, I argue that the possibility of indigenous autonomy opens a horizon beyond the nation-state form. Yet, the official process, with its attendant bureaucratic requirements, may indeed stifle the liberatory possibilities of autonomy by making indigenous forms of social, political, and economic organization more legible and, therefore, more prone to the rationalities of governance. I analyze a variety of situations encountered during the research that help flesh out this dialectical process between radical transformation and increased legibility.

The conclusion reconnects the theoretical arguments made throughout the book to examine and explain the ultimate overthrow of Evo Morales in 2019. The chapter then places the Bolivian *proceso de cambio* in conversation with the extant social scientific study of revolution in order to tease out some particularities of the Bolivian case. Scholars have debated whether the Bolivian case can be categorized as a revolution as typically defined in the social scientific literature. I argue that a reconceptualization of the idea of revolution is needed to fully understand what is indeed underway in Bolivia. During the period of transformation between 2006 and 2019, ideas of ethnicity, history, temporality, knowledge, and power were just as fundamental to the revolutionary process as the trajectories of political and economic transformation were. Using the situation in Bolivia as a springboard to think more broadly about the idea of revolution, this chapter provides an in-depth analysis of the multiply entwined components of revolutionary change in the twenty-first century.

1

HEGEMONY, SOCIAL TOTALITY, AND THE NATION-STATE

The development and expansion of the particular group are con-
ceived of, and presented, as being the motor force of a universal
expansion, of a development of all the "national" energies.
—ANTONIO GRAMSCI

Bolivia will be socialist or it will never be a modern country.
—RENÉ ZAVALETA MERCADO

This chapter provides a reading of hegemony in order to demonstrate
how this theory deeply conditions certain understandings of contemporary Bolivia while limiting the horizon of possible alternatives,
what Richard J. F. Day has labeled "the hegemony of hegemony."[1] Through
a critical treatment of the concept's development from Vladimir Lenin
through Antonio Gramsci and its transference to Latin America, I argue
that for all its utility, the theory of hegemony is wedded to the representative logic of the nation-state form. From its emergence in Marxist
political theory and practice, the concept of hegemony has been imbued
with a number of assumptions that structure the possibilities of revolutionary subjects and practices, while also delimiting the horizons of
postrevolutionary political, economic, and social forms.

Since its elaboration and expansion with Gramsci, the theory of hegemony has functioned as perhaps the most important social scientific
device for understanding social stasis and social change, on both analytic and practical levels. Yet, despite its creative potential and its historical utility, the idea of hegemony can also serve as what Luis Tapia calls
an "epistemological obstacle."[2] There are certain ideas that open up new
ways for understanding the world and push us to explore new areas of
research. Others close off intellectual reflection and limit our knowledge

and understanding of the real, impeding our ability to see and think of certain dimensions of the world around us from different perspectives. Hegemony, as a theory of politics, does both of these things. It opens up one way of understanding while obstructing others. This isn't necessarily a limit of hegemony in particular; rather, all concepts work in this way. This being the case, it is important to clarify what paths of understanding particular ideas open up, and which ones they close off.

Under the logic of hegemony, social relations unfold in what Roy Wagner calls a "syntagmatic" manner, whereby a more or less static relation between social classes places the responsibility for creating and sustaining a "universal" culture on one of the social subdivisions of society. Or, as Wagner puts it, "society invents itself as the articulation of a principle rather than as the dialectical interaction of principles."[3] For Wagner, the concept of the dialectic symbolizes a dialogue-like alternation between multiple conceptions or worldviews that are simultaneously contradictory and constitutive of one another although never formally amalgamated or synthesized. Contrary to Wagner, the logic of hegemony masks social contradictions and antagonisms in an attempt to mediate them as contributions to a collectivized totality. Hegemony, then, is a mode of social thought and action that applies the dialectic rather than embodying it.

ANTONIO GRAMSCI AND THE THEORY OF HEGEMONY

The concept of hegemony advanced by Antonio Gramsci developed out of the theoretical environment of early twentieth-century Marxism. Within Marxism, the concept of hegemony was mainly used to refer to a class alliance of the proletariat with other exploited groups, above all the peasantry, in a common struggle.[4] Gramsci elaborated and enhanced hegemony as both a theoretical concept and a political strategy during what Stuart Hall has labeled his "enforced leisure" in a Mussolini prison.[5] Since gaining wider currency during the 1970s and 1980s across the world, the theory of hegemony has been particularly useful for analyzing various social formations and prescribing strategies for change in Latin America.[6]

Gramsci's prison notebooks are notorious for their fragmentary character and coded language as they were produced in extremely difficult conditions and under the watchful eye of a prison censor. Political theorist Peter D. Thomas asserts that anyone interested in Gramsci's thought would "seem called upon not so much to read the *Prison Notebooks* as to decipher them . . . to translate their formal foreignness into a known literary convention."[7] In addition to this complication, Gramsci used theory to illuminate concrete historical cases or political questions, and, as a result, his work often appears too particular, too historically specific to be generalized at a more abstract theoretical level. Consequently, the ideas and concepts developed in the *Prison Notebooks* need to be "delicately dis-interred from their concrete and specific historical embeddedness and transplanted to new soil with considerable care and patience."[8] We therefore need to be cognizant of the historical conditions from which theory develops, and care should be taken not to run too roughshod over a concept's "original meaning" through either conceptual stretching or distortion, which would dull its analytic utility. However, viewed from a different perspective, the openness of Gramsci's ideas is what makes them so useful, and the incomplete character of his research is what has allowed his ideas to travel widely and be used in so many creative ways. All this is to say that a certain element of novel reconstruction is unavoidable in any interpretation of Gramsci.

Gramsci's theory of hegemony was largely developed through writings on the Risorgimento, the nineteenth-century process of Italian unification out of a patchwork of ancient republics and city-states. This detail is key to recognizing the centrality of the nation-state form in relation to Gramscian hegemony, but also to understanding the underlying logic inherent to processes of hegemony formation. In his early writings, Gramsci more or less adopted the idea of hegemony in its Leninist sense as a class alliance between the proletariat and the peasantry. In his 1926 essay "The Southern Question," Gramsci poses the question of the "hegemony of the proletariat" in Italy, arguing that "the proletariat can become the leading and ruling class to the extent to which it succeeds in creating a system of class alliances which enables it to mobilise the majority of the working population against capitalism and the bourgeois State; this means, in Italy, the actual relations existing in Italy, to the extent to which it succeeds in obtaining the consent of the large peasant masses."[9] However, in the *Prison Notebooks* Gramsci reconceptualizes hegemony, expanding it from a purely strategic proletarian class alliance to a more abstract theoretical concept able to analyze the forms of established bourgeois rule and state power in democratic capitalist countries. That is, whereas the term was used in Gramsci's earlier work to define the relationship between the proletariat and the peasantry during a period of revolutionary upheaval, its meaning shifted to explore the relationship between the bourgeoisie and proletariat in a consolidated western European capitalist order. Without abandoning the characteristic class alliance inherited from Lenin, the two aspects that combine to form the core of the Gramscian conceptualization of hegemony are now *coercion* and *consent*. Building on Machiavelli's Centaur, half-animal and half-human, Gramsci argues that a "dual perspective" needs to be developed in order to fully comprehend the two-sided nature of all political action.[10] In this dual perspective, seeming binaries—coercion and consent, violence and civilization, leadership/direction and domination—are articulated as interrelated levels or moments of political action. It is within this dichotomous vision that Gramsci locates hegemony, which he also labels in certain instances as intellectual and moral leadership in relation to domination. He argues: "the supremacy of a social group manifests itself in two ways, as 'domination' and as 'intellectual and moral leadership.' A social group dominates antagonistic groups, which it tends to 'liquidate,' or to subjugate perhaps even by armed force; it leads kindred and allied groups."[11] Here we can still clearly see the links with Lenin, but as Thomas points out, Gramsci's hegemony has become "an alternative, 'consensual' political strategy for the working-class movement to that of [Lenin's] dictatorship of the proletariat, which relies largely upon coercive measures."[12] Indeed, whereas Marxism has traditionally focused on forms of material domination, here hegemony moves beyond the mere economic supremacy of a corporate class to denote the moral and intellectual leadership of a group that eschews any narrow economic vision of its leading role. The hegemonic group, in effect, aims to universalize its interests (political, economic, and cultural) in order to lead. As Gramsci argues, "the development and expansion of a particular [hegemonic] group is conceived of, and presented, as being the motor force of a universal expansion, of a development of all the 'national' energies."[13] Thus, in the struggle for hegemony, differing groups "come into confrontation and conflict, until one of them, or at least a single combination of them, tends to prevail, to gain the upper hand, to propagate itself throughout society—bringing about not only a unison of economic and political aims, but also intellectual and moral unity, posing all the questions around which the struggle rages not on a corporate but on a 'universal' plane, and thus creating the hegemony of a fundamental social group over a series of subordinate groups."[14]

Gramscian hegemony is, in Marxian terms, the unification of base and superstructure. It is an always temporary and always contested fusion of material and ideological power in a hegemonic or historical bloc. In her analysis of Gramscian hegemony, Gwyn Williams highlights the elements of intellectual and moral leadership (i.e., ideology and culture) that made Gramsci's new developments so constructive. With hegemony, Williams argues, "Gramsci seems to mean a socio-political situation, in his ter-minology a 'moment,' in which the philosophy and practice of a society fuse or are in equilibrium; an order in which a certain way of life and thought is dominant, in which one concept of reality is diffused through-out society in all its institutional and private manifestations, informing with its spirit all taste, morality, customs, religious and political princi-ples, and all social relations, particularly in their intellectual and moral connotation."[15] The stress on the intellectual and moral component of hegemony is certainly an advancement, but it can be taken too far. For instance, James C. Scott, in his otherwise pathbreaking *Weapons of the Weak*, defines hegemony in purely ideological terms. "Hegemony is, after all, fundamentally about the misrepresentation of 'objective' interests," Scott argues. "Hegemony is simply the name Gramsci gave to the pro-cess of ideological domination . . . [which serves] to explain the insti-tutional basis of false consciousness."[16] While the focus on ideological leadership was a key addition to a prior materialist focus, we must not lose sight of the fact that for Gramsci hegemony was both an ideological and a material relation between social forces.[17] He argues, "the fact of hegemony presupposes that account is taken of the interests and ten-dencies of the groups over which hegemony is to be exercised, and that a certain balance of compromise should be formed—in other words that the leading group should make sacrifices of an economico-corporative kind. But there is no doubt that although hegemony is ethico-political, it must also be economic, must necessarily be based on the decisive func-tion exercised by the leading group in the decisive nucleus of economic activity."[18] In other words, while hegemony is the ideological construction of a shared worldview, or in Gramsci's terms a cultural "common sense," it is also the creation of a shared, so-called universal, consensus in the material reproduction of life. It is in these shared and common understandings between dominant and subaltern groups that hegemony is to be based largely on consent.

For Gramsci this process of creating the conditions of consent of the subordinate classes is what distinguishes "modern" states from older, "traditional" forms of rule that relied chiefly on coercion. The distinction between modern and traditional forms of state illuminates two important aspects of hegemony. The first is that modern states are what Gramsci referred to as *integral states*, meaning that there is an interwoven and reciprocal relationship between the state in its strict sense (i.e., the governmental apparatus) and civil society.[19] In contrast, in traditional social formations the state hovers over society, employing coercion to maintain the dominance of one social group over all the others. This position aligns with much of the literature on early state formation, which emphasizes the centralization of power, expansion of territorial control, and development of an integrated national market as the key markers of what eventually became modern nation-states.[20] Gramsci demonstrates this through his well-known contention that "in Russia [i.e., a traditional social formation] the State was everything, civil society was primordial and gelatinous; in the West [i.e., modern social formations] there was a proper relation between State and civil society, and when the State trembled a sturdy structure of civil society was at once revealed. The State was only an outer ditch, behind which there stood a powerful system of fortresses and earthworks."[21]

The second point to be drawn here is that only with the advent of modern, Western social formations does hegemony become possible as a form of politics. As Thomas notes, Gramscian hegemony "is a particular practice of consolidating social forces and condensing them into political power on a mass basis—the mode of production of the modern 'political.'"[22] The advent of the modern political is at the same time the advent of the modern form of the nation-state, and therefore control of the state is at the center of a Gramscian notion of hegemony. Through his discussions of what he labels "the bourgeois state," Gramsci highlights the importance of the state for constructing hegemony. He argues,

the revolution which the bourgeois class has brought into the conception of law, and hence into the function of the State, consists especially in the will to conform. . . . The previous ruling classes were essentially conservative in the sense that they did not tend to construct an organic passage from the other classes into their own, i.e. to enlarge their class sphere "technically" and ideologically: their conception was that of a closed caste. The bourgeois class poses itself as an organism in continuous movement, capable of absorbing the entire society, assimilating it to its own cultural and economic level. The entire function of the State has been transformed; the State has become an "educator," etc.[23]

It is only with the foundation of the modern state that the masses are organized politically and economically through parties, trade unions, and other entities are able to express their interests and influence the political system in new and distinct ways. This organization of the masses, Gramsci notes, "objectively reflects the fact that a new social force has been constituted, and has a weight which can no longer be ignored."[24] In other words, the new relationship between state and society represents the potential of the masses to intervene in politics, and with that potential arises the need for a new form of social management and political leadership.

In addition to clarifying the structure of class power and its maintenance, Gramsci advanced the concept of hegemony as a particular strategy of political struggle against the existing order for subordinate classes to achieve power. As Christine Buci-Glucksmann argues, hegemony "is primarily a political principle and a form of strategic leadership, that is, a guide to political action."[25] For Gramsci, the strategy to be used against an existing hegemony is, in essence, the creation of a counterhegemonic movement that can upend the current correlation of social forces and establish itself as the new dominant material and moral intellectual bloc in the state. For it to do so requires an extended "war of position" throughout civil society, where the counterhegemonic forces lay the sociocultural foundations for their leadership. As Gramsci notes, a "social group can, and indeed must, already exercise 'leadership' before winning governmental power (this indeed is one of the principal conditions for the winning of such power); it subsequently becomes dominant when it exercises power, but even if it holds it firmly in its grasp, it must continue to 'lead' as well."[26] This is the strategy to be deployed in Western capitalist democracies, as opposed to a more direct "war of maneuver" that topples the state through a concentrated physical and violent confrontation between forces, more appropriate to what Gramsci describes as traditional Eastern social formations.

The act of creating this new hegemonic bloc is not merely the yoking together of different classes with different interests (e.g., the proletariat with the peasantry) in a temporary alliance to overthrow the existing hegemony. For Gramsci, the process of aligning differing groups means a fundamental transformation in any particular group's identity and interests; it is the construction of a new homogenous political subject. Discussing the rigid aversion of some within the communist movement to the notion of compromise, or the necessity of the working class cooperating and negotiating with other subordinate classes, Gramsci states,

> there is no understanding of the fact that mass ideological factors always lag behind mass economic phenomena, and that therefore, at certain moments, the automatic thrust due to the economic factor is slowed down, obstructed or even momentarily broken by traditional ideological elements—hence that there must be a conscious, planned struggle to ensure the exigencies of the economic position of the masses, which may conflict with the traditional leadership's policies, are understood. An appropriate political initiative is always necessary to liberate the economic thrust from the dead weight of traditional policies—i.e. to change the political direction of certain forces which have to be absorbed if a new, homogeneous politico-economic historical bloc, without internal contradictions, is to be successfully formed.[27]

Accordingly, an intrinsic aspect of hegemonic struggle and the logic of hegemony more generally is the construction of homogenized political subjects that express a universal and national popular collective will to power.[28] For Gramsci, the only modern organization that is able to coalesce the diversity of identities into this new political subjectivity and challenge capitalist hegemony was the Communist Party, what he termed the "Modern Prince." The Modern Prince, according to Gramsci, is "the first cell in which there come together germs of a collective will tending to become universal and total. . . . The modern Prince must be and cannot but be the proclaimer and organiser of an intellectual and moral reform, which also means creating the terrain for a subsequent development of the national-popular collective will towards the realisation of a superior, total form of modern civilisation."[29] Yet, the formation of the party is not a seamless, organic affair where interests and identities merge without the influence of a concrete organizing force. Gramsci argues that a "Jacobin force" is necessary to awaken and organize the national popular collective will and also serve as an active and operative expression of that national popular spirit both within the party itself and throughout society more generally. Historically, it has been this Jacobin force that has founded modern states; it is an essential element of hegemonic politics.[30]

The political party, then, plays a decisive role in hegemonic struggle and is central to the organization of political force. The party mediates between the so-called objective conditions of material life, what Gramsci refers to as "stubborn reality," and the superstructures of ideological conflict.[31] The level of the party is where the degree of homogeneity, organization, and political consciousness of the conflicting social forces can be ascertained, and where we can ultimately see how the two sides of Gramscian hegemony, analytic concept and strategy, come together. Gramsci argues that it is at this level of politics that

one becomes aware that one's own corporate interests, in their present and future development, transcend the corporate limits of the purely economic class, and can and must become the interests of the other subordinate groups too. This is the most purely political phase, and marks the decisive passage from the [economic] structure to the sphere of the complex superstructures; it is the phase in which previously germinated ideologies become "party," come into confrontation and conflict, until only one of them, or at least a single combination of them, tends to prevail, to gain the upper hand, to propagate itself throughout society—bringing about not only a unison of economic and political aims, but also intellectual and moral unity, posing all the questions around which the struggle rages not on a corporate but on a "universal" plane, and thus creating the hegemony of a fundamental social group over a series of subordinate groups. It is true that the State is seen as the organ of one particular group, destined to create favorable conditions for the latter's maximum expansion. But the development and expansion of the particular group are conceived of, and presented, as being the motor force of a universal expansion, of a development of all the "national" energies. In other words, the dominant group is coordinated concretely with the general interests of the subordinate groups, and the life of the State is conceived of as a continuous process of formation and superseding of unstable equilibria (on the juridical plane) between the interests of the fundamental group and those of the subordinate groups—equilibria in which the interests of the dominant group prevail, but only up to a certain point, i.e. stopping short of narrowly corporate economic interests.[32]

THEORIZING HEGEMONY FROM BOLIVIA

With the spread of Gramsci's innovative interpretations, the concept of hegemony has become an essential tool of social analysis.[33] Perhaps the most sophisticated attempt to rework the term as a form of discursive construction came in the mid-1980s with Ernesto Laclau and Chantal Mouffe's foundational work *Hegemony and Socialist Strategy*.[34] Yet, it has been in Latin America where the concept has perhaps been most influential as a strategic guide to action for subaltern movements.[35] In Bolivia, the two most influential theorists of hegemony have been René Zavaleta Mercado (1935–84) and Álvaro García Linera, the country's vice president under Evo Morales (2006–19). Although politically active in different historical conjunctures, both Zavaleta and García Linera interpreted and theorized Bolivian reality largely in Gramscian terms to great effect.

Like with Gramsci, Zavaleta's writings are often empirically dense (focused on specific historical conjunctures), theoretically allusive, and conceptually challenging.[36] At the most abstract level, Zavaleta was attempting to understand and theorize how an underdeveloped and multicultural society like Bolivia, what he termed a *formación abigarrada* (motley social formation), could construct a common, national popular identity, which he argued was essential for becoming a modern, industrialized nation.[37] To conceive of Bolivia as a *formación abigarrada* is to see that "there are overlapping economic stages (those of common taxonomic usage) without combining much, as if feudalism belongs to one culture and capitalism belongs to another and they nevertheless occur in the same space, as if there was one country in feudalism and another in capitalism, overlapping but not combining."[38] According to Luis H. Antezana, Zavaleta developed the notion of *formación abigarrada* along the lines of concepts such as mode of production, social formation, and historical bloc. However, whereas the latter concepts sought to define the

determined relationship between economic production and sociopolitical reproduction in any society, the former was intended to highlight
the ways in which different economic, political, and cultural forms exist
within the same national geographic territory without much interrela-
tion.[39] Although more recently Zavaleta's notion of *formación abigarrada*
has been taken up in a positive sense for understanding Bolivia's multitudinous social forces,[40] Zavaleta argued that Bolivia's motley social
formation was an obstacle to be overcome if the country was to escape
its "backward," dependent position. The problem, according to Zavaleta,
is that Bolivia has historically lacked the presence of a dominant class
that could construct a leading social bloc around which a hegemonic
order could be built.[41] On the one hand, the dominant feudal classes,
what Zavaleta sometimes calls the *casta señorial* (seignorial caste), have
historically lacked the ideological vision and material power to transform
themselves into a modern bourgeoisie and consolidate a national political
and economic order under their "universal" direction and leadership. On
the other hand, rural indigenous campesinos, miners, and urban working
classes have also been incapable of forming their own hegemonic project.[42] A central element of this failure to construct a hegemonic bloc in
Bolivia is an inability to form a national popular identity. That is, dominant groups have historically failed to combine an institutionalized form
of political democracy with "the level of equality that men [*sic*] have . . .
in their carnality, in their social consumption and in their daily lives."[43]

The notion of the *national popular*, which is drawn from Gramsci,
is key to understanding Zavaleta's work and its relation to the theory of
hegemony. The national popular, according to Zavaleta, is related to the
ways in which the state and society correspond to each other. It is, he says
"the relationship between what [Max] Weber called social democratization and the form of the state."[44] Zavaleta sought to understand how the
material relations of production underpin political domination in order
to strategically theorize how a process of socialist transformation might
come about. The national popular, for Zavaleta, represents a particular
type of sociopolitical equilibrium, one where a socially and economically
inclusive state promotes equality.

Here, Zavaleta's conceptualization of the state and the process of its
transformation is important. Highlighting the link between sovereignty
and state power, he notes that "the idea of the unity of power is inherent

to the modern State, although this does not mean that the concentration of power will always be an organic unity. The historical idea of the unity of power corresponds to the notions of sovereignty and the irresistibility of legitimate power, although strictly speaking, legitimate power is that that can impose itself by its own will. The proper independence or autonomy of the State is related to the idea of unity. *There is no autonomy where there is no unity*."[45] Thus, theoretically speaking, a proper, legitimate state is one that is unified materially and ideologically under the domination and leadership of a hegemonic group, and the process of this unification has served as the historical foundation of all contemporary nation-states. Similar to Marx's argument in "The German Ideology" that "the ideas of the ruling class are in every epoch the ruling ideas. . . . The ruling ideas are nothing more than the ideal expression of the dominant material relationships, the dominant material relationships grasped as ideas," Zavaleta claims that "when a dominant class produces ideas that cannot be metabolized as civil society's own ideas, as the natural way of things, we are facing a self-righteous State. . . . In order to be durable, a dominant group has to incorporate a certain amount of the dominated group's own interests."[46] Zavaleta is here claiming that modern states are those in which a leading hegemonic bloc's particular interests and ideas are reproduced through the unification of material and ideological power in society.

Important to note is the distinction Zavaleta makes between an *apparent state* and a *national state*.[47] The former is a state that maintains an "inorganic relation" with society, one where the effective reach of the state fails to correspond to its geographic scope.[48] An apparent state, then, is an "incomplete state" or a "partial state" that fails to form a relational correspondence with civil society. It is what Zavaleta refers to as a failed social optimum.[49] A national state, on the other hand, is one where "civil society has turned into a nation and has one center of political power, or that is to say that a national state is something like the culmination of the nation."[50]

But, what is the nation? For Zavaleta there are multiple historical types of nations, but the idea of the *modern* nation is tied to the expansion of capitalism and its attendant disorganization and destruction of previously existing forms of communal life. This does not simply mean the expansion of the market economy, enclosure of the commons, increasing commodification of social life, or any other specific process of economic transformation. Material transformations are no doubt important, but they are also accompanied by moral and intellectual reform—processes that create new intersubjective national identities, whereby individuals see themselves as part of an "imagined community" (à la Benedict Anderson), which corresponds to a common internal market and a unified political system of authority. This amalgamation of structures is the modern nation-state form. The nation-state form is "the paradigmatic collective organizational form under the capitalist mode of production," which involves "the construction of a collective self . . . and . . . is an indicator of the level of correspondence between the mode of production and the social collective."[51] But, while the expansion of capitalism is seen as a somewhat objective historical process, the construction of a national intersubjective identity occurs through specific constitutive moments, particularly in conditions of *abigarramiento*. Zavaleta theorizes these nationally constitutive moments in Bolivia as historical moments of crisis, such as the 1899 Federal War, the 1930s Chaco War, and the 1952 National Revolution. On both a methodological and an ontological level, periods of general crisis "are the classic form of revelation or recognition of the reality of the social totality . . . which not only reveal what is national in Bolivia, but are at the same time a nationalizing event."[52] Thus, it is really during periods of crisis that a collective consciousness, a national intersubjectivity, is produced: "you belong to one mode of production and I belong to another, but neither you nor I are the same after the Battle of Nanawa; Nanawa is what you and I have in common."[53]

We are now in a position to understand the significance of Zavaleta's conceptualization of the national popular. It is, in essence, the construction of a collective national consciousness with a popular class content, the desire for an optimal or direct correspondence between the Bolivian state and society. In other words, Zavaleta is articulating the creation of a new historical bloc and hegemonic order under the direction and leadership of the working class (particularly Bolivian miners, the strategic center of any working-class movement for Zavaleta). He argues, "the working class is not just the most advanced class in civil society, but, on the whole, it has hegemony over civil society."[54] But, the question remains as to how a national popular hegemony actually becomes hegemonic in theoretical terms.

To understand how certain social groups construct historical blocs and become hegemonic, Zavaleta turns to Gramsci's claim, already discussed, that in the East "civil society was primordial and gelatinous," while in the West "there was a proper relation between State and civil society, and . . . the state was only an outer ditch" of the fortifications of civil society.[55] Gramsci implies here that a direct war of maneuver to overturn the state is applicable in peripheral, precapitalist societies due to their less complex stage of development, whereas in developed capitalist societies a prolonged war of position in the trenches of civil society is the necessary strategy for countering hegemony. Zavaleta flips this statement on its head and argues that peripheral, precapitalist societies are actually more complex than capitalist societies due to their heterogeneity and lack of correspondence between state and society, that is, because of their *abigarramiento*. He argues that while capitalism does transform social life and makes certain things more complex, it is also a process of social homogenization and standardization. From this point of view, precapitalist societies maintain a multitudinous sense of alterity and illegibility. "After all, social classes . . . those large, relatively uniform social units, are borne out of capitalism and, in this sense, any backward society is more motley and complex than a capitalist society."[56] The heterogeneity of "backward" societies means that radical economic, political, and social transformation is specific to any given country, but also makes that process significantly more complex. In this sense, *abigarramiento* may function as an impediment to capitalist processes of homogenization. However, at the same time and for similar reasons, heterogeneity might also hinder the development of socialism. For Zavaleta, then, the construction of a national popular intersubjectivity serves as a unifying essence among differences. Moreover, a period of systemic state crisis makes possible certain class alliances (i.e., hegemony), forming a national popular intersubjectivity that would not normally be viable.[57]

At least in his early writings, the concept of dual power explains how hegemonic change occurs for Zavaleta. Drawing on Vladimir Lenin and Leon Trotsky, he argues that the rise of a counterhegemonic social bloc against the state splits the power of the state, and thus society, into two irreconcilable camps. But, for Zavaleta, this situation of dual power is more than just abstract theory; it is the real concrete political condition of Bolivia, where multiple social relations and historical times are always in contention. He states, "The duality of power consists of that which should occur successively nevertheless occurring in a parallel manner . . . it is the contemporaneity of that which came before and that which should come after [*lo anterior y lo posterior*]."[58] When a revolutionary situation of dual power arises, the crisis only increases the instability of state power already inherent in Bolivia's *estado abigarrado*, which is by definition an apparent state.[59] But, if society and the state are in a condition of *abigarramiento*, does that not make impossible the very idea of *dual* power, the notion that there are (only) two distinct social power blocs vying for control of a unified state apparatus? Perhaps.

As Zavaleta moved away from his more orthodox Marxism, his analyses shifted from the idea of direct correspondence between base and superstructure toward a more critical analysis of the link between the economy and society in order to theorize the concrete work of constructing a counterhegemonic national popular bloc. For Zavaleta, the condition of *abigarramiento* was an obstruction, a hindrance to the creation of a national hegemonic state, in either its capitalist or its popular socialist variant. Clarifying this point, Luis Tapia notes that motley, heterogeneous societies "are characterized by having a more or less apparent state and a diversity of cultural communities and modes of production, but they are also societies where the processes of national construction, at the cultural level and above all at the level of politics, are inconclusive or partial processes."[60] Zavaleta thought that processes of struggle, accentuated by periods of crisis, could lead to the construction of a national popular historical bloc that could then implement a hegemonic order under its direction and leadership. And, for Zavaleta, this historical bloc could only be composed of the indigenous and campesino masses, undoubtedly led by the mining proletariat. Discussing the class alliance of the Popular Assembly in 1971, Zavaleta stated, "it was quite correct to lay down that there should be a working class majority, a qualitative superiority over the peasantry who are a bureaucratic and dependent class inflexibly stuck to the bourgeois-democratic acquisition of land."[61] Similarly, in *Las masas de noviembre* he argued that "there can be no doubt that the masses have been constituted by proletarian interpellation," and "what qualifies a project as democratic or not . . . is the opinion or reception of the [mining] proletariat."[62]

Overall, Zavaleta's contribution to social theory for and from the concrete historical situation of Bolivia has been extremely influential. Although his analyses did not always specifically employ the concept of hegemony, he most certainly relied on Gramsci's lexicon while similarly attempting to understand and theorize the elemental aspects of hegemonic struggle and change.[63] But, what is most important is the connection Zavaleta makes between the nation and the state for his vision of social transformation. If the state is the ultimate culmination of the nation, the construction of a national popular historical bloc and processes of hegemonic struggle hinge on the territorial structure of power that is the nation-state. In this sense, Zavaleta's analysis of hegemony and change is nation-state-centric. "The strategic aim must be to take power," Zavaleta argues, "and it is a waste of time to talk of power, organization, or anything else, if you are unable to seize the historical initiative."[64]

Building on the work of Zavaleta, Álvaro García Linera similarly views Bolivia as a motley social formation, although he theorizes this heterogeneity in terms of several overlapping civilizational systems. Drawing on Norbert Elias, García Linera views civilizations as processes of pacification to which human beings are subject through techniques of state formation and the internalization of a certain form of consciousness. In other words, civilizations can be understood as hegemonic social formations where the coercion, exploitation, and extraction of surplus by certain groups in society to the detriment of others relies less and less on the outright use of physical force and increasingly on the manufacturing of consent.[65] For García Linera, "Bolivia is a country where various civilizations coexist in a disarticulated way, but where the state only recognizes the organizational logic of one of these civilizations, modern market capitalism."[66] Apart from modern capitalist civilization, García Linera argues, Bolivia is composed of three others: the domestic, artisan, and peasant regime organized around "simple market activity"; a communal civilization based on "the strength of the masses, the management of family and communal land, and the fusion between economic and political activity"; and, finally, the Amazonian civilization "based on the itinerant nature of productive activity . . . and the absence of the state."[67] This multicivilizational structure has impeded the formation of a strictly *Bolivian* form of hegemony: the state presents itself as monoethnic, and so its legitimacy is permanently in doubt. There has historically been, in other words, a lack of correspondence between state and society. According to García Linera, in culturally and politically homogenous nationalized societies the state as a sovereign entity is viewed as a legitimate expression of the historical synthesis of society. However, in heterogeneous societies like Bolivia, "the state is not a source of hegemony, in large part due to the fact that it has not been able to generate shared beliefs and behaviors that establish a basic principle of accepted sovereignty."[68] Thus, if the relationship between state and society in Bolivia is one of noncorrespondence—and if state power is based almost exclusively on discrimination, coercion, and exploitation—then the question becomes one of how to transform this state-society relation.

How does García Linera theorize this process of transforming Bolivia's social, economic, and political reality from its contemporary capitalist form into something approaching what he calls the communist horizon? The answer to this question has shifted over time.[69] In his earlier years, particularly in the late 1980s and early 1990s, when he was attempting to foment an armed indigenous uprising against the state as a member of the Ejército Guerrillero Túpac Katari (Túpac Katari Guerrilla Army) and was writing under the nom de plume Qhanachiri,[70] García Linera's intellectual trajectory was autonomist and antistatist. For example, in the opening to his 1995 *Forma valor y forma comunidad*, he and Raquel Gutiérrez Aguilar stated:

> It is necessary to abandon, once and for all, the vulgar idea of the "conquest of power" that has resulted in the occupation of an alien power, and later an alien property and alien organization by an enlightened elite who became the administrator of that power, that property, and that organization foreign to society. What needs to be recognized is that society builds its own power to emancipate itself from the prevailing private power and establish the power of society as the only form of power throughout society. If society does not construct its power itself (from the most minute capillary level to the global and fundamental level), emancipation is a supplanting farce.[71]

Or, in *De demonios escondidos y momentos de revolución* from 1991, he argued:

In more than one hundred years the State has not been capable of producing society as an organic totality, much less of revolutionizing it; the highest moments of social organization and reform as a nation . . . are tied, on the contrary, to large movements of mass insurgency, to the self organization of society against the State, to the deployment of the organizational and revolutionary vitality of society facing the State; outside of this, and despite the attempts from above, the construction of the nation and social reform has been nothing but a seignorial, oligarchic, and landowner fiction.[72]

Compare these radically autonomist declarations to the more linear, stagist, and statist vision of revolution and social change formulated by García Linera in 2007, after he had joined the Movimiento al Socialismo (MAS, Movement Toward Socialism) and become vice president:

In the mobilizations [beginning in 2000] an enormous communitarian potential had accumulated, an enormous universalist potential, an enormous autonomist potential. The moments when I saw the greatest possibility for autonomism, self-management, and communism were the moments before the social mobilization. When the mobilizations began we saw their enormous potential but we also saw very clearly the limitations that were developing. I remember that, from 2002, we had a much clearer reading of the situation and talked about the character of the revolution as democratic and decolonizing. And we said: we do not yet see communism. Through our teaching, we saw the possibility of communism through a strong, self-organized workers movement that does not exist today, and that, in any case, could begin to emerge in twenty or thirty years. . . . The 1990s produced a total reconfiguration of the working-class condition that completely disorganized everything from before and left tiny dispersed and fragmented nuclei of working-class identity and the capacity to self-organize. In the indigenous peasant world we saw enormous vitality in terms of political transformation, achievements in equality, but also an enormous limitation and lack of possibilities for communitarian forms of management and production of wealth.

He continued:

Well, how to interpret all of this? The general horizon of the period is communist. And this communism will have to be constructed from the self-organizing capacities of society, from the processes of generating and distributing communitarian wealth through self-management. But, at this moment it is clear that it is not an immediate horizon, now we are focused on achieving equality, the redistribution of wealth, and the expansion of rights. Equality is fundamental because it breaks a chain of five centuries of structural inequality, this is the objective of the moment, until the time comes when the social forces are ready, not because we prescribed it like that but because we see it as such. To be more precise, we began looking at the movement with hopeful eyes and desires for the communist horizon. But, we were serious and objective, in the social sense of the term, to point out the limitations of the movement. . . . When I entered the government I began to operate from the position of the state from this reading of the current situation. So, where does this leave communism? What can be done from the State to support the communist horizon? A leftist State, a revolutionary State, can help deploy as much as possible the autonomous organizing capacities of society. Extend the base of the working class and the autonomy of the world of labor, strengthen the communitarian forms of economy where there are communitarian networks, articulations, and projects. Without controlling them. There are no processes of co-optation nor creation from above in communitarianism. That we will never do.[73]

In highlighting the transformation in García Linera's thinking, I do not mean to claim that the power incurred from his participation in government has somehow seduced him away from his earlier, more radical thinking and practice. This may or may not have been the case.[74] Rather, the point is to draw attention to the complexity of his thinking and also clarify that his answers to certain questions (e.g., Who are the historical subjects of revolutionary change? What is the best revolutionary strategy? What is the relationship between revolution and the state? What is the ultimate goal of revolutionary struggle?) are, like with Gramsci and Zavaleta, not meant to be ahistorical, mechanical truths, which at times makes it difficult to neatly situate García Linera ideologically.

Nevertheless, a continuous thread running through most of García Linera's thought is the attempt to understand the relationship between class, ethnicity, and the state. Seeking to apprehend the often complex and contradictory relation between class and ethnicity was, for García Linera, the great struggle to bring Marxism and Indianismo together in the specific situation of Bolivia, which he sought to do largely through engaging the work of Zavaleta and Fausto Reinaga, another important twentieth-century Bolivian social theorist. Through his work, García Linera aimed to create "a space of communication and mutual enrichment between Indianismos and Marxisms, which are likely to be the most important emancipatory conceptions in Bolivian society in the twenty-first century."[75] By combining these two theories of emancipation, García Linera argued that Bolivia's indigenous and working-class peoples would be able to put forth a new, unified vision of the Bolivian state, one with the potential for proper correspondence between state power and societal composition.

In order to define class in an open and critical manner that corresponds to Bolivian reality, García Linera pushes back against those who might define it simply as an objective, static property relation between those who own the means of production and those who do not. To simply explain social classes through the relations of property, he argues, "is to invert and mystify the problematic of classes, taking as the origin that which in a strict sense is the result, a radical critique of the social division of classes is substituted by a juridical critique of forms of property."[76] In reality, forms of property do not precede the conflicts between social classes in society; rather, forms of property are authenticated through social struggle and are crystallized in the laws, codes, and regulations that underpin the capitalist relations of property.[77] For García Linera, particularly in contexts such as Bolivia, where important communal social structures largely define themselves in relation to a burdensome state (despotic, colonial, or capitalist), these communities define themselves as a class due to the fact that their "conditions of life, consistent economic ties, cultural and political attitudes, their field of possibilities" are distinct from and subordinate to "the field of material possibilities of the holders of prevailing state power, the dominant economic activity, and the legitimate culture." He continues, "the members of a community, in any of its forms, due to their ineluctable links in the face of greater and dominant social structures, are, therefore, a social class; and the forms of going forward and challenging these links by economically, politically, and culturally dominant society will do no more than consecrate this, their class position."[78]

We can see a similarity with Zavaleta here in the way that García Linera is attempting to open up the concept of class, something that he does for two specific reasons. One is the historical period in which these ideas were being put forward, a time in which García Linera and his comrades in Grupo Comuna (Commune Group) were exposing a theoretical crisis within Bolivian Marxism (if not Marxism globally) in understanding and dealing with the triumph of neoliberal capitalism and its attendant weakening of Bolivia's working classes and their radical unionism. For García Linera, what was needed was a rearticulation of Marxist analysis and its revitalization through new critical approaches and proposals, albeit maintaining a focus on the material reproduction of life through the category of class. The second reason relates to the historical inability of certain orthodox sectors of Marxism to capture the meaning of ethnic identity in analyzing complex and heterogeneous social structures. This failure had a particularly pronounced effect in Bolivia, where many indigenous activists argued that Marxism was simply another imported Western philosophy that only subordinated and recolonized indigenous peoples.[79] Reconceptualizing class, as García Linera does, opens up the possibility of thinking of class in relational terms, not just between capital and proletariat but also between those who have political/economic/cultural capital and those who do not. Additionally, this notion of class is understood as a process that is always in construction and is formed through social struggle. García Linera argues that the concept of struggle precedes that of classes. He notes: "it is because there are struggles between social subjects that classes later develop, it is not a coincidence that in the *Communist Manifesto* Marx first talks of class struggle and only later of the classes that form part of the struggle."[80] Thus, due to the particular history of Bolivia, social classes have been constructed alongside and through indigenous ethnic identity, "social classes have been built ethnically, or, if you prefer, there is an ethnic dimension of social class."[81]

This stretching of the category of class allows García Linera to redefine the historical subject of revolutionary hegemonic change after the downfall of revolutionary nationalism and the "State of '52," with the onset of neoliberalism in the mid-1980s.[82] Whereas Bolivia's mining proletariat was to be the vanguard in the country's subaltern counter-hegemonic class alliance during the twentieth century, after the rise of neoliberalism and its disorganization and fragmentation of state-capitalist schemes of work, Bolivia's subaltern classes would henceforth congeal in various ways depending on the specific conjuncture. The economic and political importance of mining and miners' union activity has waned, and therefore the mining proletariat is no longer seen as the central driving social force of history. Instead, what has taken its place is a flexible form of organized resistance that coalesces around various struggles without an exclusive hegemonic leader. This new historical subject is what García Linera calls "the multitude," which he defines as "a bloc of collective action where organized autonomous structures of the subaltern classes articulate around discursive and symbolic constructions of hegemony that vary depending on their origin between distinct segments of the subaltern classes."[83] Unlike the more traditional union, whose form of organization is based around the workplace, the multitude lacks an explicitly defined and concentrated leadership. "At some moments the leadership of the movement is made up of coca producers, in the next moment the leadership is placed in the Aymaras, the campesinos, and in the following moment it moves to the artisans of the cities or peripheries, and in another moment it can move toward other sectors. There does not exist a [predefined] center of collective action, any group can form the center, depending on the circumstances."[84] In a sense, the multitude form is associated with the rise of and theoretical discussion around "new social movements," and was most clearly put into practice through the Coordinadora por la Defensa del Agua y de la Vida (Coordinator for the Defense of Water and Life), the central hub of organizing efforts during the Water War in 2000 in the city of Cochabamba.[85] However, where many theorists have argued that these new social movements did not aim at the conquest of state power, for García Linera the multitude has "an organizing force that is capable of putting in doubt the relevance of the existing systems of governance, the liberal democratic regime, and erecting, as of now provisionally, alternative systems of the exercise of political power and of legitimate democratic life."[86] Yet, despite this capability of challenging the contemporary order, the neoliberal policies of that same order have constituted the multitude in such a way that it lacks a permanent organizational and material structure and is a regional rather than national phenomenon. Nevertheless, the multitude has become the new revolutionary historical subject, at once an entity borne out of Bolivia's neoliberal regime and at the same time its gravedigger.

García Linera's conceptualization of class moves us away from an orthodox and economistic vision and opens up space to think about the multitude as the organized expression of contemporary Bolivia's motley society in relation to its traditionally monocultural and monocivilizational state. The question we must now ask, then, is how a multitudinous nation transforms or becomes the state. Or, in other words, how does *lo multitud abigarrado* transform the state-society nexus in order to construct a hegemony in its image? As García Linera's theoretical production has increasingly turned to the state, his answer to this question has oscillated between an idea of hegemony of difference and one of hegemony over difference.[87]

García Linera's early writings on revolutionary transformation are clearly inspired by Gramsci and his strategic notion of the war of position. He argues,

> The social revolution is not, then, an attack that exterminates bourgeois families, nor is it much less an administrative measure in which a little boss [*jefecillo*] dictates a decree of "socialization." It is a practical, historical movement, over an extended period of time, where labor is breaking down and eroding the social relations of force in the economy, politics, culture, and technology that sustain capital, long before the political overthrow of the bourgeoisie. . . . This revolutionary process is a historical process that takes decades and that begins long before the open, national fight over the monopoly of physical and symbolic violence of the State.[88]

García Linera then adds:

> The social revolution is not a putsch by a risky vanguard, nor is it a *golpe de estado* [coup d'état] that overthrows the bad functionaries of state power for others that are more selfless, committed to or educated in the "program"; it is a long process of social, economic, political, and cultural self-determination that initiates itself in each center of labor, in an isolated manner in various regions and countries, and it is capable of materially interconnecting practices, attitudes, and actions to create a practical sense of labor totalization that will positively overcome the totalization of capital.[89]

In these passages, we notice an utter lack of attention to the role of the state in the process of revolutionary transformation. "Gramsci was correct," García Linera states, "that before there can be electoral victories in the political sphere there must be cultural victories, ideological victories. There must be a displacement of the old 'common sense' and an irradiation of the new vision of the world. Only when all of these important battles are won can there be a transformation in the field of politics."[90] However, over time he increasingly turns his attention to the state and its role in social revolutionary transformation, as the 2000–2005 period of insurrection begins to overturn the common sense of neoliberalism in place since the mid-1980s. This focus on the state perhaps becomes even more central after he enters the government as Evo Morales's vice president. In "The State in Transition: Power Bloc and Point of Bifurcation," García Linera not only lays out his conceptualization of the state but also schematizes the process of its transition "from one structure of political domination and legitimation to another one."[91] The state is formulated as (1) the political correlation of social forces, (2) an institution, and (3) a general idea of collective belief. Drawing on both Zavaleta's and Gramsci's versions of the integral state while also incorporating Nicos Poulantzas's idea that the state is the material condensation of the relationship of social forces, García Linera challenges both the instrumentalist definition of the state as a fully autonomous entity separated from society and the orthodox Marxist idea of the state as simply the determined political reflection of the dominant economic class.[92] Here, the state is understood as the synthesis of the material and ideological struggles being waged in society, which are expressed in the institutional matter of the state, that is, "where ideas materialize and have a general social effect."[93]

Importantly, while García Linera's definition of the state does not necessarily imply a politics of hegemony, his theory of state transition is situated squarely within the theory of hegemony and its attendant strategy of hegemonic change. According to García Linera, when the three dimensions of the state undergo processes of transformation in form and content, we witness a multistage period of state crisis.[94] Through this schematic process, García Linera theorizes a model of social revolution based on the hegemonic struggle over the state. It is a struggle that divides society between two antagonistic political projects and visions of the future, beginning with the deterioration of an existing hegemonic order and the rise of a unified, challenging counterhegemonic power bloc. If these two blocs are roughly equal in material and symbolic power and neither is able to incorporate the other into its own project, the struggle can last for an extended period of time in a catastrophic deadlock, or what Gramsci calls an "equilibrium with catastrophic consequences."[95] However, the struggle ultimately resolves itself through the point of bifurcation, where "the direct confrontation of the material, symbolic, and economic forces [are] in conflict, without any mediating influences."[96] This is the moment when either the counterhegemonic bloc withdraws its challenge or the old power bloc accepts its defeat and the triumphant power begins to "reconstruct an order that reestablishes the state structures of political domination, leadership, and administration."[97] Similar to the thesis of dual power, García Linera conceptualizes society as ultimately being directed by a singular, unified hegemonic bloc, one that incorporates and encompasses all its sectors.

Elsewhere García Linera adds an additional phase of "creative tensions" to the revolutionary process, tensions that occur not between antagonistic and irreconcilable power blocs, as was the case during the period of state crisis (which was ultimately overcome through the construction of hegemony), but rather within the dominant power bloc itself after the point of bifurcation, which he labels as the "Jacobin moment of the revolution."[98] Of the five dialectical tensions he observes, perhaps the most important one for our purposes is the need to expand the hegemonic bloc by increasingly incorporating social sectors like the bourgeoisie that remain outside of the revolutionary alliance while making sure that the popular, indigenous, and peasant sectors maintain their vanguard position. "In all hegemonic formations," García Linera argues, "there is a nucleus, a bloc, that is capable of presenting their ideas and interests as universal. In its capacity of creating the universal, the hegemonic bloc articulates, gathers, and leads other social groups and convinces them that its interests are in fact the universal interests of society."[99] Thus, in order to expand the hegemonic order and truly universalize its ideas and interests, the bloc must incorporate the adversarial social forces. But, those adversaries should not be articulated and combined with the dominant bloc as organized and unified groups; rather, this must be done in a fragmented, dispersed, and defeated fashion.[100] Here we again see similarities with Gramsci's strategy for hegemony, where, discussing the absorption of allied and antagonistic groups by the ruling class, he states, "political leadership becomes merely an aspect of the function of domination, in as much as the absorption of the enemies' *élites* means their decapitation and annihilation."[101] For García Linera, the creative tensions internal to the now-dominant national popular hegemonic bloc serve as the transformative impulse to move forward and continually develop the revolutionary process in Hegelian fashion, with contradictions resolved and overcome through a synthesizing dialectic. However, there can be no doubt that the ultimate outcome is in the (universal) interest of the dominant and leading hegemonic power bloc in society. Put simply, García Linera's strategic definition of hegemony is *convencer, derrotar, incorporar*.[102] By this, he means one has to *convince* groups throughout society of one's political project in the process of constructing a counterhegemonic power bloc; *defeat* one's organized enemies in the antagonistic struggle for economic, cultural, ideological, and political power; and, finally, *incorporate* these others into the hegemonic power bloc not as organized social groups but in disarticulated fashion to expand the social composition of the new hegemonic order.

HEGEMONY, THE NATION-STATE, AND TOTALITY

So, what should we take away from this extended analysis of hegemony? There can be little doubt that the theory of hegemony as developed by Gramsci has proved to be extremely useful both as an analytic tool for social, political, and cultural analysis, and as the foundation of a political strategy and practice seeking social transformation. It is also undoubtedly true that Evo Morales, García Linera, and the MAS implemented or initiated a number of important economic, political, and cultural transformations during their time in power that have been beneficial for large numbers of previously excluded citizens, all inspired by a vision of hegemony and hegemonic change. Without disregarding the continued reliance on extractivism, the continuities in Bolivia's position in the global capitalist economy, and the fact that the rhetoric of the *proceso de cambio* (process of change) has never really matched its reality, the MAS project is certainly not a continuation of the status quo ante. The image of the future is at least inspired by a decolonial and communist outlook, even if that future horizon has been put off for the foreseeable future.[103]

Nevertheless, in this book I try to lay out how the government's image of Bolivia and its future is structured by the theory of hegemony, which has specific consequences for the manner and depth of change. First, despite the fact that hegemony, by definition, is always contested and never complete, the ultimate goal of any hegemonic project is to at least attempt to control if not negate social antagonism through the creation of a sutured social totality.[104] Hegemony, therefore, can be seen as an attempt to foreclose difference and heterogeneity in any particular social formation by a dominant group working in its own interests. As Richard Howson and Kylie M. Smith contend, "in hegemony, things do not always remain in a state of constant conflict and unresolved antagonism; rather, it is a process whereby the goal is to achieve the highest synthesis."[105]

Second, hegemony as a practice of politics is fundamentally tied up with the idea of the nation-state form and its attendant structures of centralized power and hierarchical domination. As Jon Beasley-Murray states, "the logic of hegemony simply identifies with the [nation-]state by taking it for granted."[106] In this way, hegemony is nation-state-centric, and its reproduction thus implies the nation-state's reproduction, albeit with the possibility of different content, although not form. But, as will be laid out in the following chapter, the nation-state is founded on a number of illusions that ultimately limit its epistemological and ontological utility and power. This does not mean that the nation-state has ceased to exist or no longer plays an influential role in politics. Rather, it is to raise the possibility that if the reality and power of the nation-state (not to say its very real material power) are illusory, then the theory of hegemony limits our understanding of social reality within the confines of those illusions.[107]

Third, the struggle for hegemony is a struggle over an existing set of cultural, economic, and political ideas and institutions, where two contending power blocs essentially mirror each other in basic outline and form, if not content, in their efforts to control those already existing apparatuses. In a sense, then, winning hegemony requires those subaltern classes and groups contesting the dominant order to become essentially like that which is already hegemonic. As Beasley-Murray argues, "there is no counterhegemony, opposed to hegemony; it is but another version of hegemony."[108] This raises questions around the possibility of thinking of and constructing alternative cultural, political, and economic forms within the limits of hegemony.

Finally, hegemony is singular in the sense that it envisions the leadership and direction of states and societies under a single, unified ideological and material image of the world. Hegemony, in its bourgeois or national popular form, is an attempt to form a universal will that either consensually incorporates or coercively eradicates understandings, interests, and knowledges that lie outside of that so-called universal construction. The modern state plays a fundamental role in this process, as Philip Corrigan and Derek Sayer note:

> Out of the vast range of human social capacities—possible ways in which social life could be lived—state activities more or less forcibly "encourage" some whilst suppressing, marginalizing, eroding, undermining others. Schooling for instance comes to stand for education, policing for order, voting for political participation. Fundamental social classifications, like age and gender, are enshrined in law, embedded in institutions, routinized in administrative procedures and symbolized in rituals of the state. Certain forms of activity are given the official seal of approval, others are situated beyond the pale. This has cumulative, and enormous, cultural consequences for how people identify . . . themselves and their "place" in the world.[109]

More than just offering a general outline of the theory of hegemony, in this chapter I have attempted to tease out a number of foundational assumptions undergirding that theory in order to raise serious questions about hegemony and its attendant form of politics. However, this is not to argue that "there is no hegemony and never has been," as does Beasley-Murray.[110] I do not mean to contend that the theory of hegemony does not help us understand political, economic, social, and cultural stasis or change, or that the struggle for hegemony fails to provide a persuasive strategy for upending any particular dominant system. My claims are more modest. I seek to show how the theory of hegemony is informed by and based on a particular vision and logic of politics and, as will be laid out in the next chapter, how the theory of plurinationality is informed by and based on a different vision and logic. More specifically, as we move into the empirical moments analyzed in later chapters, these different logics provide an interpretive framework for understanding some of the most important tensions and contradictions within contemporary Bolivia. With these factors in mind, I now turn to conceptualizing the theory of plurinationality. Despite the fact that proponents of plurinationality sometimes understand the history and social formation of Bolivia in ways similar to those struggling for hegemony, the idea of plurinationality represents a contending vision of the future state and society.

2

ARTICULATING PLURINATIONALITY

Social Asynchrony and Political Form

The idea of plurinationality emerges where the construction of a modern nation-state has not been completed.
—LUIS TAPIA

We're loosening the grip of outmoded methods and ideas in order to allow new ways of being and acting to emerge, but we're not totally abandoning the old—we're building on it. . . . Years ago we struggled with the recognition of difference within the context of commonality. Today we grapple with the recognition of commonality within the context of difference.
—GLORIA ANZALDÚA

A number of scholars, more or less assuming the hegemonic form of politics to be politics in general, have argued that Bolivia is undergoing a "passive revolution" as there has not been a complete break with capitalism and the colonial past since Evo Morales and the Movimiento al Socialismo (MAS, Movement Toward Socialism) came to power.[1] Conceptualized by Antonio Gramsci, passive revolution denotes "the constant reorganization of state power and its relationship to society to preserve control by the few over the many, and maintain a traditional lack of real control by the mass of the population over the political and economic realms."[2] According to Jeffery R. Webber, the process of passive revolution includes changes in relation to the preceding period, but these changes are "limited to such a degree that the fundamental underlying relations of domination in society persist, even if their political expressions have been altered."[3] Despite the fact that those in control of the state apparatus may have changed with the MAS, little structural change has actually taken place and any talk of radical transformation is unfounded. In fact, this position holds, rather than some type of plurinational turn, we have really witnessed the restoration of the neocolonial liberal nation-state.[4] There is much to be admired in shedding light on the structural continuities of the Morales era, yet this position fails to account for the many important changes occurring within the cracks of those continuities.

From a somewhat more optimistic perspective, others have argued that a plurinational transformation is indeed underway, although a variety of "creative tensions" remain that need to be worked through.[5] Bolivia is still in the midst of a large-scale, long-term process of change, and these beginning stages have only produced the beginnings of a new plurinational state, what Fernando Mayorga terms the *construcción minimalista del estado plurinacional* (minimal structure of a plurinational state form).[6] I identified certain elements of this view during my fieldwork, but this perspective does not adequately explain in theoretical terms how and why a plurinational state remains only a horizon.

While there was a lack of fundamental structural transformation in Bolivia during the Morales years, a number of important changes were carried out that have had profound impacts. Yet, recognizing both the changes and continuities of the Morales years does little to help us understand and theoretically interpret the tensions and contradictions between these positions. Instead of analyzing the contradictions of the contemporary conjuncture in terms of a passive revolution or as a long-term process of change still in its infancy, I interpret the Morales years as an unfolding divergence of contradictory emancipatory projects founded on the logics of hegemony and plurinationality. The logic of hegemony opens up certain possibilities for political, economic, and cultural change, while also foreclosing others. A hegemonic politics allows for certain transformative demands to become reality, as long as they can be contained within the horizon of the ostensibly homogenous nation-state. Yet, the logic and practice of hegemony falter when demands for radical transformation question the nation-state form. The inability of a hegemonic politics to adequately envision a horizon beyond the nation-state begs a better interpretation of the Morales years.

In the previous chapter I provided a genealogy of hegemony that sketched a theoretical line from the work of Antonio Gramsci through

René Zavaleta Mercado to Álvaro García Linera in order to illuminate the underlying political logic that served as official doctrine for Morales and the MAS. In this chapter I lay out an alternative theory of politics and social change, best conceptualized through the notion of plurinationality, which serves as a counterpoint to hegemony. Whereas hegemony applies the dialectic rather than expressing it, plurinationality is a mode of social action that embodies the dialectic rather than merely employing it.

Plurinationality has a much shorter history than does the concept of hegemony and, as a theoretical concept, is still in the process of construction; its definition is still very much open and contested. Thus, rather than presenting a genealogy as I did with hegemony, I envision this chapter as part of an ongoing collective act of conceptual development. By contrasting plurinationality with hegemony, I am, at least in part, defining this concept through contrast, distinguishing it through what it is not. At the same time, I also seek to conceptualize plurinationality in a generative sense as producing something new. Plurinationality, therefore, should be understood in both descriptive and prescriptive terms. On the one hand, it describes the failure of "modernity" in Bolivia, understood as the homogenization of society through the general process of universalized abstract labor and the implementation of capitalist forms of value under the political structure of the nation-state form. On the other hand, it is prescriptive in the sense that it is a positive project put forward by a variety of social groups in Bolivian society as a new horizon of intersubjectivity, value, and political form.

THE SOCIAL CONDITION OF PLURINATIONALITY

Throughout the North Atlantic, plurinationality has been used by scholars to analyze the correlation of national identity with the state, to investigate the political identity of national minorities, to examine how democracy functions in contexts of national pluralism, and to rethink the notion of national sovereignty in places such as Spain, Canada, the United Kingdom, and Belgium.[7] In this context, plurinationality has been defined as "the coexistence within a political order of more than one national identity. . . . Under plurinationalism, more than one national identity can pertain to a single group or even an individual, opening up the possibility of multiple nationalities which in turn may be nested or may overlap in less tidy ways."[8] The idea of plurinationality, it is argued, captures the more fluid and heterogeneous complexity of nationality and political order in the modern world, where the old models of state-hood based on a uniform order, whether federal or unitary, are no longer satisfactory.[9]

According to Miquel Caminal, the idea of plurinationality helps illu-minate three central illusions of the contemporary nation-state.[10] First is the notion of absolute and indivisible sovereignty. Although the holder of sovereignty has changed over time (e.g., monarch, parliament, peo-ple), the idea of indivisible sovereignty bounded by the nation-state form has remained. The second fallacy is the equivalence between state and nation, which assumes that behind every sovereign state there is also a nation. Contrastingly, when a nation is not a state it must therefore assert its right to be recognized as such. According to Caminal, as long as the idea that there must be a correspondence and equivalence between state and nation continues to exist, a vicious cycle of nationalisms in per-manent confrontation will also continue to exist.[11] Caminal quotes Lord Acton to highlight this point:

> The greatest adversary of the rights of nationality is the modern theory of nationality. By making the State and the nation commensurate with each other in theory, it reduces practically to a subject condition all other nation-alities that may be within the boundary. It cannot admit them to an equality with the ruling nation which constitutes the State, because the State would then cease to be national, which would be a contradiction of the principle of its existence. According, therefore, to the degree of humanity and civili-zation in that dominant body which claims all the rights of the community, the inferior races are exterminated, or reduced to servitude, or outlawed, or put in a condition of dependence.[12]

Thus, the illusion of a correspondence between state and nation hides the reality of a mononational state sitting atop a plurinational society. It is in this sense, according to Caminal, that "the contrast between the *political nation-state* and other nations, as *cultural nations* and members of the political nation, is incorrect, discriminatory and exclusive."[13] Relatedly, the third and final fallacy that Caminal illuminates is the cultural uniformity of the modern state. The history of the modern state is characterized by "the construction of a uniformity, of a monocultural *us*, in which diversity has been rejected and persecuted through the repression, expulsion or assimilation of those who are different."[14] Caminal correctly highlights how plurinationality challenges this monoculturalism by raising the issue of alterity, of those who practice their right to be different and to be recognized as such.

While the above scholars are correct to highlight the problematic of nation-state sovereignty, the false equivalence between the state and nation, and the deleterious effects of monoculturalism, they come to this conclusion based on the argument that globalization has exposed the deficiencies of our traditional understanding of states.[15] They also claim that due to the "complexity of advanced modern societies" the most relevant debates over plurality and difference occur "in those liberal societies where a number of the conditions for material well-being have been met for a large majority of the population."[16] Whether or not we agree with these assertions, the desire to acknowledge, understand, and sustain the plural nature of societies is certainly not a new phenomenon, nor is it one that is most pronounced in developed, modern societies. Clifford Geertz, for instance, drew our attention to the difficulties facing the newly emerging postcolonial states during the mid-twentieth century, as they tried to structure a new political order on top of the "multiplicity of communalisms" that made up those societies, a process he labeled "integrative revolution."[17] In Latin America, the potentiality of plurinationality derives not so much from globalization, although this too has been important, but rather from the fact that the ideal of sovereignty in its traditional sense as applying solely to the national state has justified an ongoing violent historical process of sociocultural homogenization on the road toward capitalist modernization and bureaucratic state formation.[18] As noted in one of the epigraphs to this chapter, the demand for plurinationality emerges from the partial openings of an incomplete nation-state project.

Much of the above discussion of plurinationality also tends to focus on the rights of minority populations in a multinational context, along with the granting of political rights to these groups. Without a doubt, the gaining of rights is an important aspect of plurinationalism, as can be seen through the expansion of rights-based language in the constitutions of those countries that have officially renamed themselves as plurinational states, such as Ecuador and Bolivia. Yet, plurinationality symbolizes a much deeper transformation of society than the conferring of minority rights. It is about the ability of different modes of economic and social production, models of political decision-making and organization, and distinct cultural forms—that is, various ways of being—to exist and reproduce themselves *as themselves* and of their own accord.

In Latin America, the concept of plurinationality attempts to theorize the heterogenous social composition of the region in ways similar to previous ideas such as *mestizaje*, hybridity, and transculturation. The notion of *mestizaje* was developed in response to the colonial Spanish caste system, based on blood purity, in order to promote mestizo national identities during the postindependence republican era. Despite the underlying idea of ethnoracial differentiation and miscegenation as the reality of Latin American identity, the language of *mestizaje* often masked a reality of racist exclusion through the promotion of national homogenization. *Mestizaje*'s syncretic lore has been in fact a pretext to marginalize indigeneity and blackness through the valuation of whiteness.[19] The ideas of hybridity and transculturation depart from the biological and essentialist discourses of *mestizaje* and center on the constructedness of culture and the syntheses resulting from cross-cultural contact and exchange. Transculturation, a term coined by Fernando Ortiz, challenges the notion of acculturation by highlighting the complex processes of cultural exchange as always bidirectional.[20] For Ortiz, when cultures come into contact, each inevitably influences the other in complex ways. As Bronislaw Malinowski writes in his introduction to Ortiz's *Cuban Counterpoint*, every exchange of culture "is a process in which something is always given in return for what one receives, a system of give and take. It is a process in which both parts of the equation are modified, a process from which a new reality emerges, transformed and complex, a reality that is not a mechanical agglomeration of traits, nor even a mosaic, but a new phenomenon, original and independent."[21] This contrapuntal vision of cultural contact draws attention to the counterhegemonic potential of secondary cultures in an uneven relation of power, and to their ability to alter the configuration of cultural exchange in ways that challenge the unidirectional understanding of cultural assimilation. Hybridity, like transculturation, according to Néstor García Canclini, is a sociocultural fusion, a process in which discrete, autonomous entities or practices are combined to generate new entities and practices. Processes of hybridization, García Canclini notes, are "socio-cultural processes in which discrete structures or practices, previously existing in separate form, are combined to generate new structures, objects, and practices."[22] In their own ways, both transculturation and hybridity emphasize the fusion of cultures as new homogenized forms are constructed. As such, the logic of hegemony is embedded in all these conceptualizations and interpretations of Latin America's varied social formations. With *mestizaje*, it is assumed that the historical plurality and illegibility of Latin American societies are obstacles to the creation of modern nation-states and homogenous national subjectivities. Differentiation is central to the analysis of hybridity and transculturation but is ultimately surmounted through a synthesis of contrasting elements into something new, a fusion of tradition and modernity that becomes *the* cultural form. Plurinationality is related to this network of concepts and grapples with similar issues but in such a way that does not essentialize race/ethnicity, nor fetishize the moment of dialectical synthesis. Rather than the converging of distinct parts into a new homogenous and coherent whole, plurinationality maintains the dialectical relation of autonomous and distinct cultural entities in creative tension with one another.

Throughout Latin American, the concept has been most influential in Bolivia and Ecuador. In Ecuador, for example, the idea of plurinationality has evolved over time but was founded on the system of social classification established during colonialism, which placed indigenous peoples, enslaved Africans, and their descendants at the lower rungs of society while white Europeans and mestizos maintained a superior social position.[23] According to Catherine Walsh, "this use of the idea of race as a permanent and conflictive matrix of power was central to the 'civilizing' domination of some peoples over others . . . [and] it assumed racial whitening as an index of 'progress,' and *mestizaje*—or racial mixing toward whiteness—as the national discourse of power."[24] This process of racialization and its associated structure of power are fundamental in understanding the contemporary state and society, and their interrelations. When a state and society are constructed according to the interests and culture of the dominant social group, the idea of a *national* state and society is an illusion, nothing more than a set of institutions that represent, reflect, and privilege this dominant group's cultural traits and interests. For Walsh, it is this noncorrespondence between nation-state form and social content that plurinationalism seeks to address. "The Ecuadorian nation," she argues, "continues to be obviated within the model of state and society conceived from uniformity." But, "the idea of the plurinational finds its primal sustenance in the literally plural character of the national . . . in those ancestral differences that continue to organize the ways of living, including the relationships with territory and nature, the exercise of authority, and the practices of law, education, health and of life itself."[25] In order to construct plurinationality, a refounding of the state is necessary, which implies a profound transformation of the state-society relationship. "Such a refounding," Walsh contends, "must not simply add diversity to the established structures (as the neoliberal Ecuadorian reform of 1998 did), but has to rethink those structures plurally and interculturally, thus encouraging politics of convergence, of conviviality, of complementarity and of a new and different form of unity."[26] In other words, it is not enough to simply alter the social composition of those who control the institutions of the nation-state. Rather, a new set of institutional structures is also necessary to both reflect and cultivate different logics of political relationality.

Similar thoughts are expressed by the prominent Confederación de las Nacionalidades Indígenas del Ecuador (CONAIE, Confederation of the National Indigenous Peoples of Ecuador), which has demanded a plurinational state since 1990. CONAIE argues that plurinationality cannot simply be implemented through a formal constitutional declaration, but rather must fundamentally transform the structure of both the state and the economy. The creation of plurinationality is part of a decolonial process that would recognize the country in its diversity and replace the "colonial State" and its monocultural organization of things with a "plurality of democratic mechanisms," including participatory, representative, and communitarian forms.[27] "It is no longer acceptable to continue assuming that there only exists one model of representation and legitimate participation. The indigenous peoples and nations of Ecuador have alternative practices to offer for the social control of the State and economy and forms of direct, collective, and organized political participation."[28]

Perhaps most importantly for CONAIE, plurinationality in Ecuador must be based on a structure of self-determination and self-governance of the country's indigenous peoples and nations. Plurinationality "promotes social and political equality, economic justice, the recognition of society's interculturality, and the right of indigenous nations and peoples to territorial control and communitarian government inside the unified State."[29] Plurinational forms of indigenous self-governance, to be clear, do not imply the fragmentation or balkanization of the state, or the isolation or enclosure of indigenous communities. Rather, they involve the political reflection of indigenous nations and the operation of their self-determination and self-governance as a condition for decolonization and the construction of interculturality and equality between the various cultures of the country.[30] The recognition of indigenous self-governance acknowledges the right of indigenous peoples to their own forms of political authority and is a form of social power, "an expression of the sovereignty of society that can and should control the administration of the State."[31] A fundamental aspect of indigenous self-governance is that indigenous communities should be incorporated into the system of state decision-making with respect to issues of natural resource extraction, particularly oil.[32] What this means in practice is the implementation of a process of "prior and informed consent" of all affected communities, *before* any form of exploration or extraction.[33] This clearly means not the end to all extractive practices, but only the inclusion of communities directly affected by these activities—which have historically contaminated the natural environment and sickened local populations—in the political decision-making process around resource extraction.

THE CONCEPTUAL ROOTS OF PLURINATIONALITY IN BOLIVIA

In Bolivia the earliest mention of plurinationality comes in 1978 from the Movimiento Indio Túpac Katari (MITKA, Túpac Katari Indian Movement), an Indianist political party that developed from the Katarista movement, which called for a new Bolivian formation, one "based on the confederation of its nations that freely and voluntarily form a Plurinational and Pluricultural State."[34] A few years later, at its 1983 national convention, the Confederación Sindical Única de Trabajadores Campesinos de Bolivia (CSUTCB, Unified Syndical Confederation of Rural Workers of Bolivia) argued that "there cannot be a true liberation if the plurinational diversity of our country and the diverse forms of self-governance of our peoples are not respected."[35] Borne of the country's colonial and neocolonial historical context, the idea of plurinationality is thus founded on the recognition and maintenance of the different cultures, economies, politics, subjectivities, and worldviews coexisting and overlapping within the geographic territory of Bolivia. It envisions the radical dispersal of power and, therefore, necessitates a fundamental transformation of the liberal nation-state.[36] Plurinationality, according to Consuelo Sanchez, requires "a radical break with liberalism . . . and questions the total structure of the nation-state and the liberal principles that sustain it."[37] Through the identification of indigenous peoples as collective political subjects, this alternative political form "transcends the liberal and monocultural State based on the individual citizen."[38] The historical failure of the modern state to fully incorporate indigenous Bolivians as citizens with equal prospects for the material and cultural reproduction of their communal lives is what has brought forward the demands to refound Bolivia along plurinational lines.[39] In this sense, "the plurinational horizon represents the possibility of democratically reconstituting the country, which would at the same time overcome the hierarchical relations between different peoples and cultures, that is, internal colonialism."[40]

In *El horizonte plurinacional* (The plurinational horizon), Luis Tapia contends that plurinationality conceptualizes a multiplicity of heterogeneous political spaces that, nevertheless, articulate with and complement one another, each forming part of the same political regime.[41] This plurality not only entails the existence of various groups that speak different languages, maintain different cultures, and practice particular spiritual traditions, but also includes these groups' distinct political structures of authority and economic forms. "In these conditions, plurinationality implies the mutual recognition of different cultures that come together to create a new form of political unity."[42] Yet, the notion of political unity here does not imply unity in the sense of a single, universal practice of politics. According to Pablo Mamani Ramírez, unity in this context is "not understood in the classic sense of the term, where one group, whether because of the Leviathan (that is, war) or others, imposes itself on others, as if this one group represented everyone." Rather, the idea of unity applied here refers to the state as a cultural, political, territorial, and economic construction—that is, a social correlation at a specific time and place in the world. The operation of unity within plurality refers to how the "nations, peoples, and actors articulate together in horizontal and open ways, in a manner where all groups respect one another."[43] However, the demand for plurinationality arose not simply as an inherent trait of Bolivia's indigenous peoples. The idea of plurinationality—along with what it means, what it challenges, and what it seeks to change—must be understood in relation to its historical and cultural context.

For Tapia, the struggle for plurinationality responds to a dual process of nation-making that has occurred in Bolivia since at least the 1970s. He argues that the process of national identification associated with the political organization of the state (i.e., the nation-state) was intended to correspond to the expansion of capitalist modernity throughout the country. The expansion of capitalism, it was thought, would transform the countryside not only technologically but also sociologically and culturally through the development of the capitalist social class structure. In order for this to actually take hold, Tapia argues, the process needed to be inclusive, which implied some form of redistribution of wealth and political power.[44] However, the historical construction of the nation-state in Bolivia "has been an extremely weak and contradictory form of unification, that is to say, it has been a process of political inclusion founded on the colonial characteristics of exploitation of and discrimination against the indigenous peoples and cultures."[45] In the process of defining and organizing the new nation-state-society matrix, the social relations of power and production remained firmly within what Anibal Quijano has conceptualized as the coloniality of power.[46] That is, when dealing with the so-called national question, constructing a homogenized Bolivian nation was to be achieved not through the fundamental expansion and democratization of social and political relations, but by the continued exclusion or limited cultural recognition of indigenous peoples.[47] In this sense, Tapia argues, "the history of the country demonstrates that the form of political unification that the Bolivian nation has experienced is really better understood as a form of national and social disarticulation and disintegration."[48]

While the project to construct a Bolivian nation-state was fragmenting, other processes of national construction were making headway among Bolivia's various ethnic groups, which Tapia labels "communitarian nations."[49] These communitarian nations are at the heart of the plurinational project. In an attempt to democratize the social and political relations of power, over the last few decades alternative processes of national formation (perhaps better understood as the political reconstitution of some peoples as nations) throughout Bolivia's indigenous populations have resulted in new demands to transform or "refound" the Bolivian nation and state. In other words, the idea of the nation, which has typically been used to theorize the cultural and political homogenization of members of a state, is today being used in Bolivia to rethink the plurality of different cultures internal to the country. The process of transforming the state would therefore require "not just the inclusion of indigenous people as individuals but also the incorporation of their forms of political action in the new governing structure of the country, in the mode of a plurinational state."[50] Plurinationality, then, is not only a question of reorganizing the state in order to incorporate other forms of political practice and authority; it also depends on constructing a new understanding of Bolivia as a nation. "In this sense," Tapia argues, "it is not only a question of transforming the state . . . above all, a substantive reform within what may be called the Bolivian nation is needed that would make possible a transformation of the relations between peoples and cultures."[51]

The most important indigenous social movements in the country pushing for plurinationality came together in the early 2000s to form the Pacto de Unidad (Unity Pact). In their proposal to the Constituent Assembly in 2006, they stated that plurinationality is "a model of political organization for the decolonization of our nations and peoples that reaffirms, recuperates, and strengthens our territorial autonomy in order to achieve a full life and to live well."[52] Plurinationality is "a way toward our own self-determination as nations and peoples, in order to define our communitarian politics, social systems, economies, political and legal systems, and in this way reaffirm our own structures of governance, election of authorities, and administration of justice, all with respect for their different ways of life and their use of space and territory."[53] In addition, they state that the concept is based on the fundamental principles of "juridical pluralism, unity, complementarity, reciprocity, equality, solidarity, and the moral and ethical principle of ending all forms of corruption."[54] Thus, we can see that for the indigenous and peasant movements who originally developed the idea of plurinationality, it fundamentally represents a path of decolonization and self-determination for those groups who have borne the brunt of historically institutionalized inequality and systemic discrimination. Additionally, the principles of reciprocity, complementarity, equality, and solidarity are key to understanding the interrelational aspect of plurinationality. Communities are not enclosed, self-sustaining entities. In order to continually produce and reproduce their forms of life, they need to form complementary and reciprocal relations with other communities and cultures. However, intercultural relations should be based on principles of respect and solidarity for each community's way of life and worldview, instead of the use of violence, subordination, exploitation, and exclusion, which the Unity Pact argues have been the predominant historical forms of intercultural exchange.

Another central feature of plurinationality is the inclusion of multiple forms of political participation. "Sovereignty resides in the people, whose collective will is the base of political authority, and should be exercised through the mechanisms of representative, participatory, communitarian, deliberative, and direct forms of democracy."[55] These mechanisms are grouped into participatory and representative forms. Practices such as referendums, plebiscites, popular recall, and communal, indigenous, and popular assemblies exemplify the former, while elections of representatives at various levels of government through the universal secret ballot as well as through *usos y costumbres* (norms and procedures) in the indigenous territories exemplify the latter. We can see that plurinationality attempts to incorporate multiple forms of political participation that ostensibly correspond to different historical temporalities, to both "modern" states and "traditional" cultures.

The final major characteristic of the plurinational state according to the Unity Pact relates to the issues of land, territory, and indigenous autonomy. While land is defined simply as property to be distributed, accessed, used, sold, and so on, the notion of territory is seen as the productive and cultural base of a community that allows for its continued reproduction and existence.[56] Therefore, without access to and control over land and territory, the idea of plurinationality as a confederation of multiple nations and cultures ceases to exist. Plurinational forms of land tenure incorporate both systems of private property and practices of collective ownership. In indigenous territories, lands are to be administered following local norms and procedures, "are collectively and communally controlled, and are nontransferrable, imprescriptible, inalienable, irreversible, indivisible, and exempt from tax."[57] Similarly, Tapia argues that collective land tenure is fundamental for plurinationality. He states that if the idea of plurinationality "is based on the cultural diversity existing in Bolivia, it can only be maintained and developed through the defense and extension of the forms of collective land tenure."[58] In relation to territory, which is meant to include subsoil resources, the Unity Pact argues that the original authorities over natural resources are the indigenous, native, and peasant nations and peoples of Bolivia. Therefore, "all extraction of both renewable and nonrenewable resources in indigenous territories is subject to processes of obligatory and prior consultation with the social organizations of the area. . . . Before any commercial exploration and/or exploitation of natural resources there should be participatory studies of the socioeconomic, environmental, and community impacts."[59] As we will see in chapter 3 on the Territorio Indígena y Parque Nacional Isiboro Sécure (TIPNIS, Isoboro Sécure Indigenous Territory and National Park) conflict, control and decision-making power over territory are a central area of conflict between plurinationality and hegemony.

Indigenous autonomy is the key characteristic of plurinationality as it encompasses all the aspects outlined above in specific territorial units. The elements that characterize indigenous autonomy are: territory; a population with a common language, culture, and history; indigenous government and administration of justice based on local norms and procedures; and control of and management over land and territory.[60] Indigenous territorial autonomies point the way toward a new form of plurinational state, the Unity Pact asserts, as they "break the vertical power structure of the contemporary State, which permits the construction of a new State 'from below.'"[61] According to Mamani, the "territorial cartography" of Bolivia—its departments, provinces, and municipalities—is based on a colonial and republican logic of spatial organization, which contrasts with the territorial logic of plurinationality. Therefore, Mamani argues, "the reconstitution of 'ancestral territories' and the redistribution of land is a central part of decolonizing the state and implementing plurinationality."[62] Thus, indigenous autonomies, despite certain limitations (which will be discussed in chapter 5 on the construction of formal *autonomías indígena originario campesina* [AIOCs, indigenous original peasant autonomies]), will play a fundamental role in territorially, institutionally, and administratively transforming the Bolivian nation-state into a plurinational state.

THE PLURINATIONAL HORIZON

Plurinationality is an attempt to conceptualize and theorize and hence understand Bolivia's *formación abigarrada* (motley social formation), to use Zavaleta's term. However, whereas for Zavaleta the plurality or motleyness of Bolivia was something to be overcome through the hegemonic articulation of a national popular identity, the idea of plurinationality contrasts with a national popular hegemony and is closer to what Raquel Gutiérrez Aguilar has termed the "communitarian popular."[63] As discussed in the previous chapter, Zavaleta's notion of the national popular can be understood as a desire to create an inclusive popular democratic national state—in other words, a hegemony created and led by the popular classes. For Gutiérrez,

> the national-popular horizon . . . [seeks to] install a series of mediations in order to establish minimally satisfactory forms of economic and political inclusion of the social heterogeneity in a comprehensive and ostensibly equal political totality. That is, if the national-popular can be understood as the general social aspiration to endow and represent itself collectively through an inclusive and democratic national State, the Bolivian struggles of 2000–2005 exceeded that horizon and tried to create different political connections that were self-regulating and new, although not exempt from difficulties, and, above all, lacking understandable and clear forms of expression and communication beyond grand radical slogans ("civil war," "refoundation of Qullasuyu," "social reappropriation of the commons," "Constituent Assembly without political party intermediation," etc.).[64]

Gutiérrez's notion of the communitarian popular, like plurinationality, attempts to go beyond the national popular perspective as it aims to rethink and experiment with the relationship between state and society through the reorganization of power and the configuration or reconstitution of the autonomous spaces where decision-making is centered locally. Political authority is based on the organization of communities themselves, where decisions surrounding the material and cultural reproduction of the community and its mode of political constitution are inseparable. In contrast to liberal representative politics, where "some govern, others are governed and, at most, periodically delegate their political voice to some authority via their votes," the communitarian popular view of politics consists of "providing the mechanisms and formats to *guarantee shared responsibility* for the totality of collective affairs."[65] According to Gutiérrez, we can see instances of the communitarian popular throughout the 2000–2005 period of upheaval as subaltern social groups in the valleys and across the *altiplano* (plateau) sought to subject decision-making over common resources to the deliberation and approval of local community authorities rather than to directives from above. This is what she labels a time of *pachakuti*.[66] These collective acts, she argues, "challenged the idea of private and/or state-owned property as the only possible options and placed the possibility of 'collective property' at the center of the political discussion, and . . . offered a radical inversion of exercising political authority, emptying the so-called 'central power' of all possibility of imposition."[67]

Elsewhere, Gutiérrez contrasts the classic revolutionary desire for hegemony and state power with the transformative desires surrounding her idea of communitarian popular struggle. National popular struggles for hegemony, she argues, have typically been theorized in terms of stability, where a previously stable and totalized society undergoes a process of social, political, and/or economic destabilization, which throws the hegemonic order into doubt and opens up space for a counterhegemonic power bloc to challenge the existing order of things.[68] Additionally, the revolutionary strategy undergirding the hegemonic struggle to take state power "consisted of building organizations that were highly internally cohesive, hierarchical, and disciplined to the point that they could organize around—and of course, direct—the set of social struggles in a particular country."[69] The ultimate goal or outcome of the hegemonic struggle from this perspective is to reach a new moment of stable totalization through the power of the state. In contrast to the above, Gutiérrez argues, "the central question [for the communitarian popular perspective] is the systematic detotalization of the existing structure, and the partial reconstruction of new realities that will be permanently detotalized, a kind of journey without end, where the future is not determined beforehand but is instead constructed piece by piece through the multilevel disputes of the here and now."[70] In other words, we need to move beyond thinking in terms of social totality and ostensible stability. Rather than attempting to re-create the impossible (a stable social totality in the context of a motley social formation), the point is to think of society in a context of instability and without any predetermined endpoint, which leaves the future open, and live within the contradictions of social life. "The will for transformation does not have to express itself in a new *totality*," Gutiérrez claims, "it requires strengthening the expression, the visibilization, and repeatedly bringing to light that which is *particular*."[71]

However, Gutiérrez's concept of the communitarian popular only goes so far in its correspondence with plurinationality. As Gutiérrez makes clear throughout her work, the communitarian popular is necessarily an antistatist perspective. "To this day, no government, be it progressive or revolutionary, has been concerned with the question of how to dissolve the structures of power—that is, allowing 'self-government,' admitting plurality, and enabling conditions for the self-regulation of society," Gutiérrez asserts.[72] As such, "the central problematic of the communitarian-popular horizon is not about—nor do I think it can be— the reconstitution of any type of state."[73] Plurinationality, on the other hand, is not antistatist *in general*, but is rather against a *particular* conceptualization and form of the state: the liberal nation-state, where the ideal of a unified nation corresponds to a sovereign state. Jorge Viaña, for instance, argues that plurinationalism refers to "a State configured by forms of direct democracy and self-representation," and should be "understood as a type of State that destructures the classic form of liberal politics and its 'State form.'"[74] If the state in its general form is understood to refer merely to the administration of social and political life through an institutional structure, there is no inherent reason the state must lead to the continued domination of some over others. We can see this in the not necessarily codified but highly institutionalized structures of communal political authority and regulation that exist in communities throughout Bolivia.[75] While these structures occasionally exist in an antagonistic position with the official state apparatus, they just as often articulate with the changing configuration of the national Bolivian state.[76] These communal structures in fact form the very foundation of the plurinational state.

Plurinationality also offers us a new conception of revolutionary social change, distinct from the one proposed by the theory of hegemony. The central distinction between these two conceptions, according to Raúl Prada, is that while hegemony "is embedded in the socialist transition toward communism, it does not challenge the horizons of modernity. Contrastingly, the pluralist transition breaks with and crosses the limits of modernity and brings forth other civilizational organizing structures."[77] The plurinational state, Prada asserts, "is constructed from the perspective of indigenous worldviews as they interpellate modernity and capitalism."[78] These indigenous worldviews are dynamic interpretative systems, (re)inventing their own histories and cultures in order to critically analyze the structures and institutions of modernity, such as the state, above all in its nation-state form. However, the fact that plurinationality questions the legitimacy of modernity does not imply that indigenous worldviews, knowledges, and movements are somehow not modern, or that they wish to return to some pure, idealized space and time before the colonial conquest. Instead, as plurinationality is founded on the historical and cultural differences inscribed in Bolivia's motley social formation and the failure of the state to adequately correspond to this heterogeneity, the plurinational horizon exposes the lie of modernity. "There is not just one modernity, there are many," Prada argues, "we exist in a heterogeneity of modernities."[79] There is not just one form of the state or one idea of the nation, nor is there only one form of economic organization or a single system of knowing the world, yet we lack the analytic and conceptual tools to properly interpret this diverse reality. Plurinationality is a conceptualization of this multiplicity and a way of theorizing how different historical temporalities coexist, overlap, and interact. Plurinationality conceptualizes "a space-time involving multiple ways of being, seeing, doing, and living in the world."[80]

However, plurinationality should not be understood simply to entail various distinct and autonomous social units increasingly separated from one another. Plurinationality is not just the expression of the historical, political, and social moment of a multiplicity of singularities. It is not mere social dispersion, but rather the articulation of the various social and cultural modes of society. In other words, plurinationality is both the recognition and incorporation of various singular nationalities as well as their complex and overlapping social, political, economic, and cultural interrelations. It is a complex unity of nations, peoples, and cultures following their own practices and forms of social and economic organization, all linked within the territorial and administrative geography of Bolivia. "It is a *Wiphala* state and society," Mamani says.[81]

Yet, despite the interconnectedness and transversality of the social structure, plurinationality is not just another reworked conceptualization of *mestizaje*, hybridity, or transculturation, all of which connote the combining of discreet elements to produce a new social synthesis. Instead of requiring a synthesis, Bolivia's motley social formation is rather more like a dialectic without synthesis. In fact, it could be seen as a demonstration of the impossibility of the very idea of social synthesis.[82] As such, the idea of plurinationality draws our attention to and challenges the historically unitary character of the Bolivian nation-state and its ultimately failed attempts at socially synthesizing and culturally homogenizing society. "The nation-state has failed in Bolivia," Prada states bluntly.[83] As distinct from the nation-state form, the plurinational state envisions a correspondence with the multisocietal condition of Bolivia. Plurinationality as a conceptualization of Bolivia's motley social formation—and the plurinational state as the political expression of that concept—"does not approve the unification of the diverse, the homogenization of difference. It opens up the possibility of combining distinct forms of Organization . . . and seeks to open up those organizational structures to contingency."[84]

CONCLUSION

The argument thus far is that plurinationality offers a contrasting logic to the theory of hegemony. Plurinationality, according to Mamani, "is different in its philosophy, in its theory, and in its practice from the oligarchic monocultural forms of power and liberal institutional politics. It is an antiracist, anti-neocolonial, anti-neoliberal, and anti-oligarchic state due to the fact that it is internally constituted by different cultures, economies, [and] desires, different civilizations and their logical systems of argumentation or thought."[85] Perhaps the plurinational, like Gutiérrez's notion of emancipation, "implies choosing what is utopian, the *future*, for that which remains to be clearly formulated against and beyond the limit of what is presented as 'possible' and put forth by the inert weight of the traditional order."[86] In this sense, the plurinational state is still only a project and is not yet a fact or a reality. At present, Bolivia remains what Teófilo Choque Mamani has termed an "apparent plurinational state," a plurinational state in name only.[87]

In this chapter I have outlined the central elements of the theory of plurinationality, while also clarifying how this theory differs from and conflicts with the theory of hegemony. These are the two most significant contending visions of social change and state transformation in contemporary Bolivia, and understanding the significant ideological differences helps us interpret the real concrete social conflicts that have transpired during Bolivia's *proceso de cambio* (process of change). Rather than just struggles over resources or political or social rights, which they most certainly also are, the prominent sociocultural and politico-economic conflicts in the country today revolve around and are best understood through these two contending theories of transformation.

Plurinationality as theory and as practice is, unsurprisingly, not a completely comprehensive nor fully coherent paradigm. There are plenty of contradictions, tensions, and conflicting currents within the plurinational project. Theoretically, the discourse on plurality can oftentimes blur with much of the theorizing on neoliberal multiculturalism, which makes it difficult to distinguish between the core theoretical tenets of plurinationalism and those of liberal pluralism.[88] In terms of strategic practice, the historical subject(s) pushing the demand for plurinationality are often pushing in different directions and in conflicting ways with one another. As Fernando Mayorga points out, the construction of the so-called indigenous native peasant (*indígena originario campesino*) subject was an attempt by the diverse bodies of the Unity Pact (highland and Amazonian indigenous groups, rural peasants, and workers) to present a unified front against the state during the 2000–2005 upheavals and the 2006–8 Constituent Assembly. Although it is impossible to determine interests based simply on identity, indigenous peoples and peasants have historically struggled to improve their lot in different strategic ways and with different goals in mind. Thus, the conceptual merging of indigenous and native peoples with peasants into a single category corresponds in contradictory ways with sociological reality.[89] As such, various tensions and conflicts have arisen surrounding the interests and political strategy of the groups fused in the indigenous native peasant trinity.[90]

Yet, despite the fact that it remains a horizon, the key here is to understand the specific ways in which the idea and practice of plurinationality relate to the theory of hegemony. If we remember that a goal of hegemony is to foreclose contestation by containing difference and plurality in any particular social formation by a dominant group working in its own interests, it is clear that plurinationality differs. A central component of plurinationality is that its literally plural structure opens it up to contingency. The goal is not to construct a totalized and homogenized social system, but rather to acknowledge and foster the multiplicity and heterogeneity of the social. From this perspective, not only is it impossible to completely contain or obviate social difference, but the act of hegemonic regulation and control actually leads to increased social exclusion, exploitation, and conflict.

Additionally, if hegemony is indeed fundamentally fixed to the nation-state form and its attendant structures of centralized power and hierarchical control, as I argue, plurinationality seeks to cut the Gordian knot that has tied the idea of the nation to the administrative and territorial apparatus of a state. Plurinationality attempts to rethink the equation of the nation with the state by highlighting the multiplicity of communal nations and cultures within the territorial borders of the state. In this way, the internal relations of each communal nation are just as important as the relations between the various nations. A plurinational form of democracy cannot simply organize based on the criteria that each nation holds a unified political position and it has the space and a clear set of procedures to articulate their differences through a common government. A plurinational democracy also needs to provide the institutional space for the plurality of subjects to be visible, the different political subjects that constitute each nation.[91] And, while plurinationality does not contest the geographic integrity of the nation-state, it challenges the nation-state's form of territorial organization through, for instance, the construction of indigenous community autonomies.

Hegemony also understands the social in a totalizing fashion. It is singular in the sense that it is an attempt to form a "universal" will that either consensually incorporates or coercively obliterates understandings, interests, practices, and knowledges that lie outside of that so-called universal construction. In contrast, plurinationality is more interested in developing the particular, or in advancing the idea of the universal understood in terms of a "multiverse" of material practices, symbolic understandings, and ideological worldviews.[92]

Finally, any hegemonic struggle is essentially a conflict over control of a series of already existing material and ideological institutions. This fact situates the conflict within a more or less predefined arena of hegemony, which, in turn, forces the subaltern power bloc to become like that which is already hegemonic if it wishes to win hegemony. This presents a particularly important puzzle for the adherents of plurinationality. It is not entirely clear whether and how the theory of plurinationality can disentangle itself completely from the hegemonic form of politics it seeks to replace. Mamani, for instance, draws our attention to an apparent paradox of the plurinational transformation of the state. He notes, "the paradox is that the state wants to reform itself and was betting on a constitutional change [i.e., the Constituent Assembly] to do so, but the operators and the statist logics of routine continue to operate outside the idea of plurinationality."[93] This indicates that despite offering a new vision for the relationship between state and society, one where the plurality of institutions corresponds to the heterogeneous nature of the Bolivian social formation, the plurinational project maintains an ontological focus on the state.

To be clear, I am not arguing that hegemony is not a successful political strategy for power or that it fails to explain social reality, as some contend.[94] Nor am I arguing that plurinationality represents a pristine form of indigenous politics or a precapitalist model of social relations, somehow outside of and in opposition to Western "modernity." It would be easy to map these two theoretical positions onto the long-running debate in Latin America between class and ethnicity, or Marxism and *indigenismo*. Yet, while this debate is important, its polemics too often ground these social categories in essentialist understandings of subjectivity. Plurinationality, at least in the context of Latin America, is certainly an indigenous proposition, but it is not based on some inherent element of indigenous peoples' ethnic composition. Rather, it is a social form and political logic from a particular cultural history, a history that is always lived in relation to others. I have tried to parse the key distinctions between plurinationality and hegemony in order to build a conceptual apparatus for interpreting many of the tensions and contradictions of the Morales era in Bolivia as a conflict between these two underlying visions of political practice and social transformation.

With the theoretico-conceptual apparatus in hand, the following three chapters examine three situations where we can see how the contending visions and strategies come into conflict and play out in concrete terms. Chapter 3 analyzes the TIPNIS conflict, where the MAS sought to build a highway to connect the eastern lowlands of the country with the western valley and highland regions. However, the highway was conceived to go through a national park and indigenous territory, which has drawn condemnations and large-scale protests from indigenous movements and urban civil society across the country and caused the government to step back, at least temporarily, from the proposed highway. While the dispute is certainly related to issues of land access and resources, it is fundamentally about a project of economic development and national integration through the expansion of infrastructure. The issue of prior and informed consultation or consent regarding development projects in indigenous territory is a key element for interpreting this historical moment.

Chapter 4 analyzes one outcome of the TIPNIS dispute through an investigation of the MAS-influenced split of the highland indigenous organization CONAMAQ. The TIPNIS affair has brought a number of smaller internal conflicts within the Unity Pact to a head, forcing the indigenous organizations Confederación de Pueblos Indígenas de Bolivia (CIDOB, Confederation of Indigenous Peoples of Bolivia) and CONAMAQ to officially cut ties with the Unity Pact and the MAS. In December 2013 and January 2014, the headquarters of CONAMAQ in La Paz was a site of open struggle between two factions within the organization. The MAS sided with the progovernment wing and provided material and police support as that faction physically ousted the elected leadership, took over the office, and proclaimed a new council of authorities. Ostensibly an internal dispute over the organization's leadership positions and ideological direction, it was also a confrontation that demonstrated the ways in which social subjectivities are materially constructed.

The final empirical chapter examines the process of creating officially sanctioned indigenous autonomy (AIOCs) in the municipality of Charagua. AIOCs, officially made possible in Articles 2, 30, and 290 of the 2009 constitution and through the 2010 Ley Marco de Autonomías y Descentralización (Framework Law of Autonomies and Decentralization), are a central component of plurinationality's vision of state transformation. Yet, since 2009 only a handful of indigenous communities have made it through all the bureaucratic hurdles and red tape to officially become autonomous. Thus, this chapter interprets the possibilities and challenges of state transformation.

Taken together, my analyses of TIPNIS, CONAMAQ, and AIOCs can be seen as an investigation into how the theoretical conflict between the political logics of hegemony and plurinationality plays out in concrete terms in the spheres of the economy, society, and state. In reality, these different levels all overlap and converge with one another, but I offer these three cases as analytic moments that crystallize the theoretical differences between hegemony and plurinationality with respect to the idea of development, state–civil society relations, and institutional transformation.

3

INFRASTRUCTURE, EXTRACTION, AND INDIGENEITY

TIPNIS and the Production of National Development

Roads and rail lines that were secondary in name but primary in fact brought the isolated patches of the countryside out of their autarky—cultural as well as economic—into the market economy and the modern world.

—EUGEN WEBER

Should this torture then torment us
Since it brings us greater pleasure?
Were not through the rule of Timur
Souls devoured without measure?

—JOHANN WOLFGANG VON GOETHE

On August 15, 2011, roughly 1,500 marchers set out from Trinidad, the capital city of the lowland department of Beni, on a march toward the national capital of La Paz, 375 miles (600 kilometers) away. The march was a protest against the construction of a highway that would link the eastern Amazonian city of Trinidad with the central valley city of Cochabamba by traversing the Territorio Indígena y Parque Nacional Isiboro Sécure (TIPNIS, Isoboro Sécure Indigenous Territory and National Park). This march was the latest in a history of indigenous peoples' marches from the lowlands to the nation's capital.[1] Beginning in 1990 with the first March for Territory and Dignity, months-long marches to the seat of governmental power had been a primary tactic in the repertoire of indigenous peoples' contentious political action. Nicole Fabricant argues that these marches have historically been an important tactic for challenging Bolivia's social hierarchy, actively presenting indigenous peoples as already fully formed citizens. Indigenous marches are, in Fabricant's words, "indigenous bodies moving visibly through space . . . in order to gain legislative rights to land, resources, and alternative ways of living."[2]

On Sunday, September 25, more than a month into the 2011 march, national police forces raided the demonstrators' encampment in the town of Chaparina, near the border of the departments of Beni and La Paz, in order to disperse the indigenous protesters and put an end to the march. With hundreds of police officers outfitted in helmets, bulletproof vests, body armor, and shields in the area to ostensibly keep the peace between the marchers and a countergroup of highway supporters, they began firing canisters of tear gas, beating the marchers with truncheons, and forcefully detaining hundreds of demonstrators, targeting the leaders of the protest. Miriam Yubánure of the Confederación Nacional de Mujeres Indígenas de Bolivia (National Confederation of Indigenous Women of Bolivia) noted, "I was beaten because the Government was looking to torture the leaders in order to say, 'there is no longer a march, just go home.'" Fernando Vargas, president of the TIPNIS Subcentral, heard an officer say as he was being detained, "we need to kill this bastard."[3] As police forces continued to raid the encampment, a number of the marchers scattered into the forest behind the camp, many running to the nearby town of San Borja, where they found shelter in the local church. Back in Chaparina, the detained marchers were loaded onto buses, with mouths taped and hands bound, to be transported to the town of Rurrenabaque, a ten-hour journey, to be loaded onto planes. Fortunately for the marchers, the townspeople of Rurrenabaque caught wind of what was happening and themselves marched on the airport, shutting down all air traffic and forcing the police to release the detained protesters.

The attack soon became national and international news, leading two government ministers and a number of other officials to resign their positions in protest. Nationwide strikes sprang up and paralyzed the country's departmental capitals. Evo Morales publicly apologized for the use of force against the protestors and asked for forgiveness, but denied responsibility for the attack, claiming the police had broken the chain of command. Days later the march resumed, now with huge national support, finally arriving in La Paz on October 19, with thousands of *paceños*

(La Paz residents) lining the streets to cheer the marchers on. Weeks after the protesters arrived in the capital, in a seeming about-face, the government gave in to their demands and passed Law 180, banning construction of the TIPNIS highway and labeling the park an "untouchable zone." Nevertheless, the TIPNIS saga continued to be a node of contention between contrasting visions of development throughout the Morales years and beyond.

At the time of the march, the TIPNIS conflict marked the most significant crisis to date for the Movimiento al Socialismo (MAS, Movement Toward Socialism) government since it took power in 2006. As such, the march and its aftermath serve as a critical moment for interpreting the distinction between the political visions and material operations of hegemony and plurinationality, specifically in relation to the extractive economy and the issue of development. As Fernando Mayorga notes, the TIPNIS episode was not simply a tactical crisis but one of political strategy. The conflict "put into question a guiding paradigm of the political identity of the MAS's official project, which was the nexus between the MAS, the indigenous movement, and a development model based on *Vivir Bien* [lit. to live well] and in harmony with the Pachamama [Mother Earth]." Moreover, the conflict "put the plurinational character of the MAS state into debate as an apparent contradiction developed between the national interest of territorial integration represented by the state and the collective rights of the indigenous native peasant nations and peoples."[4]

The ongoing efforts to build the TIPNIS highway are therefore part of a much longer historical process seeking to open up the eastern lowlands to colonization through the construction of infrastructure, agricultural expansion, and processes of accumulation and investment, all of which have been key tenets of national capitalist development in Bolivia. Importantly, therefore, despite the fact that this conflict is centered on a particular infrastructure project, it can best be interpreted through the contrasting logics of hegemony and plurinationality, each one advancing a specific vision of development. Through an examination of the TIPNIS conflict, I employ the concepts of extractivism, accumulation by dispossession, and *vivir bien*, as well as analyzing the practice of prior consultation or consent, in order to show how these two visions of development differ in practice and what that means for our understanding of social emancipation. While the projects of plurinationality and MAS hegemony both place social emancipation as a central goal, the manner through which it is achieved fundamentally differs.

TERRITORIO INDÍGENA Y PARQUE NACIONAL ISIBORO SÉCURE

Straddling the departments of Cochabamba and Beni, the TIPNIS is a triangular plot of territory covering roughly 4,600 square miles (12,000 square kilometers) that was officially designated as a national park in 1965 under the military regime of René Barrientos. Pushing back against calls to open the area up to infrastructure and highland colonization, Barrientos issued Supreme Decree 7,401 in order to protect the area as "the construction of a road on the margins of the [Amazon] jungle and plans for colonization would put the integrity of the area's natural resources at serious risk."[5] Years later, in response to the 1990 March for Territory and Dignity, President Jaime Paz Zamora decreed part of the TIPNIS as an indigenous territory of the Mojeño, Yuracaré, and Chimán (also known as Tsimané) peoples, who live in the area.[6] In 1997, under the guise of the Instituto Nacional de Reforma Agraria (National Agrarian Reform Institute), the TIPNIS indigenous territory was given the legal status of a *tierra comunitaria de orígen* (communal indigenous land, TCO), covering over 3,800 square miles (10,000 square kilometers). In 2009, the TCO received legal title and was recognized with the new official designation of a *territorio indígena originario campesino* (TIOC, indigenous, original peoples, peasant territory).

The productive activity of the park's Mojeño, Yuracaré, and Chimán inhabitants is largely subsistence based and changes seasonally. In general, during the rainy season they produce small-scale agriculture, whereas hunting and fishing occur during the dry season. Notably, this subsistence-based mode of production relies on people's ability to move throughout the territory of the park. Thus, the inhabitants' cultural and ethnic identities are directly tied to territory and their understanding and use of that territory in specific ways.[7]

Despite the legal protections entailed by the park's status as an indigenous territory, the area has not been immune to the eastward march of highland migrants in search of land. While the Barrientos regime ostensibly protected the natural environment and the rights of indigenous peoples in the area with the 1965 national park declaration, according to Deborah Yashar, "the state had little capacity (and probably little political will) to defend the park's boundaries and protect the indigenous communities therein from the new wave of Andean *colonos* [colonizers]."[8] Indeed, with the 1966 Ley General de Colonización (Colonization Law) the state encouraged highland peasants to migrate east and colonize untitled areas, particularly in the Alto Beni, north of the TIPNIS, and Yapacaní and Chapare, southeast of the park. Furthermore, in 1967 the Bolivian government created the Instituto Nacional de Colonización (National Institute of Colonization) to incentivize migration to the eastern Amazonian lowlands through the distribution of land. In the early 1970s, the *colonos* began to organize under the Confederación Sindical de Colonizadores de Bolivia (Syndicalist Confederation of Bolivian Colonizers) in order to push for further land distribution and development of infrastructure for the movement of people and commodities. Between 1967 and 1993, 11,500–19,300 square miles (30,000–50,000 square kilometers) of land were redistributed to roughly eighty thousand families in areas surrounding the TIPNIS.[9]

Alongside the distribution of smallholder plots of land to highland migrants, the regime of General Hugo Banzer also sought to expand the agro-industrial sector through the distribution of large-scale landholdings to a small number of individuals during the 1970s.[10] In many cases, these large landholdings, known as *neolatifundias*, had links to international capital or were foreign owned outright. As Patrick Bottazzi and Stephan Rist note, "land distribution was used by Banzer's military regime to satisfy a rich class of mainly foreign large-scale farmers and thereby establish ties with Western oligarchies."[11] As a result, land distribution throughout the eastern lowlands grew increasingly unequal as 40 percent of agricultural land was transferred to large enterprises that represented only 2 percent of all landowners.[12]

Increasingly, the TIPNIS itself came under migratory pressure, largely from the area south of the park. As Aymara and Quechua highland campesinos opened up the valleys outside Cochabamba, producing cacao, bananas, cassava, maize, and coca, they contributed to the expansion of the agricultural frontier, with their numbers growing increasingly larger throughout the 1970s and 1980s. In the early 1990s, the indigenous peoples in the TIPNIS and the *colonos* began a process of marking out the boundaries between indigenous lands within the park on the one hand,

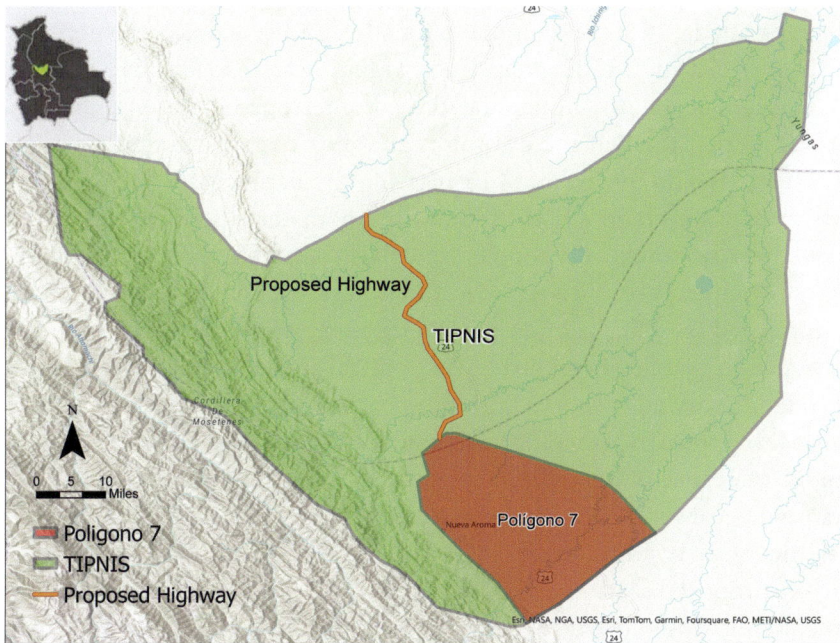

MAP 1 TIPNIS map. Created by Naomi Gutterman, based on data from DIVA-GIS.

and the area occupied by the peasant *colonos* on the other. A "red line" marked the boundary between the two territories, with the *colonos* in control of the area south of the park, known as Polígono 7 (see map 1). This southern area is populated by some twenty thousand *colono* families who are organized into fifty-two agrarian *sindicatos* (unions) affiliated with the Federación del Trópico, one of the six federations of coca producers of the Chapare. Colonization of the southern part of the park has been so intense that the number of Aymara and Quechua migrants from the Andes who reside in the park now exceeds the number of Amazonian Indians residing there.[13]

BUILDING THE NATION, ONE ROAD AT A TIME

With these historical developments in mind, we now turn to the proposed highway. Infrastructural elements such as roads are in many ways a technology of modernity in that, through their material construction, they instantiate ideas of national unification and economic prosperity.[14] As Penny Harvey and Hannah Knox argue, "whilst roads have existed in different forms for millennia, the coming together of engineering expertise, political will and economic ambition to produce standardised structures for the purposes of integrating the nation state is a particularly modern ambition."[15] More than simply material structures for the movement of goods and people, roads also generate a belief that they transform the spaces through which they pass. Particularly in the Global South, road building is often viewed as a way of helping overcome an entrenched (post)colonial history of political and economic domination through expanded access to both physical and social mobility. The contemporary construction of infrastructures like roads is interesting then not just because of the material transformations they may bring about, but also because they reveal a particular political rationality that underlies the modern nation-state.

The proposed section of the Villa Tunari–San Ignacio de Moxos road (see map 1) would traverse the park from north to south directly to the northern point of Polígono 7, the area under *colono* control. Officially, the Morales government argued that the road would play a central role in integrating the country by physically connecting eastern Amazonia with the western valleys and highlands of the Andes. It would also expand the territorial reach of the state, which would in turn help bring economic development to those indigenous groups in the TIPNIS area. As Mayorga notes, "without doubt, the idea that territorial integration would strengthen the internal market—an outstanding task of the nation-state since the liberal governments of the early twentieth century and, with more determination, since the revolution of 1952—was the main objective of the government and the campesino organizations."[16] Perhaps less explicit but no less clear a goal was that the road between Trinidad and Cochabamba would also provide an alternative to the main existing route between eastern and western Bolivia through the city of Santa Cruz, the country's most dynamic economic hub and the stronghold of the government's opposition.

From the perspective of the MAS, the need for a road connecting the Andean zone with the Amazonian region dates back more than three hundred years.[17] As such, the MAS effort to construct a road between Cochabamba and Trinidad is only the latest effort in a long historical struggle to integrate Bolivia's national territory under the control of the state by linking the Amazonian east with the Andean west. By fully linking east and west, the argument goes, the state will finally be able to establish sovereign control and provide all the protections and benefits of citizenship that the state can offer. "The Villa Tunari–San Ignacio de Moxos highway will establish the presence of the Bolivian State in the Amazon, where, in its absence, the ones who actually hold power are landlords and lumber companies (many of them foreigners)," argues Álvaro García Linera. "The highway will act as a staple that unites two regions of the country separated from each other, whose dissociation precisely permitted the loss of territories a century ago, and more recently has allowed the substitution of the State for illegal actors, hacendados and foreigners. The highway will act as a mechanism of geographic territorial control by the State and the establishment of national sovereignty."[18]

The expansion of Bolivian state power throughout the Amazonian region, according to García Linera, will help put an end to the patrimonial rule of large landowners over indigenous peoples in the area and challenge foreign capitalist imperialism. He argues, "the main enemy of the State as a protector in the Amazon region is the international imperial-corporate structure," and "the absence of the State in terms of rights and protections has given way to the formation of despotic-hacendado power over the indigenous peoples and communities and the penetration of foreign powers that, in the name of 'protecting the Amazon,' 'the lungs of the world,' etc., have extended an extraterritorial control—through some environmentalist NGOs—over the Amazonian region."[19] In this argument, the road is a technical object meant to facilitate national integration but also something that operates on the level of desire. It encodes the yearnings of both state and society to overcome a history of imperial exploitation and allow mobility, the rule of law, and citizenship to flourish.

However, the discourse of the state as a guarantor and protector of the rights of indigenous peoples in the Amazon is founded on a particular political logic, one that, as Silvia Rivera notes, exemplifies "how the hegemonic nation reproduces . . . forms of 'colonial administration' of the territory and the population that reduce the inhabitants of the Park to mere objects, domesticated and passive."[20] Lowland indigenous groups have historically been viewed as "savages" or "backward" peoples and were considered to be wards of the state up until the 1970s. Even after Bolivia's 1952 revolution, which extended citizenship rights to many indigenous people who were previously marginalized and excluded, Amazonian Indians were still not seen as full-fledged citizens. For example, the 1953 agrarian reform law stated that "forest groups of the tropical and sub-tropical plain that find themselves in a savage state and that have a primitive form of organization, will remain under the protection of the State."[21]

Proponents of the highway expressed similar tropes of the "indigenous savage" during the TIPNIS conflict. Roberto Coraite, the leader of the Confederación Sindical Única de Trabajadores Campesinos de Bolivia (CSUTCB, Unified Syndical Confederation of Rural Workers of Bolivia), the country's national peasant confederation and a main base of support for the MAS, declared that "we need to differentiate between what will provide the most benefits to our brothers in the TIPNIS; [build] the highway or remain clandestine, remain indigent . . . remain, that is to say, as savages. . . . We do not want the indigenous of the TIPNIS to continue to live as savages any longer."[22] From this perspective, the road signifies "progress" and "development," and its construction would help those indigenous communities of the TIPNIS overcome their alleged state of backwardness. Yet, this argument negates not just the validity but the very possibility of different modes of indigenous life, which is foundational to the logic of plurinationality. As Rivera states, these arguments "deny the inhabitants of the sixty-six communities of the TIPNIS their rights to territory, to their own forms of producing, signifying, and representing the world, and to self-government."[23]

DEVELOPMENT AND ITS DISCONTENTS: EXTRACTIVISM, ACCUMULATION, AND *VIVIR BIEN*

The TIPNIS conflict fits within a larger debate over development across Latin America in the twenty-first century. As leftist governments came to power across the region and commodity prices boomed, the region began a new period of heightened natural resource extraction, what Eduardo Gudynas has labeled *neoextractivismo progresista* (progressive neoextractivism).[24] Historically, Latin America's insertion into the global economy has been as a provider of primary products, so continued economic concentration on the extraction and exportation of natural resources is not a new phenomenon. However, what is new during the contemporary phase is that progressive forces control state power and are seeking to reinsert the state as a central actor in the economy. With this renewed economic role, states across the region have sought to increase their share of surplus from the extractive economy and redistribute it to society through various social programs. But, as Gudynas points out, extractivism increases environmental destruction and heightens social conflict, particularly in those sites at the point of extraction. This creates a contradiction, where "the State looks to capture the surplus from extractivism and use part of it to fund social programs, which increases the State's legitimacy, which can then be used to defend extractive activities."[25] Social programs—such as conditional cash transfers, and increased government investment in health and education based largely on Bolivia's extractive model of accumulation—have improved material well-being and helped legitimize the MAS government. Between 2006, when Morales came to power, and 2012, the size of the country's economy tripled, poverty was cut in half, and income inequality declined from 58.7 to 48.4, as measured by the Gini index.[26] According to critics, it is within this context that the MAS pushed the TIPNIS highway in order to expand the extractivist mode of accumulation undergirding Bolivia's economic growth, which is central to the MAS's development model.[27]

Extractivism, according to Alberto Acosta, is a system of socioeconomic organization that began during the developmental phases of global capitalism in the fifteenth and sixteenth centuries through the colonization of the Americas. He argues that the extractivist mode has always been determined "by the demands of the metropolitan centers of nascent capitalism. Some regions specialized in the extraction and production of raw materials—primary commodities—while others took on the role of producing manufactured goods. The former export Nature, the latter import it."[28] According to Maristella Svampa, extractivism is

a type of accumulation based on an over-exploitation of—largely non-renewable—natural resources as well as the expansion of frontiers to territories formerly considered "unproductive." This definition of an economy based on extraction is not limited to activities normally falling into the category (oil and mining), but also includes other sectors such as agribusiness or the production of biofuels. This is due to the fact that they consolidate a model that tends to follow a monoculture, the destruction of biodiversity, a concentration of landownership and a destructive reconfiguration of vast territories. In addition, it includes the transport infrastructure projects (waterways, harbors, bi-oceanic corridors, and so on), energy projects (large hydro dams) and communication infrastructure projects.[29]

Thus, more than just the actual physical extraction of natural resources, the concept of extractivism draws our attention to an entire mode of accumulation that includes the expansion of industrial agriculture for export, such as soy and palm oil, and also the construction of the physical infrastructure necessary to support and advance those extractivist industries. Critics point out how this model assumes a vision of developmental progress based on the domination of nature, which negates alternative understandings of the nature-culture interface. Specifically, scholars have highlighted how extractivism is typically implemented at the expense of indigenous territorial rights and environmental sustainability.[30]

The proposed TIPNIS roadway would be a key intermediary link in a larger highway project stretching from southeastern Brazil to the Chilean port of Arica. The Iniciativa para la Integración de la Infraestructura Regional Suramericana (IIRSA, Initiative for the Integration of the Regional Infrastructure of South America) is a plan that multiple South American governments agreed to in 2000 with the goal of increasing regional interdependence and facilitating the extraction and exportation of products, in many cases with little value added. The details of the TIPNIS highway were drawn up in 2008 between Brazil and Bolivia, and the price of construction was established at US$415 million, 80 percent of which was to be funded by Brazil's Banco Nacional de Desarrollo Económico y Social (National Bank for Economic and Social Development). The Brazilian construction company OAS was awarded the contract to build the highway.[31] According to critics of the plan, the proposed road was a reflection of the rising economic power of Brazil and would, as a consequence, induce the expansion of Brazilian agro-industrial capital into Bolivia.[32]

More important for the purposes of this chapter are the domestic politics of the conflict surrounding the model of extractivism. In addition to the expansion of Brazilian agro-industry, it was argued that the highway would induce further colonization of indigenous territory by coca growers in the south of the park, who continue to be the largest base of rural support for Morales and the MAS.[33] Additionally, critics claimed that the highway would lead to the extension of large-scale cattle farming from the north, and increased logging operations (both legal and illegal) throughout the park.[34] The park and surrounding areas have also been identified as possible sites of oil and natural gas exploration. According to the Centro de Estudios para el Desarrollo Laboral y Agrario (Center for the Study of Agrarian and Labor Development), one-third of the park has been marked out in government development plans for potential oil and gas extraction.[35] Continually expanding the extractive frontier is seen as the central means of ensuring the government's increased social expenditures. As such, there is a policy-driven demand to expand current levels of extractive production and to look for new areas that might be exploited. The road would ensure access to the currently isolated areas that hold prospective hydrocarbon deposits. Overall, according to a study from the Programa de Investigación Estratégica en Bolivia (Program of Strategic Investigation in Bolivia), a Bolivian NGO, construction of the road would lead to the deforestation of approximately 2,300 square miles (6,000 square kilometers) of the TIPNIS, or about 65 percent of the park, within twenty years.[36]

The highway, then, would extend and deepen the extractive economy and accelerate the process of what Karl Marx labeled *primitive accumulation*. Primitive accumulation, according to Marx, is the "original sin" of capitalism; it is "an accumulation which is not the result of the capitalist mode of production but its point of departure."[37] In other words, primitive accumulation is the originary process of expropriation of noncapitalist forms of production by the expanding forces of capital.[38] Marx's discussion of primitive accumulation includes descriptions of various instances of the process: the separation of peasants from their land, suppression of the commons, the slave trade, and colonialism, among others. "Primitive accumulation," Marx states, "is nothing else than the historical process of divorcing the producer from the means of production. It appears 'primitive' because it forms the pre-history of capital, and of the mode of production corresponding to capital."[39]

However, as David Harvey points out, Marx (and, he adds, classical liberal political economy) assumes that after these "original" processes have taken place, continued capitalist accumulation and reproduction proceed under new, distinct conditions, and the primitive phase is complete.[40] Harvey challenges this assumption. In order to highlight the persistence of the predatory practices of primitive accumulation within the long historical process of capital accumulation and the ongoing processes of incorporating previously noncapitalist modes of production into the sphere of capitalism, he develops the concept of "accumulation by dispossession." Harvey describes accumulation by dispossession as

> the continuation and proliferation of accumulation practices which Marx had treated as "primitive" or "original" during the rise of capitalism. These include the commodification and privatization of land and the forceful expulsion of peasant populations (compare the cases . . . of Mexico and of China, where 70 million peasants are thought to have been displaced in recent times); conversion of various forms of property rights (common, collective, state, etc.) into exclusive private property rights (most spectacularly represented by China); suppression of rights to the commons; commodification of labour power and the suppression of alternative (indigenous) forms of production and consumption; colonial, neocolonial, and imperial processes of appropriation of assets (including natural resources); monetization of exchange and taxation, particularly of land; the slave trade (which continues particularly in the sex industry); and usury, the national debt and, most devastating of all, the use of the credit system as a radical means of accumulation by dispossession.[41]

Drawing on Harvey's work, scholars have argued that the TIPNIS highway would extend the logic of (extractivist) capitalism through expanded land colonization, coca production, oil and gas exploitation, increased agro-industrial activities, and deforestation.[42] That is, the proposed highway and its corollary effects can be interpreted critically as expanding an already prevailing process of accumulation by dispossession.

Yet, for García Linera, the argument that the highway will extend the extractivist economy is wrong for a number of reasons. For example, he states that the notion of a "*cocalero* [coca leaf grower] invasion" of the park is an outright fallacy. Despite the fact that there is currently no type of coercive measure that prevents the *cocaleros* from using the existing road infrastructure to enter the park, they do not do so. Moreover, he argues, the *cocaleros* themselves voluntarily agreed in 1990 to the "red line," and they have kept their word not to cross it. He states that "the highway will not be a spearhead for any supposed '*cocalero* invasion'; nor with any of the existing sections has any 'invasion' occurred, because this is a Park and a territory of collective indigenous ownership."[43] More fundamentally, García Linera does not view the road in extractivist terms at all. He argues, "human activity is possible only through the transformation of the natural world. . . . Natural and social life necessitates processing nature in order to extract the biological components of its reproduction. . . . The human being by nature transforms and affects the surrounding natural world; that is the invariable and transhistorical condition of any mode of production."[44] For García Linera, all human societies drastically affect and modify the natural environment through some form of extraction. "All societies and modes of production have their own distinct ways of processing 'raw materials.' If we conceptualize 'extractivism' as the activity that just extracts primary materials (renewable or nonrenewable), without introducing greater transformation in the labor activity, then all societies of the world, capitalist and noncapitalist, are more or less extractivist."[45] He is correct to point out that global capitalism, because it is in fact a total *global* system, sets the limits and conditions of possibility for the horizon of social and economic transformation within any particular country. For this very reason it is important to remember that Bolivia cannot radically transform the global division of labor and mode of production of its own accord. But, García Linera's assertion that all societies' modes of production are extractivist because they extract natural resources and transform nature essentially equates the concept of extractivism with the verb *to extract*, missing the concept's fundamental critique of contemporary capitalism. It is not a question of whether societies have an organic relation with their natural surroundings (however different cultural groups understand that relation). The question is really about power and who benefits from any specific socio-environmental relation.

According to critics, the extractivist model overwhelmingly benefits transnational capital at the expense of national actors, while producing ever more isolated sectors within the national economy.[46] The model of development based on the extraction and exportation of primary resources often fails to integrate those export activities into the rest of the economy and provide benefits to society. Brent Kaup has demonstrated

how Bolivia's dependence on natural resources has shaped both the physical infrastructure of the country and the institutional and regulatory
structure, where laws, taxes, contracts, and administration all operate
to the advantage of the export sector, constraining internal economic
diversification.[47] In cases like this, the productive apparatus relies almost
entirely on external actors and, as a consequence, remains vulnerable to
the fluctuations of the global market. Additionally, extractive industries
are capital intensive and tend to generate little employment, although the
jobs they do create are well paid. As such, Acosta argues, "this [extractiv-
ist] mode of accumulation does not require a domestic market and does
not even need it."[48]

In his defense of the TIPNIS highway, García Linera also presents a
linear vision of history, where it is only through an extractive phase that
a country can then move on to an industrial phase (i.e., development).
According to García Linera, Bolivia's reliance on an extractivist mode of
accumulation is a transitional phase on the path toward development and
can only be overcome through increased extraction. "Extractivism is not
a goal in and of itself," García Linera argues, "but it can be the starting
point for overcoming it."[49] This is what García Linera labels "Andean-
Amazonian capitalism," a model of development predicated on the use
of surplus profit from oil, gas, and mineral extraction to fund domestic
social programs.[50] Through the extraction of raw materials, the Bolivian
state generates and distributes wealth to enhance the material strength
of the revolutionary social forces, a process that, in turn, "creates a new
material nonextractivist base that preserves and amplifies the benefits
of the laboring population."[51] Shuttering the mines, closing the gas wells,
and terminating the construction of highways and mega dams, the state
would in fact tie its own hands in the revolutionary process and be unable
to satisfy the basic material means of existence of the people. "Like any
emancipation, to escape extractivism we have to start from it. . . . At
present, for us as a country, this is the only technical means we have to
distribute the material wealth generated through extractivism (although,
in a different way from previous eras), and in addition allow us to have the
material, technical, and cognitive conditions to transform its technical
and productive base."[52]

In practice, however, extractivism has been a mechanism of colonial
and neocolonial plunder and appropriation for centuries, largely failing

to move on to a more advanced stage of economic development. As Raúl Prada points out, García Linera's stagist perspective fails to capture the simultaneity and complexity of the processes of economic change and development. For Prada, García Linera "fails to see that extractivism is not the condition of possibility for industrialization; it never was, they are distinct processes whose conditions of historical possibility are different."[53] On this point, García Linera's position aligns with the modernization thesis put forward by classical liberal political economists; that is, he argues that Bolivia needs to exploit the natural resources at its disposal in order to accumulate capital and, in turn, invest in the industrialization of the country. And, because there is not a national bourgeoisie sufficiently large enough or strong enough to fulfill this determined role, the state can fill this void in order to accumulate and invest in the universal interest of all Bolivians. But, while the increased role of the state in the economy is an important difference from the previous neoliberal era, the overall model of development and mode of accumulation essentially remain the same: extractivist. According to Gudynas, this mode of accumulation "is part of South America's own contemporary version of developmentalism, whereby the myth of progress and development is maintained under a new cultural and political hybridity."[54]

The view that extractivism can serve as a starting point for its own overcoming also ignores the fact that alternative projects already exist. A model of postextractivist development put forward as a challenge to extractivist capitalism is represented through the concept of *vivir bien*. Meaning "to live well," *vivir bien* is the Spanish translation of a concept that is rooted in the worldviews and ontologies of indigenous peoples of Bolivia, and Latin America more generally.[55] Despite the fact that the concept is "in permanent construction and reproduction," it should be understood not merely as a "development alternative," but rather as "an alternative to development."[56] To be clear, I am not arguing that *vivir bien* is synonymous with plurinationality or that *vivir bien* is the necessary political economic form of plurinationalism. I highlight the importance of *vivir bien* here as an alternative mode of production with a distinct set of values and desires that aligns with and complements the open and articulatory logic of plurinationalism.[57] While proponents of *vivir bien* have been unable to concretely define this alternative form, in the TIPNIS conflict perhaps its strongest impact has been to impose certain limits on the traditional developmentalist agenda by highlighting the social and cultural impacts of the highway.

The model of *vivir bien* shares a number of similarities with the idea of the moral economy developed by E. P. Thompson, James C. Scott, and others.[58] In contrast to the capitalist market economy, the moral economy functions not just on the economic imperative of surplus accumulation, but on other social assumptions about what types of economic exchange are considered moral and ethical. Similarly, the implementation of *vivir bien* would involve transforming the market system into one that subjects the economy to certain social and political criteria that would guarantee sustenance, reproduction, and subsistence for both people and the environment, nature and culture.[59] This represents a different structure of value, where economic value is embedded in networks of social relations, rather than the other way around. The moral economy, according to Thompson, "operated within a popular consensus as to what were legitimate and what were illegitimate practices in marketing, milling, baking, etc. [i.e., economic exchange]. This in its turn was grounded upon a consistent traditional view of social norms and obligations."[60] One such traditional social norm that the moral economy shares with *vivir bien* is the notion of *reciprocity*. In the context of Southeast Asia, Scott argues that the moral economy's "idea of justice and legitimacy is provided by the *norm of reciprocity* and the consequent elite obligation (that is, peasant right) to guarantee—or at least not infringe upon—the subsistence claims and arrangements of the peasantry."[61]

However, whereas the moral economy has been discussed almost exclusively as a *pre*capitalist bulwark against the increasing marketization of social relations with the rise of capitalism, *vivir bien*, while serving as a defense against the expansion of capitalist relations into previously noncapitalist spaces, is also a prefigurative proposition for an alternative *post*capitalist future. As Pablo Davalos notes, "in the same way that a plurinational State is an alternative to the liberal contractualism of the modern State . . . *sumak kawsay* [*vivir bien*] is an alternative to the capitalist mode of production, distribution, and consumption."[62] To live well, in this sense, is a different way of understanding the world. It does not deny the need to generate wealth, but the objectives to which that collective wealth should be put are radically different. *Vivir bien* "aims not only at meeting the material needs of the production of use-value, but [also at meeting] other values of emancipation. Above all, it is freedom—not reduced to a Western negative freedom—that links human beings to politics and the ability to have a direct influence on decisions that affect their lives, their natural and community context. This is cultural plurality in the broadest sense."[63]

Vivir bien is a utopian, perhaps even millenarian, vision for a future beyond extractivist capitalism. "It is difficult to re-imagine the moral assumptions of another social configuration," Thompson tells us. "It is not easy for us to conceive that there may have been a time, within a smaller and more integrated community, when it appeared to be 'unnatural' that any man should profit from the necessities of others, and when it was assumed that, in time of dearth, prices of 'necessities' should remain at a customary level, even though there might be less all around."[64] It may indeed be difficult to conceive this in a previous era, but it may also be just as challenging to envision such a time in the future for many. Nevertheless, the construction of a new socioeconomic configuration requires halting the intensification and expansion of an extractivist model based on the export of primary commodities. The extractivist mode of accumulation—"which overvalues profits from Nature and undervalues human effort, systematically destroys the environment and has serious negative effects on social and community structures, gives priority to the export market and neglects the domestic market, fosters wealth concentration and sidelines equality"—has historically failed to provide the universal benefits it declares in Bolivia, not to mention the rest of Latin America.[65] Thus, the conflict over the proposed highway through the TIPNIS is one battle in a much larger struggle over the future of Bolivian development. Whereas the proposed TIPNIS highway represents the continuation and intensification of the extractivist model of dependent development that began with the Conquest, opponents of the road envision an alternative to development.[66] In this alternative vision, development as *vivir bien*, economic growth is not disregarded but, rather, is situated within a context where other interests, such as the rights of nature and the cultural rights of indigenous peoples, are also taken into account. This new model of development, therefore, has more than just economic implications; it has social and political importance in the sense of whose voice matters, who gets to decide, and how.

WHO DECIDES? PRIOR CONSULTATION AND CONSENT

Questions of decision-making are central to the TIPNIS conflict. Who is able to make decisions and how those decisions are in fact taken have been key issues of the conflict and can be fruitfully analyzed through the international right of free, prior, and informed consultation or consent, which is laid out in both the International Labour Organization's (ILO) 1989 Convention 169 and the United Nations' 2007 Declaration on the Rights of Indigenous Peoples (UNDRIP).[67] Prior *consultation* is the collective right of indigenous communities to be consulted before any natural resource extraction or development projects take place that would affect their territory. Prior *consent* takes this consultation process one step further, requiring that those communities give their permission before any project affecting their territory may move ahead. Processes of prior consultation are seen as powerful tools to counteract the negative environmental and sociocultural impacts that characterize the extraction of natural resources across the globe. They are intended to increase effective participation, protect the rights of indigenous peoples, and democratize resource governance by giving local communities a say over decisions that affect them.[68] In Bolivia, indigenous peoples' demands for prior consultation have often been articulated in opposition to the state's traditional role as the dominant, sovereign entity, with complete control over the nation's land and resources.[69] As such, free, prior, and informed consultation/consent is a key articulatory element of plurinationalism.

ILO Convention 169 was ratified by President Jaime Paz Zamora in 1991 in response to the indigenous March for Territory and Dignity, organized by the lowland regional indigenous organization Confederación de Pueblos Indígenas de Bolivia (CIDOB, Confederation of Indigenous Peoples of Eastern Bolivia). Responding to the Guerras del Gas (Gas Wars) of the early 2000s, the 2005 Ley de Hidrocarburos (Hydrocarbons Law, Law 3058) included a section on the requirement of prior consultation, which stated that "native, indigenous and peasant communities and peoples . . . should be consulted in a prior, mandatory and timely manner when it is intended to develop any hydrocarbon activity."[70] In 2007, Supreme Decree 29,033 was promulgated by Evo Morales, further requiring the carrying out of participatory consultation in relation to development projects in indigenous territories. After the contentious

2006–8 Constituent Assembly, the right to prior and informed consultation regarding the exploitation of natural resources in indigenous territories was written into the country's 2009 constitution.[71] Denise Humphreys Bebbington argues that these various legislative victories "represented the culmination of years of mobilization, lobbying and negotiation with executive and legislative officials, bringing indigenous lowland groups closer to their goal of effective control over their territories. These mechanisms were also of enormous symbolic importance to the Morales government which heralded them as being of universal importance to indigenous societies faced with extractive activity in their territory."[72] However, despite the ratification of prior consultation in the constitution, the document does not recognize the more radical right to prior consent, even though this stronger proclamation was demanded by indigenous groups during the Constituent Assembly and is recognized by the UNDRIP, all forty-six articles of which are officially recognized as national law in Bolivia under Law 3760.

It is clear that a complex and somewhat contradictory legal foundation surrounds the rights of prior consultation and consent. Furthermore, despite the potential democratizing and participatory effects that processes of prior consultation provide, scholars have been less than optimistic about its actual impact in Bolivia.[73] According to Tulia G. Falleti and Thea Riofrancos, "its [prior consultation's] implementation has been crippled in the context of an increasing reliance on the revenues generated by the extractive sectors."[74] Nevertheless, the enactment of prior consultation in the TIPNIS in relation to the planned highway has served as a central point of contention between indigenous groups in the park and their supporters, on the one hand, and the MAS government and proponents of the road, on the other.

A central claim made by indigenous protestors against the proposed highway was that the government initially failed to carry out free, prior, and informed consultation. Indeed, the MAS only included the peasant unions and *colonos* in the early stages (2008–11) of discussion with Brazil about the highway. An official consultation process with lowland TIPNIS communities only came later, after construction of the highway had already commenced and the 2011 march against the highway had been met by the MAS's violent crackdown. Responding to the demands of a late 2011 march in favor of the highway by the Consejo Indígena del Sur

(Indigenous Council of the South), the MAS passed legislation in early 2012 to carry out a consultation in order to decide the fate of the highway construction. The consultation covered three main themes: (1) whether the TIPNIS should remain "intangible," as stated in Law 180, which originally shut down construction; (2) whether the proposed highway through the park should be constructed; and (3) what measures should be taken to prevent illegal settlements in the TIPNIS. The consultation process was completed in December 2012, with the government stating that fifty-five of the sixty-nine communities consulted favored the proposed highway. The MAS claimed that the results represented a triumph of democracy and a successful outcome of Bolivia's first experience with the *consulta previa* (prior consultation) for indigenous communities mandated by the constitution and international law.

Opposition indigenous leaders claimed that the *consulta* was a foregone conclusion, highlighting that the consultation took place after construction on the highway had already begun and included not just the indigenous groups with protected status in the park but also the local *cocalero* communities, who had been strong proponents of the road and who resided in Poligono 7.[75] Further, in October 2012, before the process concluded, Morales stated "with forty-seven communities consulted, which is more than two-thirds, and with the approval of the highway construction, it is no longer important to consult the other communities."[76] This statement demonstrates a hegemonic vision of the process, where what matters is the assemblage of a "universal" majority, rather than any actual dialogical practice that would incorporate the particular interests of all affected communities. Morales further disparaged the consultation process, while also underlining the developmentalist goals of the project, when he stated, "They [opposition indigenous groups] want the consultation to be binding. That is impossible, it is not negotiable. The Constitution and international law mandate previous consultation, and we will always respect that, but letting a group of families tell us what to do would mean paralyzing all our work on electrification, hydrocarbons, and industry." He went on to state, "Whether they want it or not, we will build the highway."[77]

Questioning the merits of the 2012 *consulta*, indigenous leaders claimed that only a minority of residents were actually consulted and that the process did not include the participation of recognized indigenous organizations and authorities. Fernando Vargas, the head of the TIP-NIS Subcentral, claimed that contrary to government assertions, at least thirty communities actually rejected the *highway as proposed*. Additionally, critics argued that the government was using clientelist practices to influence the process by promising goods, such as outboard motors, and the delivery of services, such as education, health, and transportation, which would breach the legal definition of free, prior, and informed consultation.[78]

The December 2012 findings of a fifteen-member interinstitutional commission representing the Catholic Church and the Asamblea Permanente de Derechos Humanos de Bolivia (Permanent Assembly of Human Rights in Bolivia), in association with the International Federation for Human Rights, support allegations of irregularities in the consultation process and MAS government manipulation. Of the thirty-six communities the commission visited, thirty rejected the proposed highway, three accepted it, and three others conditioned their acceptance on further study or changes in the proposed route. The commission also concluded that the *consulta* did not conform to standards of prior consultation established by national and international law as it failed to respect collective indigenous decision-making norms and did not provide information on the road's potential environmental, social, economic, and cultural impacts. Additionally, according to the commission, the government's promises of goods and services in conjunction with the consultation process severely compromised the integrity of that process.[79]

TIPNIS AND THE CONTRASTING VISIONS OF HEGEMONY AND PLURINATIONALITY

Lorenza B. Fontana and Jean Grugel argue that instances of prior consultation are often conjunctural expressions of deeper, long-standing tensions between different social and political groups over territory and access to political and economic resources.[80] In the case of TIPNIS, the conflict over prior consultation brings into stark relief the two contrasting visions of national economic development put forth by the hegemonic project of the MAS and the proponents of plurinationality: developmental state capitalism and an alternative model based on the idea of *vivir bien*, respectively. Raúl Prada correctly asserts that within the

Bolivian *proceso de cambio* (process of change), the TIPNIS conflict illuminates the fact that "there are two projects that cannot be combined and are in fact in confrontation. One is the continuation of the extractivist, capitalist, developmentalist model. It is the continuation of the republic's historical model of development until the present. . . . The other model is indigenous, the model of *vivir bien*."[81] Moreover, Prada argues, the project of the MAS government "is to conserve, continue, extend and deepen the colonial extractive model of dependent capitalism and to reestablish and consolidate the nation-state, annulling the possibilities for constructing a plurinational state."[82]

The MAS project that Prada draws our attention to is fundamentally about the construction of a new hegemonic formation in Bolivia. However, to say this is not to argue that the hegemonic project is simply a return to the status quo ante or that it is not in any sense radical or progressive. Morales and the MAS have accomplished much through a number of cultural, economic, and policy changes that have benefited Bolivia's popular indigenous majority.[83] But, social transformation is more than a checklist of socioeconomic achievements, important as those may be. The wave of social upheaval that brought the MAS to power was composed of different, often contradictory, currents. For many, support for the MAS meant support for modernization and industrialization, for increased exploitation of nationalized hydrocarbons, and for economic growth with social inclusion. In other words, for traditional understandings of "development." For others, support for the MAS meant support for development of a different kind, perhaps best conceptualized through *vivir bien*. This signified support for development of different material and ideological ways of being in the world, different understandings of the relations between people and their natural surroundings, and different systems of reproducing society. If the concept of development drawn from Western modernity is based on ideas of progress and uninterrupted growth as measured through the possession and consumption of goods, then "to live well" serves as a direct challenge to the developmentalist idea of always "living better." Thus, *vivir bien* is a rejection of a number of ideas and practices of modern Western developmental thought. Whereas modern Western ontology is dualist, creating a division between nature and society and presenting the former as an endless supply of material resources for the benefit of the latter, the ontology of *vivir bien* is relational. According to *vivir bien*, nature is not simply an entity external to humans to be exploited for the development of society; the distinction between these spheres (with nature as inert and society as active) is artificial, illusory.[84] The foundation of Western modernity is centered on the taming, harnessing, subduing, rationalizing, and understanding of the "thing" that surrounds us—that which we call nature. We objectify society or culture through our invention of "nature." This, according to Roy Wagner, is a cultural convention of Western modernity. "We create nature," Wagner notes, "and tell ourselves stories about how nature creates us!"[85] Yet, through this process of cultural objectification we conceal the actual relational association between nature and culture. From the indigenous perspective of *vivir bien*, rather than the cultural invention of nature there is instead a natural subsumption of culture. That is, if the nature/culture dichotomy still holds at all, it is interpreted through an organic totality in which the natural and the cultural worlds determine each other.

While these contrasting models of development envision different types of social transformation, *how* those transformations are managed, and *by whom*, is just as important as the transformations themselves. The manner in which the MAS has sought to construct a highway through a national park and indigenous territory has played just as important a role in the conflict over the road as its projected effects have. The top-down process of decision-making around the highway, the derision and violent repression of the marchers in Chaparina, and the failure to abide by the right of indigenous peoples to free, prior, and informed consultation/consent according to international and national legal norms all point to a hegemonic understanding of the operation of social power. The MAS's vision of revolutionary change includes a political strategy to restructure the relations of social and economic power through the organization and direction of the various social forces that constitute its base. Similarly, these events demonstrate a particular vision of what development means and how it should be implemented. For the MAS government, development means industrialization, and the strategy to achieve that objective is increased exploitation of natural resources (i.e., extractivism). The professed goal, more or less, is to provide more resources and better living conditions for the Bolivian people as a whole. Therefore, allowing a small minority group to stand in the way of national development objectives will only keep Bolivia in its dependent position within the global capitalist system.

This is precisely where the political logics of hegemony and plurinationality contrast most clearly. The operation of hegemony does not simply imply the control of society by the dominant group. The hegemonic bloc needs to recognize and continually adjust to the interests and demands of opposition groups, always seeking to incorporate them in some fashion and gain their consent, albeit always in a subordinate position. This is important to the extent that it theoretically leaves open the possibilities for resistance and change. However, when certain groups or ideas are unable to be absorbed into the hegemonic bloc and their active consent is no longer seen as a possibility, the only other option available is that of coercion, the imposition of consent through the use of force. This is what Antonio Gramsci means when he talks about the state as "hegemony protected by the armor of coercion."[86] In the case of the TIPNIS, the MAS attempt to impose its will through force was a spectacular failure. Not only did the raid at Chaparina fail to quell the protests and end the march, it had a galvanizing effect on the larger Bolivian society, inciting Bolivians to throw their support behind the protestors and against the MAS.

Similar to the logic of hegemony, a plurinational politics is also about the creation of a consensus on public matters. However, the manner in which the positions and interests of the various groups involved in any political process are expressed and taken into account and the way in which a consensus is formed differ. An important mechanism for the creation of a common consensus is the process of prior consultation. But, whereas the MAS seems to view prior consultation as a hindrance to development and an obstacle to be overcome through the will of a simple majority, for proponents of plurinationality it represents a tool for those negatively affected to voice their concerns, propose changes, and ultimately transform the practice of decision-making. Morales has generally derided the drawn-out process of prior consultation as getting in the way of the government's developmental initiatives. In 2015 he argued, "it is not possible that we lose so much time with the so-called consultations; this is a great weakness of our state, of our people. We are going to modify some norms with the single objective of accelerating investment and obtaining more natural resources to benefit the Bolivian people."[87] Yet, if plurinationality is the recognition of the histories, cultures, and, perhaps most importantly, rights of the multiple nationalities that coexist within Bolivia's geographic borders, then not only is it constitutionally required to have their demands and concerns taken into account but also this represents a radical horizon of consensus around public matters. Undoubtedly, dialogic processes of constructing consensus will take time, but if plurinationality "consists in providing the mechanisms and formats to *guarantee shared responsibility* for the totality of collective affairs," then "as a consequence, it is founded on—and necessarily requires—the availability of sufficient time to set in motion the ample and complex processes of deliberation in which, little by little, agreements are achieved which express shared decisions concerning what is to be done."[88] In essence, these processes of deliberation and the formation of a common consensus are the practices of autonomous self-government and the cornerstone of any authentic plurinational project.

CONCLUSION

This chapter began with an epigraph from Eugen Weber highlighting the role of roads in the process of national integration and capitalist market expansion that accompanied the French Revolution. "Roads that permitted carts," Weber states, "would be an emancipation as important as political revolution, probably more important."[89] Roads, he argues, facilitated the transformation of France's rural economic and social structures by providing the peasantry access to the market and "modern civilization." Weber adds, roads helped bring about "not only civilization, but national unity too. There could be no national unity before there was national circulation."[90] Yet, the expansion of "civilization" and "national unity" came at the expense of local autonomy, economies, customs, and cultures. Roads "brought ruin to local enterprises no longer protected by earlier isolation, to outdated occupational groups like the riverboatmen, and to producers of mediocre local goods or crops fated to be outmatched by specialized ones."[91] Roads played a critical role of transforming "peasants into Frenchmen," as Weber would have it. But, was that transformation actually an emancipatory one?

Underlying Weber's argument is a particular vision of emancipation bound up with the desire to develop and grow the nation-state, capitalism, and representative democracy as new forms of socioeconomic and political interaction, which, taken together, are the fundamental organizing structures of modern citizenship. This vision, of course, still remains relevant. However, there also exist other ideas of emancipation that go beyond the representative nation-state and capitalism and open up the possibility for thinking about the structures and the relations of the state, society, and economy in different ways. According to Raquel Gutiérrez,

> the politics of emancipation or, more accurately, emancipatory political action is no longer primarily, or solely, a discussion or competition regarding different ways of regulating and managing society conceived as a totality. Rather, it is a matter of the creation, care, expansion, and consolidation of a common ability to intervene—through deliberation and execution—in the issues that are incumbent on us all. Emancipation, then, is an issue both of understanding and reinforcing the sources of these abilities and of reflecting and acting on them, while simultaneously consolidating and extending them.[92]

Emancipation, then, more than something that brings the masses into "civilization," can also be understood as the capacity for people to take action and to decide public matters for themselves and, importantly, to do so through the mediums of their own traditions and customs.

Essential to any integral notion of development (beyond a narrow focus on economic growth) is the idea of emancipation. I have tried to demonstrate through an examination of the TIPNIS conflict how the theories and practices of hegemony and plurinationality advance contrasting visions of development. Thus, the conflict over the TIPNIS highway involves much more than just the technical infrastructure of the road. It underscores the differing views and desires of development within Bolivia. It is also a struggle over the relationship between society and nature, how decisions surrounding development policy are made, who benefits, and what that means in terms of social emancipation and the distribution of power.

Morales and the MAS planned the road in order to foster national unification and to spur development for indigenous peoples in the TIPNIS and the Amazon more broadly, in order to emancipate them from the yoke of patrimonial feudalism. Yet, this argument assumes that the model of state-led extractivist capitalism is a necessary stage in an inherently progressive and emancipatory trajectory. A similar idea is articulated in the second epigraph that opened this chapter. The stanza from Johann Wolfgang von Goethe is taken from an 1853 article in which Marx critiques the horrors of British colonialism in India while nevertheless extolling the advantages of the project for its obliging Indian society into capitalist modernity. "English steam and English free trade," Marx argues, broke down the traditional Indian social structures "by blowing up their economical basis, and thus produced the greatest, and to speak the truth, the only social revolution ever heard of in Asia."[93] Despite all the suffering inflicted on India by the British, Marx argues, colonialism ultimately helped bring about capitalist progress that would, eventually, lead to human emancipation. Marx asserts that the colonial expansion of bourgeois capitalism, despite its forceful coercion, is ultimately a liberating and progressive force from a previous era.[94] Thus, his use of the lines from Goethe: "Should this torture then torment us / Since it brings us greater pleasure?"

The MAS, I argue, has put forward a similar vision of development and the progressive and emancipatory future that a so-called Andean-Amazonian capitalism would bring with a highway through the TIPNIS. Evo Morales, for instance, has claimed that those who continue to oppose the highway "are enemies of the Beni. They want neither integration nor development, but instead want the people of the Beni to live like they did two hundred years ago."[95] Similarly, then vice president García Linera has argued that the Amazonian TIPNIS region is stuck in a developmental stage of feudal-like social relations and patrimonial domination, where "the despotic order of the hacendado landowner predominates and neither the indigenous organizations, nor the more recent peasant or worker organizations, have managed to create an organizational or discursive counter-power that can break down this patrimonial hacendado system."[96] Given this state of affairs, the MAS believes it incumbent on the state to reorganize this backward social structure. Despite the possibility that this process of reorganization may also bring about the dispossession of indigenous territory and the expansion of an extractivist mode of accumulation, the infrastructural fantasies accompanying the road project are entwined with a modernist belief in the human mastery of both nature and culture.[97] It is argued that this capitalist transformation is only a temporary phase on the way to a future communitarian socialist society. According to García Linera, Andean-Amazonian capitalism is the best strategic way to "improve the possibilities for the forces of worker and communitarian emancipation in the medium term," and, as such, "it is conceived as a temporary and transitional mechanism."[98] Should this torture then torment us, since it brings us greater pleasure?

Regardless of these emancipatory intentions, the decision-making process around the road was seen by many as a hegemonic imposition of a particular vision and strategy for development that conflicted with local desires. In other words, the TIPNIS highway was part of a top-down project of national unification and economic development with one goal, among many, being the emancipation of the park's indigenous peoples from above. The highway may indeed play a role in breaking down the current local power structure, but the indigenous protestors argued that it will simply be replaced by another hierarchical structure of social relations, that is to say, a new hegemonic order with similar objectives of extraction and appropriation.

Bolivia, then, like all other societies, faces questions surrounding its model of development. It is in search of a path that both preserves the natural environment and satisfies the basic needs of its people. However, Bolivia is a particularly interesting case because the idea of development itself came under question at the same time that important social changes were taking place in the early twenty-first century, opening the path toward a radically transformed country. Thus, the conflict over the highway through the TIPNIS represents a central point of contention not just between two models of development, but between two contrasting visions of what Bolivia is and ought to be.

4

PLURALITY AND POPULISM

CONAMAQ and Struggles of Indigenous Representation

They cannot represent themselves, they must be represented.
—KARL MARX

*As Indians they oppressed us and as Indians we will liberate
ourselves.*
—FAUSTO REINAGA

On my first trip to Bolivia, a two-month preliminary research stint, a colleague from Colombia, Katherine, and I were at the headquarters of the Consejo Nacional de Ayllus y Markas del Qullasuyu (CONA-MAQ, National Council of Ayllus and Markas of Qullasuyu), one of Bolivia's most important highland indigenous movement organizations. We were there to assist in the review and revision process of the organization's proposal on the law on prior and informed consultation, which was then under consideration. The process of drafting the legislation of prior and informed consultation had become increasingly antagonistic as tensions between the indigenous movement organizations of the Unity Pact and the Movimiento al Socialismo (MAS, Movement Toward Socialism) had grown due to the conflict over the Territorio Indígena y Parque Nacional Isiboro Sécure (TIPNIS, Isoboro Sécure Indigenous Territory and National Park) highway, discussed in the previous chapter. Despite the tense situation, the activists at CONAMAQ were open to a couple of graduate students trying to figure out just what the devil they were up to. They were interested in what we could offer them with the draft on prior and informed consultation, but also they allowed us access to their archives, we freely chatted with anyone and everyone in the building, and they invited us to participate in a celebratory gathering later in the week, which we gladly attended. I left that preliminary trip excited at how open the organization seemed to an unfamiliar researcher with a heap of unknowing questions.

By the time I came back for a year of fieldwork, CONAMAQ had undergone significant changes. I returned to its office headquarters in the Sopocachi neighborhood of La Paz to find a new and much more suspicious group of interlocutors. Out front three shiny new pickup trucks caught my attention, while inside a row of brand-new computers lining the administrative office wall suggested the appearance of new economic resources.

As I entered, three people from the department of Oruro sat quietly waiting to meet with someone. A young man in a leather jacket and black fedora with *wiphala* band came down the steps adjoining the entranceway and, after briefly chatting in Quechua with the *oruroeños*, directed them up the stairs. The man took a seat behind a desk facing the front door as I introduced myself. I was not sure whether my previous interlocutors would still be in La Paz, away from their communities, after more than a year since my last visit, so I asked whether Roberto or Erwin were around. They were not. I asked whether there was anyone else I could speak with. The man left, returning a few minutes later to lead me upstairs to the office of Hilarión Mamani, the new *mallku* (leader, head authority) of the organization. After introducing myself to Mamani and dropping a few names of previous contacts within the organization to hopefully signify my familiarity with CONAMAQ, I was told in no uncertain terms that those people were no longer around and that things had changed. Before I had a chance to ask anything further, Mamani told me he was too busy to talk and escorted me out of the office, telling me to come back in a month or so, after Carnaval, if I was still interested in talking.

I had been denied requests for interviews many times before and was under no illusions that an academic researcher could or should have the privilege to talk with anyone at any time. However, this instance felt different. In my previous visits to CONAMAQ I was welcome to simply sit around and hang out if no one had the time or was interested in talking. This time the entire atmosphere seemed much more regulated and restrictive. What had happened? What had changed?

In December 2013, CONAMAQ faced a serious organizational crisis as it split into two rival factions with competing parallel leaderships. Although it was an early ally of the government, Evo Morales and the MAS had encouraged the dispute between the pro-MAS and opposition factions, openly supporting the pro-MAS wing. While both factions continued to claim legitimate authority and popular support, the pro-MAS group gained control of organization headquarters, was recognized as the legal representative of the organization by the MAS government, and, as such, began receiving material support from the government and international NGOs. According to Cancio Rojas, former *mallku* of CONAMAQ from northern Potosí, this moment represented "the most profound ideological crisis in CONAMAQ's history."[1] Analyzing the conflict as a moment in the fundamental struggle between hegemony and plurinationality, I argue that the MAS has tried to construct a hegemonic form of indigeneity, which contrasts with the country's plurality of indigenous identities, as part of its particular hegemonic vision of social change and political transformation. The MAS government's intervention in CONAMAQ is, I will show, a logical outcome of a populist strategy of hegemony formation. While a populist strategy opened political space and gave a voice to many of Bolivia's dispossessed citizens during the wave of insurrections that brought Morales and the MAS to power, this chapter examines the transition from a populist moment to hegemony. More than just a struggle over representative control of the indigenous movement, this case reveals a more fundamental conflict between the MAS and its erstwhile supporters over the relationship between the state and civil society; the meaning of indigeneity; authenticity and representation; and the political logic of social transformation.

CONAMAQ AND THE RECONSTITUTION OF THE *AYLLU*

Although CONAMAQ was officially founded in a backyard meeting in the small highland town of Challapata, Oruro, in 1997, rank-and-file members and leaders alike reiterated to me over and over that they have "been around for centuries." Playing on the notion of strategic essentialism developed by Gayatri Chakravorty Spivak and Silvia Rivera Cusicanqui, CONAMAQ has underlined its pre-Columbian organizational roots and has sought to positively essentialize members' indigeneity in order to advance a political project.[2] That project involves a reinterpretation of indigenous identity and the reconstitution of *ayllus* and *markas*, which provide the territorial space to cultivate indigenous modes of being, leading, in turn, to the decolonization of Bolivian society.[3] *Ayllus* are the basic units of indigenous communities and have existed throughout the Andes since well before the arrival of Europeans in the Americas, while *markas* are a larger organizational unit composed of multiple *ayllus*. Conceptualized by John Murra as "vertical archipelagos," *ayllus* stretch over various ecological zones in order to avert the risks of high-altitude agriculture production in the Andean mountains.[4] According to María Eugenia Choque and Carlos Mamani, *ayllus* are composed of three main elements: the recognition of communally owned property (although the land can be parceled, in the final instance property belongs to the *ayllu* community as a whole); an origination in precolonial times; and, while the organizational and political systems differ depending on place, kinship as a central organizing component.[5] According to Nilda Rojas, an organization leader, CONAMAQ understands its attempts to reconstitute the precolonial system of *ayllus* as a mandate handed down from generations past.[6] *Ayllus* have been maintained throughout the Andes, although not unchanged, across the centuries of European colonialism and the ensuing republican nation-state projects of assimilating or eradicating indigenous populations. As such, according to Anders Burman, the reconstitution of the *ayllu* should be understood as a sociopolitical project that questions the legitimacy and viability of hegemonic modernity.[7]

Unlike indigenous and peasant movement organizations interested in overthrowing the state through a revolutionary uprising, CONAMAQ has historically directed its attention toward defending the rights of local communities and improving the viability of the *ayllu* form.[8] After Bolivia's 1952 National Revolution, the state sought to impose a uniform *sindicato* (union) model throughout the country in order to organize, regulate, and control the countryside. This corporatist process of state-directed unionization was intended to modernize the countryside through its economic, political, and social incorporation into the Bolivian nation-state.[9] According to Xavier Albó, this process of assimilation was an attempt to "re-baptize Indians as peasants," meaning an attempt to homogenize the heterogeneous cultural composition of Bolivian society through the imposition of a more developed capitalist hierarchy of social classes.[10]

Similar to postcolonial nation-building in Africa as traced by Mahmood Mamdani, the new State of '52 elites modeled their political imagination on the modern European nation-state, which resulted in an ahistorical nationalist dream being imposed on the reality of postcolonial social fragmentation.[11] In aiming to build a hegemonic national-popular formation, the revolutionary elites were oblivious to the ways in which their nation-building mentality internalized and mimicked their own colonial history. Nevertheless, this process of unionization and peasantization was uneven and incomplete across the country. While many *ayllu* communities did convert to the union model, others, such as in the highlands of Oruro and Potosí, continued to organize as *ayllus* and *markas*.[12] As Choque and Mamani note, "despite the presence of the peasant unions, the *ayllu* continued to express itself through symbolic representation, the territorial unity of collective land holdings, and the organizational and authority structure that still existed beneath the syndical form."[13]

During the 1980s, the contemporary movement to reconstitute the *ayllu* form began to build momentum. A severe drought and economic crisis in the early part of the decade led to the deterioration of agricultural production and worsening social conditions in many highland indigenous communities, a situation that motivated reviving the *ayllu* as a form of communal self-determination and sustainability.[14] In 1985, the "First Meeting of the *Ayllus*" was held in Potosí to discuss the viability of reconstituting the *ayllu* form as a mode of organization more representative of indigenous communities than the union model. In the early 1990s, regional *ayllu* organizations took form, such as the Federación de Ayllus Originarios del Norte de Potosí (Federation of Indigenous Ayllus of Northern Potosí), the Federación de Ayllus del Sur de Oruro (Federation of Ayllus of Southern Oruro), the Consejo Occidental de Ayllus de Jach'a Carangas (Western Ayllus Council of Jach'a Carangas), and the Federación de Ayllus y Comunidades Originarias de la Provincia Ingavi (Federation of Ayllus and Native Communities of the Ingavi Province). In 1994 these regional organizations joined together in the Comisión Impulsora para la Reconstitución de Ayllus de Bolivia (Commission for the Reconstitution of Ayllus of Bolivia), which in 1997 officially became CONAMAQ. The central goal of CONAMAQ has thus been to reconstitute the *ayllu* form in order for indigenous peoples to "institutionally practice their own cultural, economic, and political principles and values."[15]

CONAMAQ is organized at ascending levels from the local *ayllu*, through the *marka*, to the regional *suyu*. The organizational *ayllu* network is composed of primarily Aymara and Quechua communities in the departments of La Paz, Oruro, Potosí, Cochabamba, and Chuquisaca. Although organizational structures differ across CONAMAQ's member communities, the general authority structure of rotational leadership known as *thaki* (paths of increasing leadership demonstrating community membership) and the use of consensus-based decision-making are common to *ayllus* and to CONAMAQ itself. *Jach'a tantachawis*, or communal assemblies, are convened every year or every other year; they bring together authorities from the network of *ayllus* to discuss issues facing communities, deliberate and decide on CONAMAQ actions, and select new leaders.[16]

The growth of the *ayllu* movement and the creation of CONAMAQ were aided by both international and Bolivian NGOs, and spurred by a set of political reforms during the 1990s. International groups such as Oxfam America, the Inter-American Foundation, and the Denmark Foreign Aid Agency opted to fund projects working with *ayllus* and not unions, while Bolivian NGOs such as the Taller de Historia Oral Andina (Andean Oral History Workshop) worked to revitalize knowledge and recognition of the *ayllu* form. Additionally, national reforms such as the 1994 Ley de Participación Popular (Law of Popular Participation) and the 1996 Ley INRA (Instituto Nacional de Reforma Agraria, National Agrarian Reform Institute) provided legal standing to indigenous communities, which allowed *ayllus* to officially register with the state as *personería juridical* (juridical persons). Despite its many flaws, INRA did recognize indigenous communally held land tenure rights, giving these communities a material basis of subsistence and reproduction.[17] According to José Antonio Lucero, "given these new political, economic, and cultural benefits, many communities that previously identified as 'peasant communities' now opted for 'reconstituting' themselves as *ayllus*."[18]

CONAMAQ IN THE ERA OF EVO

Early on, CONAMAQ was quick to distinguish itself from other social movement organizations like the Confederación Sindical Única de Trabajadores Campesinos de Bolivia (CSUTCB, Unified Syndical

Confederation of Rural Workers of Bolivia) that employed more aggressive and confrontational tactics of struggle.[19] In 2000, when protests erupted in Cochabamba over a plan to privatize water—and then spread across the country, with the CSUTCB playing a central role in a more general repudiation of neoliberalism—the *mallkus* of CONAMAQ were pictured in the press showing support for then president Hugo Banzer (also a military dictator in the 1970s) by presenting him with a poncho and an emblem of leadership (*bastón de mando*, staff of power). At the time, only fifty-six miles (ninety kilometers) from La Paz, the military was using tanks to fire on indigenous protesters blockading highways, while the leaders of CONAMAQ, for their part, claimed that *ayllus*, unlike unions, were made not for protesting but rather for negotiation and dialogue.[20] Reaction from the organization's base was swift, and soon a new, more militant leadership was selected.

In the early twenty-first century, CONAMAQ took a more confrontational stance and began participating in protests and road blockades as the country entered a period of serious social and political upheaval.[21] CONAMAQ joined the eastern lowland indigenous organization Confederación de Pueblos Indígenas de Bolivia (CIDOB, Confederation of Indigenous Peoples of Bolivia) in calling not only for an overthrow of the existing political system and an end to neoliberal policies, but also for a Constituent Assembly to "refound" Bolivia as a plurinational state. With the election in 2002 of Gonzalo Sánchez de Lozada, a former president whose government had implemented the latest round of neoliberal reforms in the 1990s, CONAMAQ was quick to voice its opposition; the organization played an important role in the protests leading to his resignation and flight to the United States in October 2003.

As protests, marches, and road blockades continued to rack the country, plaguing the ensuing government of Carlos Mesa, CONAMAQ joined with various other movement organizations to form the Unity Pact. Like his predecessor, Mesa was ultimately forced to resign in June 2005 due to the constant state of insurrection, which he said made the country ungovernable. With a new round of elections in December 2005, CONAMAQ and the Unity Pact provided a crucial base of support that brought Evo Morales and the MAS to state power.

After Morales's election, the Unity Pact's demands to rewrite the constitution and refound the country along plurinational lines increased, leading Morales to call in 2006 for a Constituent Assembly, which featured a significant number of campesino and indigenous representatives. Over the ensuing three years, while the new constitution was being debated and drafted, Bolivia faced the risk of outright civil war as the old elite based in the eastern half of the country (known as the *media luna*) tried to impede the assembly and violently clashed with supporters of the Unity Pact and the MAS. While disagreements arose between some member organizations of the Unity Pact and the government during the assembly debates, particularly around issues of resource extraction and indigenous autonomy, the threat coming from the opposition in the *media luna* was enough to stave off any significant fissures internal to the ruling coalition for the time being.[22]

After a referendum on the new constitution in 2009 passed with 61 percent approval, Morales was reelected with nearly 65 percent of the vote, and the MAS gained a majority in both chambers of the national legislature, the threat from the elite opposition subsided. According to Fernando Mayorga, this electoral victory marked a strategic shift in the MAS's vision and practice of social transformation. While during Morales's first term (2006–9) the MAS relied on the supportive action of its base in the streets to defend the government against the opposition and to push forward the process of change, with a clear electoral majority the locus of attention turned toward the institutional political arena.[23]

The effects of this shift on the relationship between the government and its indigenous movement supporters were most clearly demonstrated during the TIPNIS conflict discussed in the previous chapter, which led CONAMAQ and CIDOB to withdraw from the Unity Pact. The choice of CONAMAQ and CIDOB to formally leave the Unity Pact and oppose the MAS government was a strategic one, although it was contested. Factions within each organization thought it better to remain strategically aligned with the MAS, despite seemingly contradictory goals.[24] These internal disagreements would ultimately provide an opportunity for the MAS to intervene, in an effort to control dissent. According to Cancio Rojas, "after the success of the TIPNIS march [and CONAMAQ and CIDOB's withdrawal of support of the government], the MAS divided CIDOB with a parallel organization. After that, they strategized how to do the same thing to us in CONAMAQ, which has severely affected us."[25]

In December 2013, a dispute between the two factions over the election of new organizational leaders led to a police siege of CONAMAQ's headquarters, followed by a number of violent confrontations, hunger strikes, and blockades. After the initial row, the office sat unoccupied for a month as police dressed in riot gear secured the building and denied access to both factions, while members of the CONAMAQ *orgánico* faction set up a vigil outside in the street.[26] On January 15, members of the so-called CONAMAS faction led by Hilarión Mamani marched on the two-story building, where another violent confrontation ensued. During the skirmish the police stepped aside to allow CONAMAS to take the building.[27]

The CONAMAS faction received strategic support from the government that allowed it to violently take control of the organization's building. Afterward, CONAMAS received significant legal support and funding from the government for development projects, services, and organizational goods like trucks and computers.[28] While the MAS government revoked the legal status of CONAMAQ *orgánico*, the parallel group was reinstated in the Unity Pact and installed in the directorate of the national indigenous development fund, the Fondo para el Desarrollo de los Pueblos Indígenas, Originarios y Campesinos (Fund for the Development of Indigenous, Native, and Peasant Peoples). CONAMAS leader Mamani was also appointed the head of the Coordinadora Nacional por el Cambio (National Coordinator for Change). These material and representational resources gave the CONAMAS faction the ability to buy support from local *ayllu* communities, while leaving CONAMAQ *orgánico* economically debilitated and increasingly isolated.

If there was any doubt that the MAS was exploiting the internal division in an attempt to repress the dissent of CONAMAQ *orgánico*, only two days after the initial ouster police occupied the offices of the Asamblea Permanente de Derechos Humanos de Bolivia (Permanent Assembly of Human Rights in Bolivia), which was providing office space to the displaced faction, and once again expelled CONAMAQ *orgánico*.[29] The transformation of the CONAMAQ building (see figure 1) offers a clear visual representation of the intervention and its outcome. What used to be a brick and stucco outer wall was painted in the blue and white colors of the MAS, with the slogan "President Evo" added above the entry gate. MAS flags flew in place of what used to be the *wiphala* and Bolivian tricolor, while a banner picturing Evo and MAS legislative candidate Sonia Brito hung prominently on the face of the building.

FIGURE 1. CONAMAQ headquarters, before (2013, *top*) and after (2014) the MAS take-over. Photographs by Samy Schwartz.

The upshot of the situation was the demobilization of CONAMAQ as an indigenous movement organization. As Pavlína Springerová and Barbora Vališková explain, the intervention significantly reduced CONA-MAQ's autonomy, "as the state became the almost exclusive source of resources for social and economic development, the allocation of which was conditioned by loyalty to the MAS government. . . . The result is the demobilization of the organization, as can be seen in the decline of protest activity since 2013, for the organic part lacks the grassroots, while the parallel part remains pacified through patronage and co-optation."[30]

While the MAS has been labeled authoritarian by critics for its inter-vention, we can understand the government's action as a logical con-sequence of the MAS's vision and practice of social transformation based on the logic of hegemony and hegemonic change. This moment represents an empirical expression of the underlying theoretical differ-ence between the MAS government and some of its erstwhile indigenous supporters over the relationship between state and society, the politics of indigenous identity, and the way these issues relate to processes of social change. In order to further explain my argument, I now turn to an analysis of populism, which, in an abstract sense, operates as an integral mode of representational political action within the logic of hegemony.

POPULISM

The literature on populism has consistently lamented the concept's lack of clarity and resulting lack of utility for political analysis. As Ernesto Laclau has noted, few terms have been so widely used yet so imprecisely defined. "We know intuitively to what we refer when we call a movement or an ideology populist, but we have the greatest difficulty in translating the intuition into concepts."[31] This is nowhere clearer than in the schol-arly research on Latin American politics, where the practice of populism has perhaps been most widespread and where the concept has been most analytically applied.

Debates over how best to define and theorize populism have largely focused on the phenomenon's economic and political ideological con-tent. Based on the wave of populist leaders throughout Latin America in the middle of the twentieth century, many scholars highlighted the economic determinants of the trend. Populism was identified with a par-ticular stage of economic development.[32] In contrast, the failures of the institutional political system were given prominence with the rise of neo-populism in the 1990s. In essence, populism was understood as a failure to properly incorporate citizens into political life through strong and stable political parties.[33] From this position, without proper democratic incorporation through the representative institutions of political soci-ety, citizens are drawn to charismatic populist leaders outside the main-stream political institutions as the only way to be represented. According to Kenneth M. Roberts, populism thrives during crises of representation, times when political institutions are incapable of marshaling the loyalty and allegiance of citizens.[34]

Others have analyzed populism and its relationship with democracy.[35] Where some analysts view populism as a fundamentally democratizing force, others see the critique and abandonment of political institutions as an authoritarian threat to democracy. Populism's relationship with democracy in Latin America has been debated since the first wave of populist leaders; during the rise of left-leaning governments in the early 2000s, the discussion intensified. Largely focusing on the governments of Rafael Correa in Ecuador, Hugo Chávez in Venezuela, and Evo Morales in Bolivia, critics have argued that these populist leaders threatened the political stability and democratic expansion that many countries in the region achieved through the 1980s. Kurt Weyland, for instance, argues that populism "inherently stands in tension with democracy and the value that it places upon pluralism, open debate, and fair competition," and that Correa, Chávez, and Morales "set about strangling democracy and putting competitive authoritarianism in its place."[36] Critics also argue that populist economic policies create commodity shortages, hyperinflation, capital flight, and economic ruin, similar to that witnessed in the period before neoliberal stabilization.[37] What is more, even if populist leaders are able to implement policies that temporarily improve the welfare of the people, these advancements become politicized; often suffer from inefficiency, problematic design, and implementation; and in the end are not sustainable.[38]

Contrastingly, it has also been argued that populism opens a path toward democratic popular sovereignty by placing "the people" at the center of political action. According to Peter Worsley, "insofar as populism plumps for the rights of majorities to make sure—by 'intervening'— that they are not ignored (as they commonly are) populism is profoundly compatible with democracy."[39] In a similar vein, Enrique Peruzzotti claims that populism offers a necessary check on the elitist logic that dominates contemporary representative democracy.[40]

Scholars have debated whether populism ideologically aligns more with the Left or the Right. Similar to the discussion of populism's relationship with democracy and its central causal determinants, populism's ideological content is ambiguous and elastic. Whereas many leaders of

Latin America's Left Turn have been identified as populists, "neopopulists" of the 1980s and 1990s such as Carlos Menem in Argentina, Alberto Fujimori in Peru, and Fernando Collor de Mello in Brazil implemented neoliberal policies and were aligned with the political Right. Thus, while we may be able to identify specific populist movements as left wing or right wing, populism as a political practice lacks any innate or essential ideological correspondence.

Following the work of Ernesto Laclau and Robert S. Jansen, I argue that populism is best understood as a political *logic*, a specific type of politics that is situated as an internal periphery of hegemonic political practice.[41] That is, rather than trying to define populism based on its economic or political ideological *content*, I wish to highlight the *form* itself as the key defining feature of populism. Doing so allows us to see how the political field is conceptually organized in such a way that obscures the malleability of identity categories, their constructedness, and expresses them as something essential. Populist practice delimits subjectivities, in this case indigeneity, reducing them to dualities and implying a politics of domination of one over the other.

POPULIST LOGIC AND PRACTICE

Following Laclau, the meaning of populism "is not to be found in any political or ideological content entering into the description of the practices of any particular group, but in a particular *mode of articulation* of whatever social, political, or ideological contents."[42] In order to more fully grasp this idea and show its conceptual utility, we need to analyze Laclau's theoretical apparatus further.

To begin, Laclau focuses on how social demands are expressed and whether those demands are satisfied, leaving aside the political or ideological substance of the demands themselves. If, for instance, a group makes a particular demand and that demand is then satisfied, we are in an instance of what Laclau calls a *logic of difference*. That is, all social actors accept the legitimacy of the process, and nobody questions the right to make the demand or the right of those in power to make a decision on whether to satisfy the demand. Logics of difference "presuppose that there is no social division and that any legitimate demand can be satisfied in a non-antagonistic, administrative way."[43] But, what happens when a variety of social demands are expressed and are not satisfied but are instead met with silence? In this case, while the contents of the demands substantively differ, they share a similarity in that they have all been negated. A situation such as this is what Laclau labels a *logic of equivalence*. If these unsatisfied demands, despite their differential character, are seen as related due to their unfulfilled status by the social subjects making them, we have what Laclau calls an *equivalential chain* or a *chain of equivalence*. The demands within a chain of equivalence are linked based on their negative character (their lack of fulfillment), which requires the source of that negativity to be identified. Thus, the formation of a chain of equivalence divides the social into two distinct camps: those with the power the negate or fulfill demands (the elite, the oligarchy, the ancien régime, etc.), and those without power (e.g., *el pueblo* [the people]). Here we have the structural components of populism understood as a form of political practice. "The more social demands tend to be differentially absorbed within a successful institutional system, the weaker the equivalential links will be and the more unlikely the constitution of a popular subjectivity; conversely, a situation in which a plurality of unsatisfied demands and an increasing inability of the institutional system to absorb them differentially co-exist, creates the conditions leading to a populist rupture."[44] Independent of the actual political or ideological contents of any particular movement, populism is understood to operate here as a mode of articulating social demands through an equivalential rather than differential logic.

Notably, the appeals of various groups that link up to create the overarching equivalential chain of demands (and thereby split the social into two contending camps) do not come from some preconstituted social group (i.e., "the people") with an already existing defined set of interests. Rather, those groups' action of making the demands and forming a chain of equivalence is what constitutes the historical subject of "the people."[45] According to Francisco Panizza, populism is "a mode of identification in which the relation between its form (the people as signifier) and its content (the people as signified) is given by the very process of naming— that is, of establishing who the enemies of the people (and therefore the people itself) are."[46] From Laclau's perspective, populism is the political practice of constituting a national popular "universal will" with the ultimate goal of "creating hegemonically a unity—a homogeneity—out of an irreducible heterogeneity."[47]

It is from this view of populism, as a political logic within the realm of hegemony, that I would like to interpret the MAS government's intervention in CONAMAQ. The following section examines two contradictions of populist hegemonic politics that are made apparent through the moment of CONAMAQ's separation: the internal contradictions of the logic of populist hegemony, and the issue of representation as an indicator of difference between populist hegemony and plurinationality. The analysis demonstrates that despite the claims of Laclau and others, populism and hegemony are not synonymous with politics in general.[48] According to the overarching argument I am making in this book, plurinationality represents one such political logic and practice outside of populism and hegemony.

POPULIST CONTRADICTIONS

As outlined above, the central feature of populism as a political logic is the creation of a chain of equivalence that brings together various disparate demands, thereby assembling a unified historical popular subject, "the people," which, in turn, splits the social space into two opposing camps. From a strategic point of view, this political act makes sense in a context where the goal is to challenge an existing power bloc that is perceived to control a unified economic, political, and cultural space through the extension of its universal will throughout that social terrain. The process by which "the people" is constituted and struggles against the existing power bloc for economic, political, and cultural control of society is the political practice of hegemony. But, what happens when the chain of equivalence that is "the people" moves beyond the moment of counterhegemonic potential and actually assumes hegemonic power? Despite the argument that the act of hegemonic formation itself changes the interests and demands of the groups involved, is it possible that the chain of equivalence that discursively binds the people together dissolves after hegemony is attained, leaving the new hegemonic bloc in an ambiguous and contradictory position? What happens when the negated dimension of the social demands no longer holds the equivalential chain together against the previous hegemonic system? This is the contradictory moment of populist hegemony that leads to a reconfiguration of the equilibrium between coercion and consent in the equation of hegemony. We can see how this process unfolds in the situation under examination here, in CONAMAQ's revocation of support of the MAS government over the 2011 TIPNIS conflict and the indigenous organization's subsequent division.

During the period extending from the formation of the Unity Pact in 2004, through the ascension of the MAS to state power in 2006 and the Constituent Assembly (2006–9), until the TIPNIS conflict in 2011, the discourse around indigeneity functioned as an *empty signifier*. That is, indigeneity was conceptualized not simply as an ethnic identification but rather as a symbolic representation of the Bolivian people against the ruling neoliberal elite regime. As an empty signifier, indigeneity linked together the chain of equivalence composed of the multitude of peasants, indigenous groups, neighborhood associations, labor unions, and other civil society organizations that challenged the old neoliberal elite and brought Morales and the MAS to power.

The discourse around indigeneity and indigenous representation has always been a contested field, but after Morales took power as the first indigenous president of Bolivia it became an even more important terrain of social struggle. Rather than serving as an empty signifier that operated to strategically homogenize what in reality was a heterogeneous social subject, indigenous identity more and more began to split into (at least) two contending camps. For instance, scholars have analyzed how Morales and the MAS attempted to define who and what was "indigenous" based on distinctions between highland and lowland regions, and between territorialized and deterritorialized groups.[49]

A key defining feature of indigenous identity revolves around the questions of land tenure and social organization. According to Burman, compared to peasant groups organized along syndical lines, who view land as individual cultivable plots, indigenous peoples understand land as territory under the collective management of self-governed communities. "While the struggle of peasant unions for many years has been one for land, that is, the right to individual parcels of cultivable land, the process of reconstituting the *ayllu* has become a struggle for territory, that is to say, the right to extensive areas of collective management, including the administration of natural resources and free political, social, and economic determination."[50] This distinction between land and territory is often presented as a distinction between western highland and eastern lowland indigenous groups.[51] For many highland Aymara and Quechua peasants, the argument goes, land is meant to be a productive entity and should belong to those who put it to productive use, while lowland groups need access to vast territories to reproduce themselves through hunting, fishing, and foraging. These differences have led to conflict, as western highland people migrated east in search of more arable land after their *minifundios* (small parcels of land) secured through the 1953 agrarian reform law gave way to parcelization over several generations, to such an extent that many referred to their landholdings as *surcofundios* (single rows of crops). For land-hungry highland Aymara and Quechua peasants, lowland indigenous groups who control large tracts of seemingly idle land are sometimes labeled as the new *latifundistas* (large landowners). Yet, this same land/territory fissure occurs internally in both the highlands and lowlands, making this geographic distinction untenable.

Others have interpreted this distinction in the system of land use in terms of indigeneity, arguing that those who communally hold the land, are subsistence based, and maintain traditional forms of social organization (*ayllu, marka, capitanía,* etc.) are real, authentic Indians, while those who view land in terms of smallholder private property, are more thoroughly integrated into the market, and have been organized on the basis of unionism are not really indigenous people. For instance, in an otherwise insightful and reflective piece on the notion of "strategic ethnicity" as a political strategy, Silvia Rivera Cusicanqui states, "even though the coca growers use the Indian flag [the *wiphala*] for their organization and they speak largely in Quechua, this is not enough to consider them 'indigenous,'" due to the fact that they want to open up eastern lands for colonization, separate the land into smallholder plots, and connect with the commodity chains of the global market.[52] What this debate makes clear is that an important characteristic of contemporary indigeneity involves a material conflict between (at least) two cultural groups who have distinct relations to land or territory and who both identify as indigenous. This finding sheds light not only on the divergent positions of these groups' material relations, but also on the ambiguities of indigenous subject formation.

Importantly, distinctions between varying groups are representational, and what it means to be "indigenous" is open to contestation and change. Critiquing the notion of essentialism, Lucero calls our attention to the processes by which identities are constructed relationally and, through this process, become visible and representable. He states, "the subject of representation is always contingent and contested, even when certain formations become dominant. . . . Representation (political or otherwise), on this view, has what Foucault and others would call a productive role in fabricating the very thing it supposedly represents. . . . Whatever the subject of representation has been (e.g., interest, will, or popular sovereignty), it has not existed prior to the particular machinery of representation, but was produced with and in part, by that machinery. The political subject itself is a product of representation."[53] It is through the machinery of representation—whether of nations, political parties, or social movement organizations—that these subjectivities are actually brought into being.

Problems arise when a concept like indigeneity is universalized on the representational plane, obviating internal differentiation. One way of countering the tendency to essentialize indigenous identity is to understand the multiplicity within the category of indigeneity itself. Andrew Canessa, for instance, argues that in contemporary Bolivia there are two currents within indigeneity: "one sees indigenous people and values as the foundation of the nation-state and seeks to create an ecumenical indigeneity for a majority of Bolivia's citizens, and the other seeks to respect cultural difference in its multiple forms and protection of marginal peoples *from* the state."[54] This latter group, whose discourse is more about autonomy and territorial control, Canessa labels as "territorialized." Those in the former group, who are much more interested in a Bolivian national identity that puts themselves at the center, and who argue that the nation's resources should be exploited for their benefit in particular, are labeled "deterritorialized." Xavier Albó makes a similar argument in the context of the 1970s downfall of the so-called Military-Peasant Pact and the rise of Katarismo and the independent organization of highland indigenous peasants in the CSUTCB. Highlighting two distinct currents within this movement, Albó notes, "the first tendency has been that of winning autonomous terrain in the face of a state considered inefficient . . . a theoretically symmetrical, although subordinate, relationship regulated by an implicit contract between an autonomous body (the *ayllu*) and the state. The peasant project, then, appears to point to a plurinational state. The second tendency seeks full participation in the state as a means of controlling the government."[55] Morales and the MAS, through laws, policies, and discourse, have linked the latter of these forms to a universal indigeneity, but their attempt to construct a hegemonic indigenous identity has come at the expense of a nonessentialized plurinational indigenous subject.[56] For Burman, "hegemonic indigeneity" is "intimately tied to notions of Bolivian nationhood and a strong Bolivian state" and emphasizes an indigenous identity that helps maintain traditional systems of state power.[57] This hegemonic indigeneity is in some ways similar to what Charles Hale has labeled the *indio permitido* (permitted Indian).[58] The version of indigeneity that is being put forth by Morales and the MAS is hegemonic not because it is necessarily dominant, but rather in the theoretical sense that it is not interested in projecting territorial and political visions beyond the Bolivian nation-state—that is, beyond the logic of hegemony. As Nicole Fabricant and Nancy Postero point out, the MAS government has used indigeneity "as a part of the tools of sovereignty to reinforce indigenous groups who cleave to the state line and support capitalist accumulation and extractive industries and to punish those who fail to acculturate to the workings of the market."[59] Morales and the MAS have claimed to represent indigenous people, but in the process have sought to define what indigeneity means. The MAS's hegemonic indigeneity "constitutes no threat to the established notion of *la patria* [the national homeland]; rather it gives *la patria* indigenous legitimacy."[60]

This duality of indigenous identities was demonstrated to me in conversations with leaders from both CONAMAQ and the CSUTCB, Bolivia's national peasant union organization. Fidel, a CONAMAQ activist, told me that at the root of the government intervention lies an ideological and strategic difference between the politics of the MAS and those of the *ayllus* and *suyus* of CONAMAQ. Sitting in a small apartment that had served as CONAMAQ *orgánico's* office since the faction's eviction from the old headquarters, Fidel told me that the MAS "holds a position of centralizing power, which includes defining us indigenous people in ways that are in contrast with our own aspirations." He continued, "we have our own political forms, but with the MAS we continue to see how they attempt to control indigenous and original peoples and steer the indigenous movements toward their own goals of the party and political power, not the desires and aspirations of our indigenous communities."[61] For Fidel, Morales and the MAS employ a rhetoric of indigenous peoples' rights for an international audience, but change their tune when it comes to their policies regarding indigenous peoples within Bolivia. The MAS, Fidel said, uses indigenous ideas and language to promote the continued expansion of natural resource extraction and large-scale capitalist agricultural production in an attempt to "develop and modernize" Bolivia as a nation-state. Yet, Fidel sees the MAS project in historical terms as only the latest attempt in a long line of nation-building schemes that have ultimately been unsuccessful. Echoing Fidel, Postero argues that "Morales continues to invoke indigenous history and culture, but he does so in performances of a state-controlled version of indigeneity that legitimizes state power. . . . Moreover, the MAS government has made it clear that it will sacrifice some indigenous communities to its national development project."[62]

Other conversations with members of CONAMAQ *orgánico* revealed similar ideas. One afternoon, Esther, Raúl, and I left the apartment/office for lunch at a restaurant across the street. As we waited for our *sopa de fideo* (noodle soup), I explained to them that I was still trying to comprehend who the term *indigenous* actually referred to in the contemporary context of struggles over its meaning. Esther laughed and, with a mixture of what I took to be understanding and pity, began describing a number of traditions for different territorially situated groups. She pointed out that while the community she was from in southern Oruro wore particular hats, for instance, and chose their communal leaders through their own *usos y costumbres* (norms and procedures), this was different from other places in the *altiplano* (plateau) and even more so in the Amazonian east. "This word is a very interesting word," she said. "Despite the differences, the thing that unites us all is a shared history, one that is based on our common difference with the West and colonialism." Raúl chimed in, "there are thirty-six different nations here, and many, many more communities. CONAMAQ doesn't speak for all indigenous peoples, but neither does the MAS. We represent those communities that follow our form of organization [the *ayllu*], while others follow their own forms. We have our own way of socially organizing, of controlling land, but we acknowledge the ways of others. This is how it has always been here."[63] While they were perhaps essentializing a bit to make their point clear, what I took Esther and Raúl's comments to mean was that the concept of indigenous was socially expansive, that there is no singularly authentic indigenous identity. Indigenous identity is historically constructed, as the comment from Esther about shared history implies, and, as such, changes over time and across space. Esther and Raúl's comments express a plurinational articulation of indigenous identity.

While CONAMAQ *orgánico* is critical of the government's developmental model and its attempt at circumscribing indigenous identity to fit its own goals, the influential indigenous organization CSUTCB maintains a vision of hegemonic indigeneity.[64] Mauricio Choque, the head of the CSUTCB's Commission on Land and Territory, told me, "Evo Morales is our indigenous brother, he is our brother president, he is our leader, he represents us. While we [the CSUTCB] maintain our independence, we support and follow our indigenous president. . . . We support Evo and the MAS government because they represent Bolivia's indigenous people." When asked about the relationship between the CSUTCB and CONAMAQ, Choque explained that the visions of the two movement organizations were very different. He described how the CSUTCB had fought and struggled to achieve indigenous rights and to make Bolivia a more democratic country through protests, marches, strikes, and blockades, while CONAMAQ had historically done none of these things. CONAMAQ, he said, wasn't interested in democratizing Bolivia because it wasn't a "national" organization and was only interested in local struggles. "What do they mean when they talk about 'reconstitution'? What are they going to reconstitute? They don't want to reconstitute Bolivia. They want to split Bolivia apart. With their vision of social change, Bolivia as a nation wouldn't exist."[65] What is important to note here is Choque's focus on the nation as the locus of struggle. The local struggles of CONAMAQ (i.e., the reconstitution of the *ayllu*) come at the expense of the nation itself. He stated, "CONAMAQ calls themselves *originarias* [native, indigenous]. Indigenous to where/ what [*originaria de que*]? To me, and I say this with all due respect to CONAMAQ, they are not our indigenous brothers." For Choque and the contemporary CSUTCB, imagining an indigenous identity outside the territorial confines of the Bolivian nation-state is analogous to not being indigenous at all. To be indigenous from the perspective of hegemonic indigeneity means to be one of the original inhabitants of the Bolivian nation, and to struggle for indigenous peoples is to struggle for Bolivian sovereignty at the level of the nation-state.

INDIGENEITY, POPULISM, AND REPRESENTATION

The different visions of indigeneity discussed above are central to the issue of populism because they are the very substance of who and what is represented through the MAS's populist politics. Representation, according to Hanna Pitkin, is the "making present of something that is nevertheless absent." Representation entails "acting for others," which "means acting in the interests of the represented, in a manner responsive to them."[66] The absent something is made present through an intermediary, such as a name, a symbol, or an agent that acts in the name of the represented. Accordingly, representation is a set of social and cultural processes through which identities are constructed by linking certain political subjects with larger political communities.

Populism, as an act of representation, brings into existence the subject it seeks to represent: "the people." According to Lucero, "populism depends on a representation that claims to mirror a certain reality, yet is more important in producing a version of reality."[67] Rather than reflecting an already existing social subject, populism works to bring into existence a specific social subject that corresponds to a particular situation. In the case of CONAMAQ, the MAS government not only attempted to quell criticisms of a formerly supportive indigenous movement organization, but also sought to produce a particular type of indigenous subject that could be represented within the confines of *el pueblo Boliviano*. The production of subjects that become "the people" is the very essence of populism, and this can only be accomplished through the mechanisms of representation. Similar to Karl Marx's critique of the French peasantry in his "Eighteenth Brumaire," which serves as one of the epigraphs to this chapter, Morales and the MAS assume that a certain type of indigenous subject cannot represent themselves but instead must be represented.[68] The populism of the MAS assumes that the Bolivian people are indigenous, that they have been exploited and divided for centuries, and that for them to be liberated, they must be unified, organized, and represented by the nation's first indigenous president.

The whole idea of representation presupposes a distinction between the represented and the representative, between the symbolized and the symbol. This bifurcation distinguishes representation from self-government, which presents an issue for populism and hegemony. If hegemony is about the creation of a universal will that guides a society through mechanisms of coercion and consent, populism is the political practice through which that universal subjectivity is constructed and projected in the form of "the people." However, there is a contradiction in this process when the populist leader is seen to embody the immediacy of the people while at the same time acting for them. There is an incongruity between the populist leader acting *as* the people and their acting *for* the people.[69] In other words, populism seeks to suspend the distance between the people and their representative while at the same time maintaining the authority and control that representative politics provides. This contradiction displayed itself when CONAMAQ questioned the MAS government in the name of indigenous people. Guided by a hegemonic political logic, the MAS sought to construct an indigenous subject in its own image.

CONCLUSION

The CONAMAQ intervention was a populist moment embedded within the MAS's overarching theory and practice of hegemonic social transformation. We can see that this episode is more than just a conflict over the direction of an indigenous movement organization; rather, it highlights a distinction between how the MAS and proponents of plurinationality separately understand indigeneity, intersubjectivity, and representation in the context of state-society relations. When CONAMAQ rescinded its support for the government due to what it claimed were anti-indigenous policies, the MAS was threatened not only by a waning base of support, but more importantly by a challenge to its symbolic association with indigenous identity—an indigeneity that served as the empty signifier and chain of equivalence that brought Bolivians together against the ruling neoliberal elite during the 2000–2005 insurrectionary period, which ultimately carried Morales and the MAS to power. CONAMAQ's grow-ing opposition to the government threatened the MAS's control over the symbol of indigenous identity, which, in turn, compromised the MAS's entire hegemonic project, one founded on an indigenous president governing an indigenous state. When the MAS was unable to maintain CONAMAQ's consent, the party was compelled to use the mechanisms of coercion at its disposal to secure its hegemonic project. "By creating the parallel organization," Springerová and Vališková argue, "the govern-ment was able to eliminate its indigenous opponents and maintain the illusion of indigenous representativeness in state structures."[70] Attempt-ing to eradicate the heterogeneity of indigenous subjectivity and placing the weight of state power behind a particular vision of indigeneity, the MAS acted as if there were a consensus on what it means to be indige-nous and who counts as being indigenous.

The government's intervention in CONAMAQ was a strategic choice based on a reading of the political conjuncture structured by the MAS's theoretical vision of hegemonic social transformation. For theorists like Laclau, the logic of populist and hegemonic politics is the univer-sal form of politics. Laclau asks, "if populism consists in postulating a radical alternative within the communitarian space, a choice at a cross-roads on which the future of a given society hinges, does not populism become synonymous with politics?" He responds that "the answer can only be affirmative," adding, "the end of populism coincides with the end of politics."[71] Elsewhere he claims, "hegemony is, in the final instance, an inherent dimension to all social practice."[72] From Laclau's perspective, then, it is possible to question the strategic effectiveness of the MAS's intervention, but the underlying political logic that, in the final instance, determines what is politically imaginable remains outside the realm of examination. But, there are other political logics that do not rely on split-ting the social space into two camps that contend for power over an imagined social totality.

This chapter has offered a critical reading of the MAS's involvement in an internal dispute within CONAMAQ through the concepts of pop-ulism, subjectivity, and representation. While I am critical of MAS pop-ulism, I am not arguing that populism leads to economic instability or democratic backsliding, as others claim.[73] Populism is, in fact, an inher-ent aspect of electoral representative democratic politics; it is a reflec-tion of democracy.[74] I am arguing that democracy is more than simply procedural—more than just voters, political parties, and elections—and that the systems of representation intrinsic to populism and hegemony inhibit the expression of alternative forms of democracy and democratic politics.

Scholars such as Paolo Virno, Michael Hardt, and Antonio Negri have attempted to theorize a different form of politics through the concept of the multitude.[75] For Virno, the multitude is a plurality that persists as such in the public sphere, without converging into a unified One, "which allows for the political-social existence of the *many* seen as being *many*."[76] The multitude, then, provides us with a possibility where a political logic does not necessitate the homogenization of social heterogeneity. Instead, the multitude is a collection of singularities without equivalence, a plurality without unification. This is not to claim that the work of articulating various demands and identities together is useless. Articulation remains an important political task in any process of social transformation, but the concept of the multitude shows that there are other ways to conceive of articulation beyond populism and hegemony.

In Bolivia, similar to the notion of the multitude, the theory of plurinationality offers an alternative politics. Like the multitude, plurinationality attempts to rethink society outside the confines of a hegemonic social totality. The underlying logic of plurinationalism is related not to the construction of a universal will expressed through "the people," but rather to the proliferation of various "peoples" with the ability to express their own demands through their own forms of representation. In this sense, plurinationality also offers a different view of indigeneity. Whereas the MAS has attempted to construct a hegemonic indigeneity, proponents of plurinationality such as CONAMAQ recognize the plurality of indigenous identity and its varying forms of representations. CONAMAQ's effort to reconstitute the *ayllu* has been one avenue of building plurinationality, as the *ayllu* provides the institutional structure for cultural recognition and the territorial basis for cultural reproduction in the highlands. As such, the *ayllu* is a foundational element for the construction of a plurinational democracy. It is through the *ayllu* that certain indigenous communities govern themselves directly, a practice that does not eliminate the system of political representation but alters the possibilities of who or what is represented, and how. As Burman argues, "CONAMAQ has the potential to create another cartography of power and, thus, another political project—the Indianismo of the *ayllu*—for the future."[77]

5

TRANSFORMING THE STATE?

Indigenous Autonomy in *El Estado Plurinacional*

We disembark from the bus at the large *casco minero* (miner's helmet) monument in the middle of a roadway roundabout on the outskirts of the city of Oruro. There is a cool breeze at this morning hour, but the sun is starting to warm the air as it rises overhead. My colleague Paul and I wander around asking where we can find the minibus to San Pedro de Totora and get different, often contradictory, answers. After twenty minutes or so, we manage to find a minibus a few blocks away, waiting to fill up with passengers before it can head out to the village. We cram ourselves into the back corner, and we are soon rumbling out of town along a gravel road. As we travel, the concrete and adobe houses of Oruro become sparser and the dry brown rolling hills of the *altiplano* (plateau) take over, foregrounded by the snow-covered mountain peaks in the distance.

After a couple hours of drifting in and out of sleep, we pull into the central plaza of Totora. The plaza is nearly empty, apart from a few kids playing and a small group of people milling about in a far corner. I am a little surprised and wonder whether we got the date right, or whether perhaps the event was changed. This is our first visit to Totora, and we have come for a state-run discussion of the village's attempt to reorganize itself as an autonomous indigenous community, or *autonomía indígena originario campesina* (AIOC, indigenous original peasant autonomy), according to the official codification laid out in the 2009 constitution and ensuing legislation. Referred to as *talleres de socialización* (socialization workshops), these events are meant to be opportunities for the community to come together with NGO advisers and state officials to comb through the details of the long and onerously bureaucratic road to autonomy. I had assumed this to be a big event for this small community and thought it would be a good opportunity to get to know the town and meet some central proponents of the AIOC initiative. We made our way across the plaza and joined the small group in the corner, who were also there for the event and waiting for it to get underway. After about an hour of us loitering around, a small caravan of three cars pulled into the plaza. Edwin, a local man in his midfifties with whom I had been talking, pointed at the cars and said, "This is what autonomy brings, recognition." As he was saying this, Gonzalo Vargas, the vice minister of autonomies, and Adolfo Mendoza, a well-known Movimiento al Socialismo (MAS, Movement Toward Socialism) politico and AIOC advocate, were stepping out from one of the cars that had just arrived.

I must admit that I didn't put a lot of thought into Edwin's comment at the time. I jotted it down in my field notes later that evening, but my attention that day was focused on trying to get a sense of the community. It was only later, after I had returned from fieldwork and was going back over my notes, that Edwin's remark really caught my attention. It is an interesting and astute observation that, I think, gets at one of the central contradictions of the MAS era and the *proceso de cambio* (process of change) in Bolivia, not to mention the more general demand for indigenous autonomy across Latin America. The potential to legally create autonomous, self-governing indigenous communities recognizes that indigenous groups exist as distinct subjects within larger contemporary nation-state formations. But, who (or what) is actually doing the recognizing, and what does that acknowledgment mean for the ability of any given community to make decisions and autonomously govern itself? Edwin was highlighting the recognition that Totora had been accorded from high-level state administrators, and the fact that the community's demand for autonomy had indeed brought about that recognition. The implication was that acknowledging Totora as an indigenous community was historically important, but also that recognition could result in benefits, both material and ideological, for the community. Yet, does the process of recognition itself require the thing being recognized (i.e., indigenous communities) to be recognizable on the same epistemological and ontological register as that of the provider of recognition (i.e., the state)? And, if that is in fact the case, how might that fact affect the actual construction and operation of autonomous self-governance? Could the attempt to carve out autonomous space for indigenous communities to reproduce themselves and their cultures on their own terms actually create the conditions for the further penetration of the state, leading to new forms of regulation and control? Or, in the terms of the argument being developed in this book, how might the plurinational demand for indigenous autonomy challenge, contradict, or align with the political logic of hegemony?

In this chapter I analyze the struggle for indigenous autonomy in order to further flesh out the material and ideological contrasts between the political forms of hegemony and plurinationality. Indigenous communities' free determination and self-government ostensibly allow them to control their own territories and make decisions about how resources in their territories are exploited (or not) and by whom, presenting a potential obstacle to the territorial reach of the state, the expansion of which has been central to the MAS's notion of revolutionary transformation.

If Bolivia is to actually reconfigure both the nation and the state along plurinational lines, indigenous autonomy is a necessary element of these transformations. As José Luis Exeni Rodríguez argues, "indigenous autonomies constitute the essence of plurinationality" because they "are not only about the redistribution of power, decision-making, and resources to the local community level, but also about something much more substantial: the exercise of the rights to free determination and self-government."[1] However, I also want to think about the possible contradictions and unintended consequences that might come about through the construction of official, state-sanctioned indigenous autonomies. Charles Hale has suggested that the demand for indigenous autonomy as a form of resistance "is losing traction as a path towards expansive political change, because it is increasingly entangled with the very structures of dominance that these communities intend to resist."[2] James C. Scott's notion of *legibility* provides a conceptual apparatus through which to consider this ambiguity. For Scott, all states have historically tried to simplify unwieldy and diverse societies in order to more easily understand, manipulate, and govern them.[3] Similarly, Peter Miller and Nikolas Rose describe "rationalities of government," whereby certain "objects" are constituted and become knowable, therefore opening up to intervention and regulation.[4] Thus, I am interested in the ways that AIOCs operate as an instance of fundamental state transformation while simultaneously making indigenous community practices more legible to the state and thus more open to the rationalities of governance.

However, this inquiry should not be taken to imply that the state's only role is to regulate society and ensure compliance with its dictates. While the state is most certainly a regulatory apparatus, it is also a provider of goods and services and can be a powerful mechanism in any process of social transformation. In fact, these two ostensibly distinct visions of the state are really just two sides of the same coin. In order for services to be rendered by the state, groups receiving those services must be legible to it. As Kirk Dombrowski argues, "recognition by power can, and increasingly does, involve as many problems as the neglect and marginalization that comes from an absence of state interest."[5] By thinking in terms of legibility, recognition, and the rationalities of government, I am thinking about the state not as a unilaterally negative and controlling force, but rather as an institutionalized social relationship that opens up certain possibilities at certain times in certain places while partially foreclosing others. That is, the social relations that comprise the state tend to ossify in such a way that then structures social life for a period of time, until those relations break down and the process moves anew. However, the process of structural ossification is always already temporally and spatially contingent, open to social intervention and alteration.

WHAT IS THE STATE?

Before moving on to examine AIOC as a critical component in the process of state transformation in contemporary Bolivia, it is worth pausing to lay out what exactly I mean by "the state." It is by now well known that theorizing the state is a rather difficult task. According to Philip Abrams, the state, "conceived of as a substantial entity separate from society has proved a remarkably elusive object of analysis," and "like *the* town and *the* family, is a spurious object of sociological concern."[6] Similarly, Ralph Miliband has argued that "there is one preliminary problem about the state which is very seldom considered, yet which requires attention if the discussion of its nature and role is to be properly focused. This is the fact that 'the state' is not a thing, that it does not, as such, exist."[7] Nevertheless, the state—understood as a coherently ordered center of power through which society is regulated—remains a reified illusion, perhaps nowhere more than in the discipline of political science, where it persists as a reified unit of analysis. In fact, within political science, at least since the publication of Peter B. Evans, Dietrich Rueschemeyer, and Theda Skocpol's *Bringing the State Back In* in the mid-1980s, the state has largely been viewed as an autonomous entity separate from society with its own interests and drive.[8] Even in disciplines like anthropology and sociology, where the social foundations of the state are taken as a given, empirical analysis of the state tends to fall back on a view of the state as separate from social relations. Specifically in relation to indigenous autonomy in Latin America, there two general schools of thought, both of which, despite their different arguments, present similar understandings of the state. One, from a more Foucauldian position, sees the struggle for autonomy as simply one more way of ensnaring local communities in networks of bureaucratic state power.[9] The other, from a more horizontalist position, argues that autonomy is by its very nature antistatist.[10] Both approaches hold elements of truth and are useful in understanding indigenous autonomy in contemporary Latin America. Yet, they also both present the state as a reified thing that either engrosses communities in webs of governmentality or can be struggled against and escaped from. The distinction between state and society needs to instead be perceived as permeable and contingent, embedded within a complex web of social relations. Any attempt to analyze the state as an autonomous entity outside of and above society reifies the state, hindering both an analysis of the phenomenon itself and the possibilities of its transformation.

Anthropologist Nancy Postero offers a different approach. She demonstrates how constructing indigenous autonomy at the local level in Bolivia, while falling short of completely overturning the liberal nation-state, has nonetheless altered the political scene and the social relations of politics.[11] Following Postero, I am interested in the ways that indigenous autonomy might transform the equilibrium of social relations that, once congealed and solidified for a period of time, form "the state." Yet, unlike Postero, I am less interested in the question of whether the mechanisms of the liberal nation-state can be used to overturn the colonial social relations that the liberal state has put into place.[12] This way of seeing the problem reproduces an essential dichotomy between society and state. It is not that the liberal state has imposed a colonial form of social relations, but rather that the colonial structure of social relations has given rise to the liberal nation-state.

In this chapter I draw from a theoretical tradition that understands the state as the material correlation of social forces at a given time. According to Nicos Poulantzas, the state is not an entity with its own preferences and interests. Rather, it is "a relationship of forces, or more precisely the material condensation of such a relationship among classes and class fractions, such as this is expressed with the State in a necessarily specific form."[13] Drawing on Poulantzas, Álvaro García Linera argues that the state is a mechanism where the correlation of social forces and a collective and shared moral consensus are institutionalized.[14] In this view, the state is formed and defined through a process of social struggle, whereby the social relations of economic and cultural production in a specific place and time are consolidated into a temporary yet durable political relationship of domination and subordination.

Yet, the state as such is not simply a tool of the dominant class or hegemonic bloc, what Ben Fallaw and David Nugent refer to as "a mask of rule."[15] Too often the state is conceptualized as an ahistorical and universal entity of governance, devoid of specific cultural characteristics and historical trajectories.[16] Conceptualizing the state in this way, as an apparatus utilized to dominate and control subordinate groups, fails to account for the many apparent contradictions within the state itself. In fact, due to its contingent and relational nature, the state, or at least parts of the state apparatus, may become accessible and open to the intervention of opposition or popular social forces at certain times.[17] The empirical focus of this chapter, the creation of indigenous autonomy, is just one such example. As Timothy Mitchell notes, "such conflict is an important indication of the permeability of state boundaries because it enables one to trace how wider social differences reproduce themselves with the processes of the state."[18]

This theory of the state also has important implications for the idea of resistance. Resistance is not a social or political practice emanating from a location external to and independent of the state; it is an interwoven, constituent part of the social relations of the state. "Political subjects and their modes of resistance are formed as much within the organizational terrain we call the state," Mitchell argues, "rather than in some wholly exterior social space."[19] Thus, the demand for indigenous autonomy does not arise from a pre-Conquest, indigenous space completely outside the sphere of the (post)colonial state. Nor does the demand look to a territorial horizon beyond the reach of the state, a return to some idealized precolonial society against the state.[20] Rather, indigenous autonomy is indeed a modern dispute within the changing field of relations between various social forces in contemporary Bolivia. The indigenous organizations that helped bring Evo Morales and the MAS to power and that have made indigenous autonomy a central political issue are proposing a new state form, one in which distinct political collectivities are able to make their own decisions about the core issues that affect their livelihoods. According to Fernando Garcés, this type of demand "puts into question the idea that the state has unique and absolute sovereignty over its territory and raises the possibility of creating plural forms of self-government (within indigenous peoples' territories) and co-government (between the indigenous peoples and the plurinational state)."[21] It is precisely this conceptualization of the state as a terrain of social struggle that has informed and motivated activists to mobilize for local autonomy through the construction of AIOCs.

Indigenous demands for autonomy, therefore, are a form of resistance not against "the state" in general, but rather against a particular historical form of the state, one in which indigenous Bolivians have consistently been situated in a subaltern position. Through their demands for a Constituent Assembly to "refound" Bolivia as a plurinational state with indigenous autonomies, Bolivia's indigenous peoples proposed an alternative form of the state. This new state form is significant, according to Garcés, because it represents "a departure from the classical sense of the struggle against the state, or the struggle to take or capture state power. The issues are *which* kind of state the people will make and whether and how it might be constructed—whether they can construct an Other kind of state that resolves the historical discrimination and exclusion to which they have been subjected since the creation of the colonial republic."[22] The relational view of the state and resistance pushes us to rethink the analytic division between the state and society while also clarifying the seeming contradiction between constructing indigenous autonomy and further incorporating autonomous municipalities into the regulatory apparatus of the state.

INDIGENOUS AUTONOMY AND THE PLURINATIONAL STATE

Autonomy and self-governance for indigenous groups have been recurring demands throughout the course of Bolivian history.[23] However, as Xavier Albó notes, the demand for indigenous autonomy has often conflicted with a contrasting transformative desire for popular control over the state. The former advocates for the "winning of autonomous terrain in the face of a state considered inefficient, if not allied with the capitalist sectors," while latter "seeks full participation in the state as a means of controlling the government."[24] Both of these seemingly opposed tendencies have influenced Bolivia's indigenous movements. The most recent wave of demands for indigenous autonomy began in the 1980s and were articulated largely by indigenous peoples in the eastern lowlands. Throughout the 1990s and into the 2000–2005 insurrectionary period, the demand for indigenous autonomy expanded territorially to encompass indigenous groups across the country.

The Bolivian state responded to these demands, in part, through the implementation of political decentralization and policies of neoliberal multiculturalism. The 1994 Ley de Participación Popular (Law of Popular Participation) was the cornerstone of Bolivia's neoliberal decentralization plan. While critics argued that this law shifted responsibilities and accountability from the national to the subnational level as a pretext for reducing public services, the law contained certain important measures for indigenous autonomy, such as recognizing peasant and indigenous communities.[25] In addition, the 1996 Ley INRA (Instituto Nacional de Reforma Agraria, National Agrarian Reform Institute) established and offered formal recognition to *tierras comunitarias de origen* (TCOs, communal indigenous lands). While these initiatives were certainly a response to indigenous demands for autonomy and self-determination, they were nonetheless partial concessions in a larger process of restructuring the Bolivian state along (neo)liberal representative lines.

AIOCs, conversely, challenge the liberal form of the nation-state and seek to move beyond it. According to Jason Tockman and John Cameron, indigenous autonomy implies a radical break with liberalism and questions the entire edifice of the nation-state and the liberal principles that sustain it.[26] Similarly, Pablo Regalsky argues that indigenous autonomy "represents a challenge to the culturally homogenizing forms of the nation-state . . . [and] presupposes the end of a type of government based on the fundamental principles of cultural homogeneity and juridical monism."[27] AIOCs thus form one aspect of a much larger project of transforming the state structure in contemporary Bolivia along plurinational lines.

The 2009 constitution recognizes the right of indigenous peoples to govern their territories and officially established the process for indigenous municipalities to become AIOCs.[28] The 2010 Ley Marco de Autonomías y Descentralización (Framework Law of Autonomies and Decentralization) further clarifies the requirements for the creation and jurisdiction of AIOCs. The administrative and territorial boundaries of AIOCs correspond with the municipal system of government already in place, which somewhat constricts the transformative possibilities of spatial organization. Additionally, while AIOCs are legally accorded certain rights such as jurisdiction over indigenous justice and the ability to design their own governing institutions, AIOC control over nonrenewable natural resources remains an issue of debate. Article 349 of the 2009 constitution gives control over natural resources to the national state, but indigenous groups have challenged this with reference to other parts of the document that recognize the existence of indigenous territory, and the right to prior and informed consultation. Therefore, a central factor in determining the depth of indigenous autonomy in plurinational Bolivia is the degree to which the state practices meaningful informed and prior consultation or consent, particularly when it comes to natural resource extraction. Since indigenous notions of territory include subsoil resources, control over these resources could seriously challenge the MAS government's extractive model of development, its political power, and its hegemonic project. Whether or not the consultation process includes consent and the power of veto for AIOCs is an important factor determining the actuality of indigenous autonomy and, in turn, plurinationality.

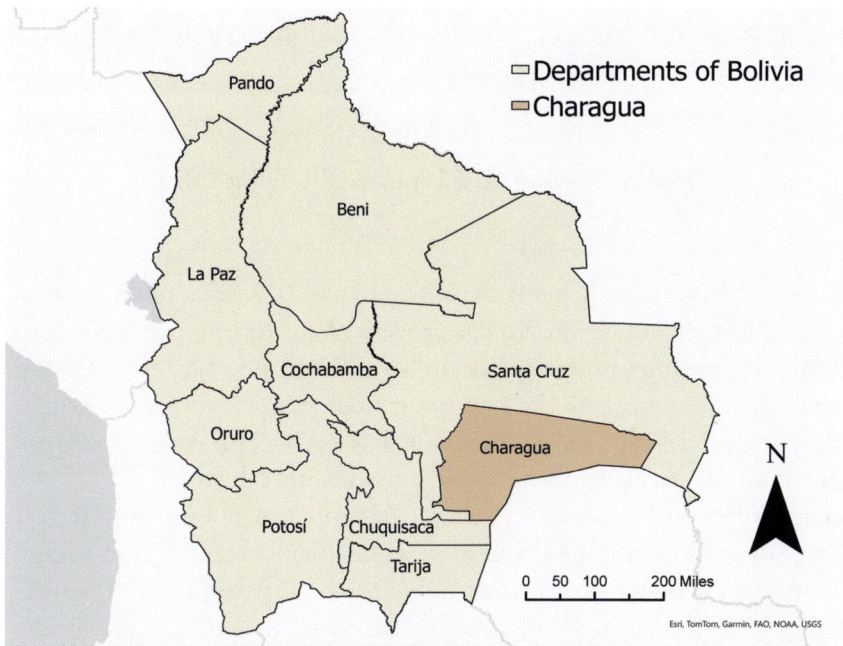

MAP 2. Departmental map of Bolivia with Charagua highlighted. Created by Naomi Gutterman, based on data from DIVA-GIS.

Ethnographic fieldwork for this chapter was carried out in three separate indigenous municipalities across the country: Totora, Jesús de Machaca, and Charagua. While the path toward AIOCs has failed in Totora and has been more or less abandoned in Jesús de Machaca, Charagua was the first indigenous community in the country to successfully become a *gobierno autonomo indígena originaria campesina* (GAIOC, indigenous native peasant autonomous government).[29] Although the chapter draws on research in all three communities, the focus is specifically on Charagua (see map 2) in order to draw out the various demands, desires, accomplishments, and contradictions of the process in depth. As with the previous two chapters, a discussion of indigenous autonomy offers a concrete empirical entry point into the contending theoretical and political-strategic ideologies of revolutionary transformation at play in contemporary Bolivia. Exploring the transformation of Charagua from a municipality to an AIOC allows us to understand both the possibilities and the ambiguities of AIOCs in contemporary Bolivia, and the meaning of indigenous autonomy in processes of revolutionary state transformation in Latin America more generally.

CHARAGUA IYAMBAE: IN PURSUIT OF LIVING WELL, AUTONOMOUSLY

HISTORY AND SOCIAL STRUCTURE

In 2009, *charagueños* (Charagua residents) passed a referendum with 56 percent of the vote to initiate the process of converting into an autonomous indigenous municipality. In 2015, Charagua passed a second referendum and became the first indigenous municipality in Bolivia to successfully fulfill all the requirements of the AIOC process—what Pere Morell i Torra has aptly termed "the bureaucratic odyssey."[30]

According to 2012 census figures, Charagua has an estimated thirty-two thousand inhabitants, and at 28,500 square miles (74,000 square kilometers) it is Bolivia's largest municipality. Territorially, the municipality is divided into six separate zones, four rural (Charagua Norte, Parapitiguasu, Alto Isoso, and Bajo Isoso) and two urban (Charagua Pueblo and Charagua Estación). It is also one of the most ethnically and linguistically diverse municipalities in the country, such that it is often referred to as "Bolivia chica" as it mirrors the social heterogeneity of the country. Sixty-seven percent of Charagua's population identify as indigenous, the largest group being the Guaraní. Most Guaraní work in agriculture, mainly growing corn and other staples for local consumption, although since the mid-twentieth century a number have entered into cattle farming.[31] There is also a growing population of Quechua and Aymara speakers who have migrated east to the Chaco region from the western highlands. Making up roughly 7–10 percent of the municipal population, Aymara and Quechua speakers migrated into the area in significant numbers beginning in the 1950s through the 1970s, mainly from Chuquisaca and Potosí.[32] They established rural communities as part of a 1970s government-sponsored agricultural development scheme called the Programa Abapó-Izozog, which attempted to alleviate highland poverty and overcrowding by enticing peasants to migrate to the more sparsely populated eastern lowlands, although they now mostly reside in the urban centers of Charagua Pueblo and Estación. Though some of these urban dwellers have maintained small parcels of land and cattle, most are now concentrated in local commerce and transport. These *colla* (highland indigenous) migrants have organized themselves in the Asociación de Comerciantes (Traders Association), the Sindicato de Transporte 12 de Octubre (Transportation Union of October 12), and, to a lesser degree, the Asociación de Juntas Vecinales (Association of Neighborhood Boards) to influence municipal planning and political power. There is also a minority of white/mestizo people, known locally as *karai*, who are largely located in the urban areas of Charagua and have historically dominated the municipality's political power. They have organized through a variety of social clubs such as the Club Deportivo 21 de Abril (April 21 Sports Club), the Club Cuape Uai, and the Centro de Amigos del Pueblo (Center of Friends of the People); the largest and most influential of these clubs is the Comité Civico de Charagua (Charagua Civic Committee). Besides their involvement in the Comité Civico, mestizo cattle ranchers have been organized in the Cooperativa de Riego (Irrigation Cooperative) and the Asociación de Ganaderos de Cordillera (Cordillera Cattlemen's Association), both of which have sought to extend private property through the regularization and legalization of land tenure titling. A further important social group that arrived later on the scene is the Mennonite community, of low German descent. Since the mid-1980s, Mennonites have migrated into the area; they currently make up a sizable 20 percent of the population. Mennonites have purposely remained on the margins of political and social life, although they have had a large influence on the local land market in terms of how much land they actually own and their pressure to legalize and regularize tenancy. They have also affected local patterns of commerce and transport, introduced genetic modification of crops and animals, and supported a new network of precarious and temporary labor for non-Mennonite *charagueños*. However, despite their rising economic power and impact on local markets, Mennonites have remained politically detached from the municipality and chose not to participate in the AIOC process.[33]

THE ASAMBLEA DEL PUEBLO GUARANÍ AND THE PATH TOWARD AIOC

The Guaraní demand for autonomy and self-governance according to their own *usos y costumbres* (norms and procedures) has a long history.[34] Resistance to the Spanish Crown and to missionary incursions was common throughout the colonial and republican periods until the infamous massacre at Kuruyuki in 1892, in which the military intervened to quell a Guaraní uprising and more than six thousand Guaraní (at that time known as Chiriguano) were killed.[35] The Chaco War (1932–35) between Paraguay and Bolivia again altered the social landscape of Charagua, as Paraguay took control of the area. After Bolivian forces regained control of Charagua and the war ended, the Bolivian Regimiento Boquerón (Boqueron Regiment) built a base there; the military regiment remained in the municipality and has played an influential role in the reconfiguration of local land tenure. According to Oscar Bazoberry, "since the Chaco War, through the Revolution of '52 and the ensuing civil and military regimes until the end of the twentieth century, the State distributed territories and rights of land possession as political favors, despite the fact that this has often signified the violent expulsion of the previous [Guaraní] landholders."[36] It was in this context, in the 1960s, that the Guaraní again began to organize around issues of territorial autonomy and the contesting of *karai* hegemony in the lowlands. Particularly with the founding in Charagua of the Asamblea del Pueblo Guaraní (APG, Assembly of the Guaraní People) in February 1987, demands for indigenous autonomy were placed front and center.

The APG is an organization that represents southeast Bolivia's Guaraní nation, which comprises more than 360 communities in the departments of Santa Cruz, Chuquisaca, and Tarija.[37] Formally part of the Confederación de Pueblos Indígenas de Bolivia (CIDOB, Confederation of Indigenous Peoples of Bolivia), the APG was created, according to a founding member, "with the objective of expanding and recuperating our territory and improving the life conditions of the Guaraní communities. . . . In this way, [the APG] was organized to make the *karais* respect [the Guaraní people]."[38] According to Ruben Ortiz, a contemporary APG leader from Charagua Norte, "autonomy for the Guaraní people signifies self-governance combined with control over territory and economic resources."[39] The term *territory* is key here. According to Alvaro Díez Astete and David Murillo, the concept of territory for the Guaraní "symbolizes more than just land for agriculture or raising cattle. It also includes the ability and space to hunt and fish, to collect fruit and medicinal plants, while also representing a natural sacred space that allows people to communicate with the supranatural world of their ancestors."[40]

In Charagua, the APG is made up of the four rural *capitanías* (communal indigenous territories): Charagua Norte (twenty-six communities), Alto Isoso (thirteen communities), Bajo Isoso (sixteen communities), and Parapitiguasu (also known as Charagua Sur, eleven communities). With the passage of the Ley de Participación Popular in 1994, the APG began actively participating in local municipal politics, although each *zonal capitanía* has the ability to decide exactly how to participate. Partially through this process, the APG played a key role in the 1990s as the four indigenous *capitanías* were configured as TCOs, which would serve as the territorial foundation of indigenous autonomy.[41] In 2009, not long after the new plurinational constitution took effect, the APG decided to move forward with an AIOC project in Charagua, with the *capitanías* of Charagua Norte and Parapitiguasu leading the effort to the present day.

While the APG has been the central indigenous organization pushing for AIOC, both the Ministry of Autonomy and a number of NGOs have contributed a wide range of human and material resources to assist the process. During my fieldwork in Charagua, as well as in Jesús de Machaca and Totora Marka, it was clear that certain officials in the Ministry of Autonomy and the now-defunct Vice Ministry of Indigenous Autonomies had worked extremely hard in promoting AIOC at the local and national level. In general, the MAS has played an ambiguous role in the AIOC process in municipalities across the country, at times impeding the construction of indigenous autonomy while at others providing useful support.[42] In the case of Charagua, despite the fact that AIOC raises the specter of resistance to the central government's continued access to hydrocarbon rents in the region, the MAS aligned with the APG in support of indigenous autonomy as a political tactic to counter the demands for departmental autonomy put forward by the rightist opposition centered in the city of Santa Cruz.[43]

In the NGO sphere, two key AIOC proponents situated in Charagua Pueblo have been the Centro de Investigación y Promoción del Campesinado (CIPCA, Center for Research and Promotion of the Peasantry) and the Fundación Centro Arakuaarenda (Arakuaarenda Center Foundation). CIPCA is a nationally based organization with seven regional offices across Bolivia that was founded by three Jesuit priests—Xavier Albó, Luís Alegre, and Francisco Javier Santiago—in 1971. It has played a vital role in helping define, articulate, and support indigenous and campesino communities and organizations. CIPCA opened a regional office in Charagua in 1976 with the goals of contributing to the defense and consolidation of Guaraní territory, and helping put an end to the relations of debt peonage between many *charagueño* peasant families and local landowning elites.[44]

The Centro Arakuaarenda, which means the "space/place of knowledge," was originally a Jesuit institution and was formed to "accompany" the indigenous peoples of Charagua and help combat social inequality in the municipality. Organized as a technical school, it has focused largely on issues of education, agricultural production, land tenure, and, more recently, autonomy. Marcelo Alberto, the director, told me that not only had many of the indigenous community leaders advocating for AIOC passed through the center's education programs but the APG was officially created in a meeting at the center, demonstrating the formative nature of the institution and showing "how the vision of Guaraní autonomy comes from inside, not from the outside and above like other NGOs."[45] Both CIPCA and the Centro Arakuaarenda provided important technical support during the writing and revisions of the AIOC statute while also hosting workshops, meetings, and "spaces of reflection" for community members to debate issues related to AIOC and its implementation.

Inevitably, these linkages between the local community, the state and its functionaries, and NGOs have not come without tensions and contradictions. While Maximo Quisbert Q. correctly argues that "there can be no doubt that indigenous peoples need a central government that helps produce the minimal conditions to create autonomous indigenous institutions," Tockman and Cameron point out that on a general level, the MAS-led state, apart from the Ministry of Autonomy, has not only failed to support indigenous autonomy but also acted in some instances to undermine it.[46] This conflict was very much in evidence in a planning meeting I attended in October 2015. Local people listened, stone faced, to recitations by state officials and NGO representatives who lectured them on the need to deeply familiarize themselves with all the technical details of the statutes; these community members only became animated when the discussion turned to community issues that they perceived to be important. Sitting in a covered gymnasium, government *técnicos* (experts) went through a number of policy and legal details in an effort to clarify the structure and language necessary for the AIOC statute, while a woman from the United Nations and an agent from an international NGO gave a presentation on the possible external funding that AIOC status might bring. Almost no one in the audience commented on the technical presentations, and only a few people had questions about how external funds would be distributed. After lunch the meeting resumed with a period of open discussion. Here, the roles were almost completely reversed, as the community members held forth on the meaning of autonomy for them, the importance of land reform, the economic possibilities of gas extraction for the community, the environmental ramifications of gas exploration and extraction, the impact of autonomy on access to national resources, autonomy and education, and, finally, autonomy's possible impact on tourism. Those who had given the morning presentations chimed in a few times, but they did not have many straight answers to community members' questions and offered scarcely little to the discussion. After the meeting, I approached a young lawyer affiliated with the MAS government who had given a talk on the importance of aligning the language between the constitution and the autonomy statute. I asked her how she thought the meeting went, specifically what she made of the discussion after lunch. She was not from Charagua and said that it was interesting to hear what was viewed as important locally, but also that much of what was voiced by locals was not relevant at the moment. What was important was for Charagua to get through the process and actually become autonomous. Despite the fact that the community had already voted in favor of AIOC, it was only after AIOC was formalized that all the local demands and desires could then be realized. "Without AIOC," she said, "nothing else can happen."[47] Scholars have made similar observations in other municipalities across the country embarking on the path toward AIOC, where the formal promotion and socialization meetings tended to focus on the technical and legal details of the statutes, at the expense of the politics of the community.[48] As Bolivian scholar Wilfredo Plata emphasized to me, such meetings need to articulate more convincingly how AIOC can address and alleviate poverty and help indigenous cultural forms and traditions flourish, rather than focusing on the legalistic details of how the statutes align (or not) with the 2009 constitution.[49]

In conversations with various Ministry of Autonomy officials, they expressed real concern regarding the perceived failure of local people not only to take the statutes seriously but also to make progress on those aspects of the statutes that remain vague and in need of further elaboration according to the enabling legislation. However, conversations with local Guaraní revealed a different set of concerns, such as a desire to exert more control over oil companies working within the municipality, without losing access to revenues from natural resource extraction. As one member of the APG told me, the extraction of hydrocarbons is now a central element of the local economy, but it benefits companies and workers not from the area more than it does Charagua itself. Moreover, the economic benefits need to be weighed against the environmental impacts and the loss of land. He said, "we aren't totally against extraction, it can serve a purpose. But, we demand to participate in and have our voices heard in how areas of extraction are designed, how the contracts are organized, who the gas companies negotiate with, who gets jobs. We need to be part of the whole process."[50] This tension between the focus of government *técnicos* on fulfilling the bureaucratic and legal procedures of the AIOC process and the desire of local community members to be in charge of the process and have it meet and accomplish local needs and desires demonstrates a central paradox in attempts to create autonomy.

In addition, there was outright opposition within the municipality to the multiple cultural, ideological, and material implications of AIOC.[51] The opposition was largely composed of the *karai* population living in Charagua Pueblo, organized through the Verdes party (Verdad y Democracia Social, Truth and Social Democracy) and linked with the conservative Comité Cívico de Charagua, which was supported by the then governor of Santa Cruz, Rubén Costas, a well-known opponent of the MAS. There was also opposition from a significant part of the Aymara and Quechua populations in Charagua Estación, who mostly live along the railway line. In the 2009 referendum, 61 percent of Charagua Estación residents voted against indigenous autonomy, out of concern that AIOC would favor the Guaraní.[52]

After the 2009 referendum, the Asamblea Constituyente para el Estatuto AIOC (AIOC Constituent Assembly) was formed to draft a statute outlining the institutional organization of AIOC and its relationship to the nation-state. While the assembly was initially organized in such a way as to provide representation for the various territories that make up Charagua, representatives from Charagua Pueblo did not participate, while those from Estación did so only intermittently. René Gómez, president of the assembly, argued that "the *karai* chose not to participate because they did not want to legitimize a new order that they no longer dominated."[53] The absence of representatives from Charagua Pueblo, combined with the partial representation of Aymara and Quechua populations and the self-exclusion of the Mennonites, meant that "the composition of the Assembly did not reflect the diversity of social actors" in the municipality.[54]

A number of arguments were put forward against AIOC. According to Plata, the two most consistent arguments were that AIOC would "take away the right of the citizenry to a universal vote," and that it "would break the unity, harmony, and social peace" that Charagua had enjoyed for over a hundred years.[55] Another argument, put forward by local landholders, was a concern that AIOC would lead to the expropriation of private lands. Informal conversations with *karai* middle-class professionals and business owners often revealed the concern that indigenous autonomy would put into power people who lacked the necessary knowledge and public policy experience. For instance, an employee of Save the Children International, discussing the possibility of AIOC, laid out a number of issues his organization had regarding the use of funds that had been administered by the *capitanías*. He also accused various indigenous leaders of incompetence, corruption, and nepotism but either could not or would not substantiate his claims with specific examples.[56] Nevertheless, according to Ambrosio Choquindi, the *capitán grande* (head authority) of Alto Isoso, despite all the arguments against AIOC, the opposition's critiques failed to coalesce into a persuasive alternative project. As such, the unity of the Guaraní populations under the leadership of the APG was the deciding factor in making AIOC an actuality.[57]

FROM MUNICIPALITY TO GAIOC

Despite the difficulties and social conflicts involved in the process, the AIOC statute was approved in the final referendum in Charagua on September 20, 2015, with a vote of 53 percent, and the municipality officially transitioned to a GAIOC on January 8, 2017. The GAIOC organization of power fundamentally transforms the institutional structure of the local

government and is based on the territorial organization of the municipality. Additionally, the GAIOC is heavily influenced by the indigenous
capitanías' model of decision-making, which is articulated on three levels: the communal (families), the zonal (individual *capitanías*), and the
interzonal (the four *capitanías* in coordination).

According to Magaly Gutiérrez, a longtime CIPCA employee and current GAIOC official, the principal innovation of the new institutional
system of self-government is the creation of the Ñemboati Reta, or the
communal mechanism of collective decision-making.[58] There are twenty-
seven members of the Ñemboati Reta: four representatives (two men and
two women) from each of the six zones and one representative from each
of the three national parks located within the municipality. In Bolivia,
national parks—such as the Kaa Iya del Gran Chaco, Otuquis, and Ñembi
Guasu in Charagua—are inhabited territory and are therefore accorded
representation under the autonomous government. Each zone is free to
elect members according to its own norms and procedures, which means
that leaders in the *capitanías* and park areas are chosen through their
own *usos y costumbres*, while the secret ballot is used in the two urban
zones. The Ñemboati Reta, which is defined in Article 19 of the statute as
"the maximum instance of decision-making of the Gobierno Autónomo
Guaraní Charagua Iyambae," is explicitly designed to be a deliberative
body, meaning that it is to be a space where debate occurs and communal
decisions are made.

The institutional structure of Charagua's GAIOC is different from
other indigenous communities on the path toward autonomy, in the
altiplano for example, as there is no ultimate authority in the form of a
rotating *mallku* or *cazique* (indigenous community leaders), or even a
rotation of power between socioterritorial units. The GAIOC replaces
the accumulation of power in one person (for instance, a mayor) with a
decentralized power structure that attempts to represent the diversity
of the municipality. Article 47 of the statute stipulates that the executive function, the Tëtarembiokuai Reta, comprises six executive representatives, one from each zone, known as "coordinators." But, as Magaly Gutiérrez pointed out, the Tëtarembiokuai Reta does not have any
actual decision-making power. As an executive body, it can only ratify
and implement decisions that have already been made by the real locus
of power, the deliberative Ñemboati Reta.[59]

Take, for example, the Proyecto de Construcción Carretero El Espino–
Charagua–Boyuibe, a 99-mile (159-kilometer) highway construction
project funded by a US$215 million loan from the Export-Import Bank
of China that is planned to extend from El Espino in the north, through
Charagua heading south to Boyuibe and, eventually, Paraguay. A community assembly I attended in the urban mestizo enclave of Charagua
Pueblo in July 2022 was called to discuss a land dispute involving the
road. Construction of the highway was well underway to the north, and
the proposed route heading south through Charagua was planned to
pass through private land. Twenty-six families had already given permission for the construction to proceed on their land, while one, the
Mocoa family, had steadfastly held out in hopes of better terms. The
assembly, attended by around 130 people, brought members of the community together with an envoy of technicians and lawyers from the
Administración Boliviana de Carreteras (ABC, Bolivian Administration
of Highways) and three representatives of the China Railway Group Limited (previously China Railway Engineering Corporation, CREC), which
had been contracted to build the road. The meeting began with a long,
winding presentation by a lawyer from ABC on the technical requirements of road construction, the benefits this highway would provide to
Charagua and surrounding areas, and the legality of the state's capacity
to expropriate land in situations where "development projects promote
the common good of all Bolivians, and in this case *charagueños.*" Most
in attendance nodded in agreement with much of what the lawyer had to
say, and when it came time for community members to speak the majority supported the highway, demanding that the Mocoa family acquiesce
and allow access through their land. Yet, a small group of Mocoa family
members and supporters pushed back, demanding compensation from
either ABC or CREC for a broken fence and lost cattle (resulting from
preconstruction activity), before they would even consider allowing the
road to pass through their property. Both CREC and ABC claimed that
they had not received any formal grievances from the Mocoa family
requiring compensation, while the Mocoas alleged that they had received
verbal assurances from both agencies to no avail. The discussion dragged
on for hours, with allegations of unaccountable power and unfulfilled
promises meeting accusations of greed and selfishness. As the assembly
ended, no consensus was reached concerning the continuation of the

highway, apart from community members scheduling another meeting, one where representatives of ABC and CREC would not be present.

Land and property disputes like this one are central nodes of contention in infrastructure development projects throughout Latin America. Yet, what is interesting in this case is the manner in which the conflict has been mediated, which sheds important light on the operation of indigenous autonomy in Charagua. As the lawyer from ABC made clear, the Bolivian state could certainly assert eminent domain, expropriate the property needed to build the highway, and get on with things regardless of local views. The fact that this is not what has been happening demonstrates, I think, the real power and potential of autonomy. Not only is the state recognizing the local sovereignty of the GAIOC by at least entering into discussions over the highway, but the consensus-building process is one that has more or less always operated at the local level but is now being acknowledged as a legitimate form by participants and state officials alike. Policy is not necessarily something to be dictated; it is rather a consensual product of deliberation among ostensible equals. This shows, at least on a small scale, the transformative possibilities that AIOCs have for the Bolivian state as a political institution.

THE AMBIGUITIES OF AUTONOMY

NEUTRALIZATION THROUGH BUREAUCRATIZATION

Miguel González has argued that Bolivia has the most advanced and comprehensive conceptualization of territorial autonomies in Latin America. However, "despite the innovative legislation, and partly due to the restrictions imposed under the constitutional provisions through secondary/enabling legislation, the actual operation of autonomies . . . has been an uphill and a winding terrain."[60] Tockman, Cameron, and Plata similarly argue that the future of indigenous autonomy has been substantially limited by language adopted in AIOC statutes.[61] They reason that state functionaries influenced the adoption of statutes that have made it difficult, if not impossible, to meaningfully depart from the municipal model put in place during the 1990s decentralization program. Most importantly, they argue that the statutes undermine the ability of local indigenous communities to exert robust territorial control and free, prior, and informed consent as called for by the United Nations Declaration on the Rights of Indigenous Peoples (UNDRIP) and International Labour Organization (ILO) Convention 169.

These critiques of indigenous autonomy raise important questions: In what ways might AIOCs operate to make indigenous community practices more legible to the state and invite increased state oversight, thus making those communities prone to the rationalities of government? In other words, how might state-sanctioned and state-administered processes of constructing indigenous autonomy transform and "domesticate" indigenous demands for self-governance "into a state reform that deepens the mechanisms of indigenous participation in the state but does so through their subordination, without changing the structures of the state itself?"[62] These questions are particularly important in Bolivia, given the historical experience of previous attempts at political transformation. The expansion of union structures into the countryside after the 1952 revolution was an attempt to transform the Bolivian state-society relation and open up avenues for increased democratic participation by the previously excluded indigenous peasantry.[63] Yet, at the same time, the Bolivian state also sought to control and manage that participation in a top-down, hierarchical fashion.

After the 1952 revolution, the Movimiento Nacionalista Revolucionario (MNR, Revolutionary Nationalist Movement) sought to transform indigenous people into peasants. There was a concerted effort to incorporate and assimilate the largely rural indigenous communities within the country's newly burgeoning national identity. Indigenous peoples, through a variety of mechanisms, were urged to cast off their languages, forms of dress, and ritual cultures in order to modernize and become "Bolivian." Through the 1953 agrarian reform and the creation of the Ministry of Peasant Affairs, indigenous agricultural production was increasingly incorporated into the national market. Further, indigenous forms of political and social organization were replaced with rural unions (*sindicatos*), expanding the territorial reach of the state. In many areas, especially where large agricultural estates (haciendas) did not exist or had failed to stamp out traditional communal organizations, such as northern Potosí, the *sindicatos* were basically grafted onto existing indigenous social structures.[64] In others, such as parts of La Paz and the valleys of Cochabamba, where the expansion of haciendas had resulted in the decomposition of traditional communal organization, the union structures took hold more easily. As Laura Gotkowitz describes, after the revolution, "the MNR and other outside organizers played a fundamental part in the formation of rural unions and militias: the party's agents were sent virtually everywhere after 1952."[65] MNR involvement in their expansion helped arrange communities in a top-down, corporatist fashion.

In the eastern part of the country, the agrarian reform failed to fundamentally alter the social relations of production; rather, it deepened the inequality in land distribution and agriculture, which remained essentially semifeudal. While it is commonly believed that the 1953 reform was not applied in the east, a number of scholars have shown how the reform had important real impacts. Miguel Urioste and Cristóbal Kay, for example, demonstrate how the agrarian reform promoted a new structure of large estates (*latifundio*) and created a new rural elite sector in the eastern lowlands.[66] Gabriela Valdivia argues that the reform in the east laid the foundation for the development of agro-industrial capitalism from the 1970s to the present.[67]

Attempting to develop the country's agriculture production, the MNR state tried to fundamentally alter the countryside and "modernize" it by transforming the existing systems of land tenure and relations of production. It also sought to incorporate the indigenous peasantry into the Bolivian nation, albeit in a manner that made these rural communities legible to the MNR-led state. Thus, instead of maintaining the extensive and varied systems of *ayllus* and *markas* and their communally owned forms of land tenure and modes of production, which had structured the Andean countryside prior to the hacienda system, the MNR wanted to reorganize these communities in a hierarchical and corporatist structure of rural *sindicatos* that were similar across various communities. While unions certainly addressed the grievances of rural populations under hacienda domination, they were also an expression of the cultural hegemony of the mestizo elite and were conceived as a means of transforming and overcoming the indigenous society's forms of social organization.[68] This is not to claim that the agrarian reform was solely developed and implemented from above. Indeed, as Carmen Soliz demonstrates, the timing, depth, and ultimate outcomes of the land reform process were also defined by local and community forces.[69] This example demonstrates that the form of reorganization made it easier for the state to interact with communities in order to implement the agrarian reform, which also had the effect of increasing the state's ability to direct and govern from above.

The point of examining this past experiment in political transformation is not to claim that some "traditional," untouched sphere of indigenous relations external to the rest of Bolivian society was opened up and compromised by a "modern," universalizing state attempting to implant a new capitalist market logic. Rather, the point is to highlight how reforms that at least theoretically present the possibility of radical social transformation may in fact also extend the rationalities of governance.

Chantal Mouffe has conceptualized these types of situations as "hegemony through neutralization," which occurs when demands that might challenge the hegemonic order are "recuperated by the existing system by satisfying them in a way that neutralizes their subversive potential."[70] Can we see the practice of hegemony through neutralization unfolding in the case of AIOCs in plurinational Bolivia? The AIOC process thus far has largely been organized by government bureaucrats, lawyers, and consultants, and it has relied heavily on their technical capabilities and know-how, which has shaped the debate about what autonomy actually means, how it should be organized, and how it operates in practice. This reliance on *técnicos*, in addition to the overarching legal framework structuring the autonomy process, has dulled the transformative potentials of indigenous autonomy and, according to critics, predisposes AIOCs to function as little more than *municipios con poncho*, or modestly reformed municipalities with a token indigenous facade.

TERRITORIAL CONTROL AND THE *PUENTE CLANDESTINO*

The bureaucratic process of aligning AIOCs with the constitution and the structure of a hierarchical nation-state surely, it would seem, dulls the transformative edge of indigenous autonomy. Yet, from another direction has recently come a different challenge, one that raises questions about the autonomous government's ability and right to control its territory. Over the course of 2021, during the depths of the COVID-19 pandemic, a 492-yard (150-meter) bridge was covertly constructed over the Parapetí River in Bajo Isoso by a Mennonite community seeking access to nearly 54 square miles (140 square kilometers) of land it had privately purchased on the east side of the river. Flowing east-northeast from the Andean foothills, the river meanders through a number of provinces in southeast Bolivia until it empties out in the marshes of the Bañados de Isoso, an internationally protected wetlands site based on the Ramsar Convention. Although there were debates about whether the land was privately owned property or a TCO communally held by Guaraní of Isoso and thus unable to be sold, the clearing of land began in November 2021 and construction was completed in October 2022, costing half a million dollars. The so-called *puente clandestino* (clandestine bridge) was built without the autonomous government's knowledge or recognition—and without any type of environmental impact analysis, according to José Ávila, the director of the Office of Protected Areas of Charagua. And it was not simply a bridge, but also miles of road to arrive at the river from the west and more on the east side to open up the land for a new community of two hundred Mennonite families. The central issue, according to Ávila, was that the bridge would open land to deforestation and expand the agricultural frontier in one of the most biodiverse areas of the country, inside the Bañados de Isoso and the Kaa Iya del Gran Chaco National Park. "These lands are prized," said Ávila, "because they are one of the only locations in the Chaco, which is extremely dry, that reliably has water year round."[71] Additionally, while there are certainly environmental risks, Kaa Iya is home to one of Bolivia's only remaining uncontacted indigenous groups. There is even now a sign on the road to the bridge that says "AIOC Charagua Iyambae: Indigenous peoples living in isolation, do not contact them or approach them." Opening up access to this part of the Chaco forest will not only increase the likelihood of deforestation but also increase the pressure on these uncontacted groups.

Despite the apparent risks posed by the bridge, it has its defenders. For their part, the Mennonites have claimed that the bridge's location was chosen at least partially because of the indigenous communities in the area, as it will allow them to cross the river, especially in the rainy season, more freely. Jhonny García, a Guaraní community leader in the village of Cuarirenda, which gave the Mennonites permission to build an access to the bridge through their land, said that the entire 1,800-person community was happy with the bridge. "When one of our brothers would get sick, we had to cross the river holding on to a rope to get to a hospital. Now it is possible to use the ambulance we have here in Cuarirenda."[72]

Beyond the immediate area of impact were also supporters. Rosanna Berril, a restaurant owner in Charagua Pueblo, was enthusiastic about the developmental prospects the bridge would offer, even if they would not directly affect her. "We need more projects like this, more roads, bridges, schools. Look around, the roads are full of potholes and transportation is difficult. If the government won't do it, let them [Mennonites], they know what they are doing, and it will be useful for everybody."[73]

Huberto Rivero, the *mburuvicha* (lead authority) of Bajo Isoso, has stated that while there was never any written permission for the bridge, a verbal agreement was given by the people of Bajo Isoso to allow the Mennonites to construct the bridge. Yet, Bajo Isoso is one of six zones that make up Charagua's autonomous government, and the other five zones were not consulted. Representatives from the other zones have pushed back against the ability of Bajo Isoso to make decisions without conferring with the larger GAIOC. Other zonal leaders from the GAIOC have argued that the bridge was clearly envisioned "to exploit the territory on the other side of the Parapetí River." More forcefully, they have claimed that "the Mennonites have a system of production that just destroys everything."[74] In this sense, the bridge is more than just a river crossing that allows a fairly small number of families access to a plot of land. Rather, the construction of the bridge has implications for the GAIOC's decision-making power (in terms of who gets to make decisions that affect local communities and how those decisions are made) and territorial control, that is, the GAIOC's ability to administer biodiverse areas and manage the expansion of the agricultural frontier, a critical and ongoing concern in the Chaco.

Sitting on a bench under a tree, shaded from the midday sun, Marcelino Cuellar of Alto Isoso maintained that the bridge is a criminal act against the Guaraní people and their long struggle to protect their territory and should be taken down. "We fought long and hard for our territory, for it to be protected [under the system of national parks and protected areas], so how can we let this happen? It wasn't built according to our norms or laws, it is illegal." Moreover, for Cuellar, the entire situation is a demonstration of the failure of local Guaraní leaders and the GAIOC to actually enforce its own power. "We say we are autonomous, but we are only autonomous in words, not deeds."[75] A number of people expressed similar sentiments when asked about the bridge, while others argued that the bridge issue was actually a successful demonstration of autonomy in action, even if they personally disagreed with the current state of affairs. "Personally, I see the risks but I don't live in the community that sold the land or the one that gave them [Mennonites] access to the river," said Cerino Justiniano, the *capitán grande* of Charagua Norte. "It was their choice and they made it according to their own systems. This is how GAIOC functions here in Charagua Iyambae; the base decides." The lawyer sitting next to him, Liseth Pardo, intoned, "look, most people probably want a bridge over the Parapetí, but a bridge just isn't a bridge, it depends on context. In this context, the bridge was built clandestinely, without proper paperwork and environmental analysis. It was also built to benefit a certain group at the expense of others. These are the problems, not necessarily the bridge itself."[76]

CONCLUSION

This chapter has outlined both the possibilities and the ambiguities of constructing officially sanctioned indigenous autonomies in contemporary Bolivia. I have argued that indigenous autonomy is an essential aspect of any plurinational project and that without the creation of territories under indigenous control the realization of plurinationality and a plurinational state will remain only a possibility, an enduring future horizon. The construction of indigenous autonomy opens up possibilities for a radical transformation of the Bolivian state and society, which was a driving factor in the 2000–2005 period of social upheaval that brought Evo Morales and the MAS to power. As the first indigenous municipality to officially gain AIOC status, Charagua is in the process of creating new material, ideological, and institutional structures that have the potential to transform the historical social and political relations of exploitation and exclusion that have kept Bolivia's indigenous majority population in a subaltern position.[77] As such, AIOCs are an important part of the continuing struggle to decolonize Bolivia and construct a novel plurinational form of politics, a new and distinct political logic that contrasts with the hegemony of the nation-state form. Yet, indigenous autonomy does not, and cannot, exist as a space completely external to that of the state. Rather, AIOCs are intricately bound up with the state as sites of an ongoing struggle of social forces with differing visions of the relationship between the governing apparatus and society. As such, the demand for indigenous autonomy has also opened the way, however unintentionally, for expanding the bureaucratic power of the state by making autonomous indigenous communities more legible to, and increasingly mediating local affairs through, the state, however reconfigured. Perhaps, as Hale has argued in the context of Central America, indigenous autonomy as a path toward radical social and political change in Bolivia is increasingly becoming entangled in the very structures of dominance it was originally attempting to resist.[78] A relational view of the state helps us understand the seemingly contradictory outcomes of achieving indigenous autonomy in Charagua, while at the same time further incorporating autonomous indigenous municipalities into a regulatory governing apparatus that impedes radical, decolonial social transformation.

Nevertheless, if Bolivia is to institutionalize a new state form and actualize the idea of plurinationality, meaningful expressions of indigenous autonomy are an indispensable element in this process. What, then, does this tell us about the conflict between hegemonic and plurinational visions of social change in contemporary Bolivia? To be sure, indigenous autonomy is still an open terrain of struggle, and how it relates to the nation-state and operates in practice in any given local situation can only be determined in the process of its construction. However, there is certainly a disjuncture between the rhetoric of plurinationality articulated by the MAS government and outlined in the Bolivian constitution and its actual implementation and practice on the ground thus far. Without a more expansive implementation of AIOCs throughout the country, the construction of MAS hegemony will have come at the expense of not only indigenous autonomy but also an actualized form of plurinationalism, which would represent a missed opportunity to fundamentally transform the institutions of the Bolivian state.

CONCLUSION

Rethinking Revolution from Bolivia

It is not that nothing has happened, that a new era has not been entered. Rather, that era having been entered, it is necessary now to live in it rather than merely imagine it, and that is inevitably a deflating experience.

—CLIFFORD GEERTZ

Nayrapacha means ancient times. But not in the sense of a past that is dead, incapable of renovation. It implies that this world can be changed, a past that can also be the future.

—CARLOS MAMANI CONDORI

Just as the material relations through which we produce and reproduce ourselves are inherited from the past, the theories and concepts we use to interpret the world around us "do not develop out of nothing, nor drop from the sky, nor from the womb of the self-positing Idea."[1] Rather, they emerge from within the preexisting material and ideological conditions in which we find ourselves. Much as the theory of hegemony emerged in response to the formation and expansion of the nation-state and its territorial structure of power, plurinationality emerges from within and in response to a particular historical conjuncture composed of two overlapping historical developments in Bolivia, one long term and one short term. The former refers to the ongoing processes of political, economic, and cultural subsumption of colonialism, while the latter refers to the mediated forms of political representation and economic austerity of the neoliberal period. The theory of plurinationality speaks directly to these overlapping processes and posits an image of state, society, and economy that draws from the past in order to transform the present for an alternative future. As such, it offers a distinct vision of revolutionary change from the conventional one proposed in the social sciences since at least the late eighteenth century.

The preceding chapters have sought to develop the theoretical and conceptual perspectives of hegemony and plurinationality in order to interpret a number of recent empirical moments in Bolivia's ongoing *proceso de cambio* (process of change). In this final chapter I would like to tie everything together through a brief concrete analysis of the 2019 forced resignation of Evo Morales on the heels of a contested election, before returning to a theoretical discussion of hegemony and plurinationality in order to think through what these contrasting visions of social change mean for the social scientific category of revolution. Like with the discussions of the Territorio Indígena y Parque Nacional Isiboro Sécure (TIPNIS, Isoboro Sécure Indigenous Territory and National Park), Consejo Nacional de Ayllus y Markas del Qullasuyu (CONAMAQ, National Council of Ayllus and Markas of Qullasuyu), and indigenous autonomy, the contrasting logics of hegemony and plurinationality provide an interpretative framework for understanding the 2019 coup d'état that forced Morales and the Movimiento al Socialismo (MAS, Movement Toward Socialism) from power. The 2019 crisis arose from a complex array of structural and conjunctural factors all linked to the struggle for hegemony as the guiding political logic of Morales and the MAS.

Turning to the concept of revolution, as well as the manner and apparent ease by which Morales was overthrown and the conservative opposition was seemingly able to temporarily suspend the *proceso de cambio*, I believe, requires us to consider the type and extent of social, economic, cultural, and political changes typically associated with cases of revolutionary transformation in the social scientific literature. The theory of plurinationality opens up new vantage points from which to conceptualize the category of revolution and interpret revolutionary change. Specifically, it offers a distinct notion of temporality that challenges much revolutionary thinking since the 1789 French Revolution, while also urging us to consider the ways in which many conventional analyses of revolution are abstractly bounded by the nation-state form and a particular understanding of state power.

THE YEAR 2019: CONTRADICTIONS AND CRISIS

The forced resignation of Evo Morales from the presidency in November 2019 seemed to announce the end to a fifteen-year period of social, political, economic, and cultural change in Bolivia, popularly known as the *proceso de cambio*. Morales and the MAS swept into state power on the heels of the 2000–2005 revolutionary upheavals, promising to implement the deep-seated demands being put forth by the country's multitudinous civil society. Morales was elected with outright majorities in three presidential elections, while the MAS became the dominant political party and has continuously controlled the legislature. Evo and the MAS oversaw the longest period of economic growth and political stability in the country's history, resulting in a variety of social welfare gains, expanded political rights, and legislative and cultural changes to combat racism, discrimination, and exclusion. Indeed, the Morales government achieved a great deal by way of economic, social, and cultural reforms. Yet, despite these historical accomplishments and seeming hegemonic control, Morales and the MAS's command over the institutions of political power quickly disintegrated as a revanchist opposition sought to reverse fifteen years of social change through the government of a previously little-known senator from Beni, Jeanine Áñez. While Morales's overthrow was exceptional, the underlying conditions that made the coup possible had been accumulating during the MAS's decade and a half of rule. Beyond the short-term catalysts of the coup—allegations of electoral fraud on top of the overturned 2016 referendum against a constitutional amendment to allow Morales to run for a fourth term—the 2019 election was not the cause of the ensuing crisis but rather a tragic outcome of longer-term fissures in Bolivian society. Just as antagonisms between hegemony and plurinationality help us make sense of the TIPNIS conflict, the CONAMAQ intervention, and indigenous autonomy, these contradictory perspectives also allow us to interpret the 2019 coup d'état as an outcome of divergent political logics.

Scholars and analysts have pointed to a number of structural factors, MAS missteps, conflicts, corruption, and conspiracies that laid the way for the 2019 political crisis.[2] Going from the specific to the more structural, I think three contradictions of the Morales government laid the foundation for a contested election to develop into a coup. As I explain below, each can be tied to the logic of hegemony that served as the ideological orientation for Morales, Álvaro García Linera, and the MAS during their years in power. At the level of tactics was the choice for Morales to run for president for a fourth time, while at the level of strategy was the MAS alliance with old elite classes and fractions of capital. Directly related to those alliances, the final contradiction is a more general continuation of the existing mode of accumulation, which created conflicts within the MAS and factions of the Left more broadly.

The MAS was originally founded as a "political instrument" of the Chapare coca growers and the larger peasant union federation, the Confederación Sindical Única de Trabajadores Campesinos de Bolivia (CSUTCB, Unified Syndical Confederation of Rural Workers of Bolivia), in the 1980s.[3] In contrast with traditional political parties, the MAS was envisioned as the political wing of various peasant and indigenous social movements, which would operate collectively to guide the party as it contested elections. Yet, as the MAS became more entrenched as the dominant political force in the country, it transformed into a more traditional political party, distinct from the social organizations and movements whose political instrument it once was. Even as it maintained certain internal democratic structures, the MAS was not immune to the populist caudillismo so prevalent across much of Latin America's history, and the persona of Evo increasingly became symbolically important for the MAS and the process of change more broadly.[4] As Robert Cavooris notes, "identification with Evo as a symbolic figure, while not without reason, began to stand in for an organic process that would have deepened the MAS's hegemony through a constant process of organizing, mobilizing, and participating. Grassroots organizations that once steered the MAS ended up being steered by a layer of political leaders and party functionaries."[5] For the MAS as a "political instrument" meant to mobilize a variety of social organizations, many of which rely on systems of leadership rotation themselves, the party made a tactical mistake in putting Evo forward for a fourth presidential term. This had been an ongoing criticism of the MAS for years, as Pablo Solón, former Bolivian ambassador to the United Nations under Morales, argued in 2017. "The cult of personality around Evo has grown for a number of reasons, rightist opposition, foreign imperialism, etc., but it is a serious error. The process of change is more than just one person, it is about the transformation of life for millions."[6] It was also an acknowledged issue within the party leadership itself, as then vice president García Linera noted. "Renewing leadership is absolutely necessary," he stated just before the 2019 elections. "We made a big mistake in not training new leaders sooner."[7] This tactical mistake opened the door to opposition claims of authoritarianism and liberal allegations of democratic backsliding, as well as accusations that Morales and the MAS were not in fact revolutionaries intent on foundational change but were simply politicians replaying historical political trends with an updated indigenous veneer. Whether such accusations were truthful is up for debate, but their degree of truthfulness was somewhat beside the point in 2019. The fact that they could be made at all influenced the trajectory of events by bringing people into the streets to protest Morales's reelection and shaping the domestic and international media representations of the situation.

While the fantasy that the *proceso de cambio* depended on the individual character of Evo was a significant tactical blunder, the MAS also made a strategic error in its failure or inability to transform the institutional apparatus of the state in such a way as to further entrench the revolutionary process throughout society. A significant amount has been written about the maintenance of a centralized, presidential political system and what that means for the composition of a plurinational political regime.[8] Questions of whether a parliamentary system would better correspond to a plurinational state than does a presidential model, or whether proportional representation would be a more adept electoral system than majority first-past-the-post, are important to consider. Yet, with the new constitution, the Plurinational State of Bolivia remained a majoritarian presidential system. The reliance on (and retention of) a liberal system of political institutions to overcome colonialism and neoliberalism and actualize plurinationalism, according to Nancy Postero, has been a key source of tension within Bolivia's process of change.[9] For Luis Tapia, more than just a tension, "the combination of presidentialism with the legislature elected through single-member majority is the worst way of constituting a plurinational state, it is in fact not possible."[10] The formal political system is of course only one indicator of state form, but the failure to alter this system during the Constituent Assembly signaled the MAS's lack of resolve to transform other components of the state as well. Although a number of ministries and vice ministries were indeed created, such as the Vice Ministry of Indigenous Autonomies and the Ministry of Decolonization and Depatriarchalization, their seemingly endless permutations and lack of adequate funding have reduced their impact.

As described in chapter 5, the equivocal if not outright hostile reaction of the MAS to the idea of indigenous autonomy was a missed opportunity to significantly reconfigure the structure of political power across the country. Indigenous autonomy proposes a complete reconfiguration of the state that would allow indigenous communities and peoples to employ their own norms and procedures to govern themselves and their territories. Sanctioning and empowering indigenous communities through autonomy would, contends Pablo Regalsky, "restrict the power of the timber, mining, and oil multinationals and their landowning allies who exploited their [indigenous communities'] resources and destroyed their territories."[11] Indigenous autonomy is not simply about "decentralizing" political power, but also about lessening the power of traditional elites and transforming the balance of social forces. While the MAS could not predict the specifics of the 2019 crisis, it was well aware of opponents' desire to retake state power by any means. The failure to promote indigenous autonomy on a broad scale, combined with the slowing of large-scale agrarian reform after 2011, represents an "opportunity squandered," according to Linda Farthing, for the MAS to advance a project of state transformation.[12] Efforts to build indigenous autonomy should have been situated within a larger set of institutional reforms and innovations meant to transition the Bolivian state form toward plurinationalism. The failure to do so stunted the MAS's ability to grow a mass base of popular power with real material capacity and interests, something that could protect against conservative retrenchment. Certain parallels can be drawn here with what happened in Chile in 1973, even if the outcomes were significantly different. According to Ralph Miliband, Salvador Allende's government failed to sufficiently reorganize the political system and encourage the construction of alternative organs of power that would "mesh" with the state. As Miliband argues, any revolutionary regime bent on fundamental changes in the economic, social, and political structures "must from the start begin to build and encourage the building of a network of organs of power, parallel to and complementing state power, and constituting a solid infrastructure for the timely 'mobilization of the masses' and the effective direction of its actions."[13] Vanguardist logic aside, Miliband makes an important point about the reconfiguration of the state and the building of popular power being part of the same process. Rather than reconfiguring the state, which could have at the same time grown a base of popular power to mobilize against would-be putschists and protect the reforms already achieved, the MAS chose a more expedient strategy of accommodating elites in order to exercise power. This ties into the third main contradiction that laid the foundation for the 2019 putsch.

The MAS government's continued reliance on an extractivist mode of accumulation set the conditions for a variety of conjunctural tensions to coalesce into an organic crisis of state legitimacy. This was a structural contradiction in the sense that the MAS's ability to maneuver within its economic model was always shackled in large part by the historical conditions and expansion of capitalism.[14] As discussed in chapter 3, the MAS's development model did not merely maintain an extractivist form but deepened it based on the belief that doing so would provide the necessary resources for improved social welfare, thereby laying the basis for a future transition beyond capitalism. The extractivist model of the MAS did represent a break with the neoliberalism of the recent past as the state became an important locus of economic activity and distribution. Nevertheless, a transformation of the social relations of production never materialized to actually democratize or pluralize the economy, let alone implement a model of socio-ecological development akin to *vivir bien* (lit. to live well). Plurinationalism, at least in the Bolivian context, proposes an alternative development paradigm based on indigenous cosmovisions that embodies human and nonhuman relational well-being, while the hegemonic project of the MAS meant a developmental model focused on industrialization. This model conflicted with the collective rights of indigenous peoples as laid out in the 2009 constitution and, more specifically, in the 2012 Ley Marco de la Madre Tierra y Desarrollo Integral (Framework Law of Mother Earth and Comprehensive Development).

In what Fernando Mayorga describes as a "programmatic turn," the MAS attempted to find a strategic balance between economic continuity and transformation by combining the rhetoric of Pachamama (Mother Earth) and *vivir bien* with the maintenance of an extractivist mode of accumulation to generate industrialization.[15] The Morales government did this by forming strategic alliances with certain fractions of capital in order to incorporate them into the MAS hegemonic bloc. Around 2008–9, coalitions were formed with the dominant economic classes, particularly those in the eastern lowlands, in order to both quell their opposition and expand hegemonic control over those adversarial groups.[16] As García Linera noted, "we [the MAS] knew they [eastern lowland opposition] did not have an alternative program for Bolivia, but they held significant economic power that could hurt us, hurt the country. We needed their conditional support and compromised with them to bring them into our orbit so we could use their economic power for our own transformative ends. We incorporated them, but not as organized classes, we brought them in as disaggregated groups and individuals."[17] A similar process occurred with other fractions of capital, including transnational mining companies, natural gas and oil industries, and sectors of finance. This strategy was meant to stabilize and consolidate MAS rule but came at the expense of allowing the right-wing opposition to maintain its economic position. While these alliances, in combination with the commodities boom, certainly played a role in Bolivia's economic growth and the MAS's ability to generate profits and redistribute wealth during the Morales years, traditionally dominant classes were able to expand their economic power and reproduce themselves.[18] These elite classes, organized in many of the main cities' civic committees and coalescing around the figure of Luis Fernando Camacho in 2019, took advantage of what was originally a largely urban, middle-class protest against Morales's reelection and channeled it toward a more radical, violent, and racist revolt against the MAS, its supporters, and the entire *proceso de cambio*. Although benefiting economically during the Morales era, the oligarchic elite sought a return to a previous period when their economic interests were consolidated under their own political power. The maintenance of an extractivist mode of accumulation provided the economic base for the reproduction of these class fractions, while the alliance with the MAS gave them access to political decision-making power.

The MAS government assumed that an anticapitalist future must first pass through an extractive capitalist present, and that the MAS, as *the* expression of the national general will, would lead that process of change in a hierarchically organized manner. Yet, the *neoextractivismo* of the MAS, like that of the other Latin American Pink Tide governments, generated a number of economic contradictions and social conflicts that, taken together, weakened the links between the MAS and sectors of its original base of political support.[19] The popular economic achievements during the Morales years are undeniable and in many respects originated from the increased rents garnered from the renegotiation of hydrocarbon contracts with transnational companies during an era of high prices. Yet, the expansion of an export-oriented mode of accumulation has hindered the development of other sectors of the so-called plural economy, namely the cooperative and communitarian.[20] Additionally, the increasing industrialization of agriculture and the expansion of the agricultural frontier, particularly in the eastern lowlands, have led to environmental degradation and growing social conflict over land and territory.[21] Favorable policies promoting mining operations and hydrocarbon exploration and extraction have created a contradictory legal framework of conflicting rights over access to land and resources such as water. In turn, this has led to disputes between extractive industries and indigenous communities, as well as tensions within indigenous communities around resource extraction.[22] Morales and the MAS thus continued the historical capitalist movement of enclosure, expropriation, and dispossession that had driven many popular, campesino, and indigenous sectors, seeking a better future, to originally support the MAS.

The maintenance of the extractivist mode of production, the MAS's failure to institutionally transform the state apparatus, and the tactical reliance on the persona of Evo were the underlying conditions of the coup in November 2019. What had been Bolivia's longest period of democratic political stability and macroeconomic stability abruptly came to a halt over an electoral dispute that most likely could have been easily managed only a few years prior. The tactical mistake of failing to renew or rotate MAS leadership gave political opponents the opportunity to assert claims of authoritarianism, regardless of the party's and Morales's democratic credentials. The end of the commodities boom in 2015–17 made the MAS less useful to those traditional economic elite classes with whom they had aligned, who then took advantage of the 2019 protests to push for Morales's ouster. Without the organized support in the streets that had helped the MAS break the conservative opposition in 2006–8, there was little it could do to maintain control of the state apparatus, especially after the police began to mutiny in support of the opposition.

The military soon followed suit, and on November 10 the commander of the armed forces, General Williams Kaliman, "suggested" that Morales step down.

The 2019 crisis was neither the result of a spontaneous uprising nor a preplanned coup d'état. Without doubt there were spontaneous protests and a coup indeed took place, but the same type of tensions between hegemony and plurinationality I have examined in relation to TIPNIS, CONAMAQ, and indigenous autonomy also helped create the conditions for the 2019 overthrow of Morales and the MAS. But in recognizing the tensions, contradictions, and perceived failures of the Morales era, I do not mean to imply approval of his antidemocratic removal from office. Rather, we cannot understand the 2019 crisis without grasping the underlying theoretical and material contradictions of the *proceso de cambio*. As I have argued, an accumulation of economic and political contradictions created important social antagonisms that, on a conceptual plane, can be viewed as the outcome of a struggle between MAS attempts to construct hegemony and other social subjects' desires to actualize plurinationality. When the crisis erupted in October 2019, the MAS could no longer automatically count on the power of an organized social base to materially and ideologically defend the government, as it had during the early years of the Morales presidency. The process of social articulation during the late 1990s that resulted in the popular insurrections of the early 2000s and the rise of the MAS was gradually reversed after 2011, as the *proceso de cambio* became more and more disembedded from the projects and organizations of popular and indigenous sectors. I have tried to demonstrate this process of disarticulation during three specific moments through the logics of hegemony and plurinationality. These and a number of similar situations generated enduring conflicts within the governing social bloc, as is demonstrated by how quickly Morales was overthrown. It was a mistake for the MAS to overturn the outcome of the 2016 referendum and for Evo to run for a fourth term in 2019. A resurgent conservative opposition encouraged questions of electoral integrity and took advantage of the ensuing protests to push for a return to power under Jeanine Áñez's government. The above factors might have been necessary elements for the 2019 overthrow of Morales, but it was only in conjunction with the structural continuity of the extractivist mode of accumulation and the resulting disarticulation of the MAS's social base that historical conditions were sufficient to turn a contested election into a full-blown crisis.

The revanchist violence of the Áñez government and the ultimate return of the MAS to power in late 2020 under Luis Arce, Morales's former finance minister, are somewhat outside the scope of this book yet remain understandable through the interpretive frame of plurinationality and hegemony. Áñez's year in power demonstrated to many the dire consequences of an oligarchic hegemonic project for plurinationalism. Yet, the return of the rightist opposition to power was not tied to a widespread social base and therefore lacked a clear hegemonic link between political leaders and mass society.[23] In that sense, the discussion about Bolivia's future continued to revolve around the projects of revolutionary transformation envisioned by MAS hegemony and plurinationality. The return to power of the MAS through the October 2020 elections, which Arce and his running mate, David Choquehuanca, won with over 55 percent of the vote (more than 26 percent points beyond Arce's closest rival), was an important moment of social articulation to overcome an electoral opponent. However, the change in MAS leadership from Morales to Arce does not reveal a deeper ideological change in the party's vision. The MAS, although composed of various competing factions, still operates under the logic of hegemony. In that sense, the struggle between modernizing the Bolivian nation-state toward future socialism and refounding the country as a plurinational state continues to be the central tension driving questions of what Bolivia is and should be.

RETHINKING REVOLUTION

The above analysis helps explain how Morales and the MAS were overthrown seemingly with such ease after nearly fifteen years in power. Yet, the 2019 crisis also sheds light on the larger MAS project in relation to the notion of revolution and revolutionary transformation. The hegemonic logic of the MAS opened up certain avenues for taking state power and implementing a number of important social, political, cultural, and economic changes. Yet, at the same time, that logic limited the possibilities for a plurinational revolution, the consequences of which unfolded in October and November 2019. The failure to transform Bolivia's economic mode of accumulation and attendant social relations of production was structured by a global economic system that hemmed in their capacity to maneuver. Such transformation would have been, and remains, a tall task for any would-be revolutionary government. Nevertheless, a number of other potential changes were constrained by the MAS's understanding of politics as hegemonic. The theory of hegemony understands identities to be malleable over time, but they remain unified singularities; the theory of plurinationality, in contrast, sees identities as contingent multiplicities. Moreover, while the nation-state form is the given political terrain of hegemony, plurinationality envisions a different state form, one that decenters the unified political hierarchy and disperses power in radically plural ways. The failure of the MAS to institutionally refound the state on plurinational terms was a grave mistake, especially when an opportunity arose for the oligarchic and neoliberal opposition to once again challenge MAS hegemony. Not only did erstwhile MAS supporters fail to sufficiently defend the Morales government in the streets, but when the opposition took power it was bequeathed a more or less identical political apparatus to the one Morales and the MAS inherited in 2005. For the MAS, the concept of plurinationality came to symbolize the distribution of wealth backed by increased popular political representation rather than a truly revolutionary transformation of social power and political institutions. The failure to open up and transform the institutional structure of the nation-state in such a way that would have diffused power downward and outward to local communities was perhaps the most critical error of the Morales years. This would have gone some way toward actualizing the plurinational demand for state transformation and, in the process, built a more entrenched territorial configuration of support for the MAS's "democratic and cultural revolution."

Comparing and contrasting the theories of hegemony and plurinationality thus offers a way to understand key moments of conflict during Bolivia's *proceso de cambio*, including the ultimate downfall of Evo Morales. But, the manner in which these two theoretical approaches overlapped, combined, and conflicted during the Morales years also provokes a new analysis of the social scientific conceptualization of revolution. The Bolivian *proceso de cambio*, what Adolfo Gilly labeled the "first revolution in the 21st century," has sparked a reevaluation of what actually constitutes a revolution.[24] In twenty-first-century Bolivia, Igor Cherstich, Martin Holbraad, and Nico Tassi note, "revolution features not as an ideology-changing operation but as an occasion for Bolivians to free themselves from the need to change, a chance to see the world as they currently see it."[25] Revolution, in this context, is a process that allows indigenous Bolivians the possibility to be themselves and reproduce themselves *as indigenous peoples*. While Antonio Gramsci's development of hegemony opened up new ways of envisioning and interpreting revolutionary processes and practices, it did so largely within a modernist frame. The theory of plurinationality pushes us to further rethink, from a different historical and cultural vantage point, what a revolution is and how it unfolds. To conclude this book, I want to focus on two specific challenges that the theory of plurinationality poses for our conceptualization of revolution: historical temporality and the apparatus of the (nation-)state.

Both the conventional social scientific and Marxist conceptualizations of revolution assume a linear temporality, where the revolution represents a sudden break, a rupture in chronological time that generates a distinctly new present and future. A plurinational theory of revolution forces us to rethink this temporal sense, to incorporate modes of temporality in which the past plays a central, defining role in the present and future. Plurinationality seeks not a return to the past, but rather an incorporation of the past as a principal force in the present. Similarly, most analyses of revolution focus largely on violent seizures of state power. This concentration on the state, though useful, has given less attention to some of the more culturally and symbolically significant transformations that imbue revolutionary change. While the theory of hegemony offers a more nuanced approach to revolution than does much orthodox Marxism or mainstream social scientific literature, it remains ontologically fixated on the modern nation-state and its sovereignty as the terrain over which revolutionary struggle occurs. Plurinationality, on the other hand, questions the nation-state form and raises the prospect of rethinking revolution as more than just gaining control over the state. Revolution, according to plurinationality, entails reimagining what exactly the state is and how societies relate to it, the natural world, and one another.

ASYNCHRONIES IN TIME AND REVOLUTION

The idea of revolution as a process of social emancipation developed over the course of the eighteenth century. Before the era of the Enlightenment, according to Reinhart Koselleck, the term *revolution* "signified a turning over, a return of the movement to the point of departure, as in the original Latin usage. A revolution initially signified, in keeping with its lexical sense, circulation."[26] Similarly, Raymond Williams notes that revolution was traditionally understood in social and historical terms as a process of circular movement. "In the simplest sense, [revolution meant] men [*sic*] revolved, or more strictly were revolved, on Fortune's wheel, setting them now up, now down."[27] Revolution as social change was understood in terms of natural evolution, similar to the rotation of the stars, of fate entwined in the cosmological visions of different cultures. This understanding of revolution with a naturalistic origin assumed that history and time were uniform, cyclical, and repeatable.

Our contemporary conceptualization of revolution comes directly out of the French Revolution. It was in France that "the term 'revolution' took on its modern social scientific significance because an event exploded existing perceptions about politics, society, and economy and, at the same time, destroyed previous beliefs in the uniqueness of events."[28] Not only did the French Revolution change people's conceptions about the world and their place within it, but it also presented the possibility of historical change occurring in observable and measurable scales. That is, the French Revolution transformed notions of historical time, opening up an unknowable future that would be distinctly different from the past. Martin Malia claims that with the French Revolution, "Europe's sense of time changed from a supernatural to a this-worldly perspective on the future. History's providential course to the Second Coming and the Final Days was replaced by belief in human progress in the here and now."[29] A new world could be purposefully built by overcoming the past. Revolutions now became associated with reorienting temporality from the past, through the present and toward the future, thereby wedding linear ideas of time with processes of social and political transformation. Since 1789, Koselleck notes, revolution as a concept has referred not to a return of the past but rather to "a general impulse to plan the social future. . . . The social revolution must write off the past and create its substance out of the future."[30] Time became malleable through the desires and actions of people, people who are able to propel humanity out of the past and into a new, liberated future. The revolutionary event produces a rupture in time, necessarily separating it from the past and reorienting it in the direction of the future. For Koselleck, during the French Revolution history was "temporalized" as the present and even more so the future were intended to be superior to preceding times. History ceased being a circularity and became instead a linear progression. Revolution no longer denoted a circular *re*turning; rather, it meant an idea of *over*turning and a radical new point of departure.

According to Lynn Hunt, this new relationship to time was perhaps the most significant innovation of the French Revolution. Beginning in 1789, "a new temporal schema took shape in which revolutionary time pulverized the foundations of the old order. . . . In that schema, those in the present would constantly endeavor to create something new, modern, up-to-date and future-oriented. The past would no longer serve as a reservoir of exemplars for present behavior; the past would be what had to be overcome in order to make a better future."[31] Thus, with a new understanding of revolution came a new understanding of time, one in which the past was seen as a hindrance, a barrier to the future. It is in this sense that Karl Marx refers to the past as an impediment to real revolutionary change. "The social revolution of the nineteenth century cannot take its poetry from the past, but only from the future. It cannot begin with itself, before it has stripped away all superstition about the past. Earlier revolutions required world-historical recollections in order to drug themselves concerning their own content. In order to arrive at its content, the revolution of the nineteenth century must let the dead bury their dead."[32]

These same conceptualizations of time continue to underlie our conventional views of revolution. Revolutionary ruptures are understood as unfolding within the linear chronological coordinates of time, a present break between past and future that sweeps away the "muck of ages" and implements a new social and political order, one that is incommensurable with what came before. Yet, the theory of plurinationality invites us to question this modernist revolutionary temporality by highlighting the ancestral past as a central actor in the present and a guide for the future. Plurinationalism is not a restoration of the past but rather a demonstration that the past need not be eradicated on the path to liberation. As the previous chapters on CONAMAQ and indigenous autonomy reveal, a plurinational theory of revolution is built on attempts to reconstitute modes of social, political, and economic organization that have historically been viewed as obstacles to the modern nation, electoral democracy, and the market.

As I briefly noted in chapter 2, a plurinational theory of revolution aligns with the indigenous notion of *pachakuti*. Meaning a turning over (*kuti*) of time and space (*pacha*), *pachakuti* is often translated as "the return of time/space" or "the world turned upside down."[33] Remaining untranslated, *pachakuti* is more than just a new term for revolution; it also functions as a discursive intervention that indexes indigenous difference on a metaphysical plane.[34] Through a concept expressed in indigenous code, a different reality—an alternative time/space—is opened up and becomes thinkable, and therefore also possible. The myth of *pachakuti* invokes a time/space cycle corresponding to the five hundred years since the Spanish Conquest. If the arrival of Europeans symbolized an initial rotation of time and space that produced European domination with indigenous subordination, then the insurrections of 2000–2005 and the construction of a plurinational Bolivia have been interpreted as the completion of the historical cycle, a turning of the world right side up. Closer to the original notion of revolution, *pachakuti* symbolizes not a linear march toward an enlightened future but a return of the previously marginalized, an upending of once-dominant social relations. As Cherstich, Holbraad, and Tassi argue, "*Pachakuti* not only changes the rhythms and directions of time . . . but also brings about an immanent space or cosmos. In practice, it takes the semblance of a cosmological transformation, an emergence in all its intensity of an indigenous world that has previously been rendered invisible and relegated to the social and political margins."[35] A plurinational notion of revolution, then, is deeply inflected with a cosmological character. It alludes to a process that brings about or reconstitutes a world, unfolding and refolding the coordinates of human existence and transforming not just the state, society, and economy, but styles, systems of thought, spiritual beliefs, notions of time, and multiple other symbolic dimensions of everyday life.

Instead of a transcendent horizon of universal freedom and equality, a plurinational revolution is driven by an immanent metaphysical reconfiguration that alters the material and spiritual coordinates of life. Freedom and equality remain important goals, but there are other elements on the horizon too. Such a reconfiguration is created not by a sudden rupture with tradition but rather through a potentiation of traditional worldviews and practices that activate and infuse, often in uneven and contradictory ways, the revolution.[36] Whereas the transcendence of hegemony leads to the construction of a new hegemonic bloc that ossifies into a social, political, and economic order that lasts until the process starts anew, the immanence of plurinationality maintains the moment of the dialectic instead of seeking to overcome it.

As Forrest Hylton and Sinclair Thomson point out, this vision of revolution draws extensively on Bolivia's historical cultural of insurrectionary politics. Arguing that the ascent of Morales and the MAS to power was the result of Bolivia's third great revolution, Hylton and Thomson maintain that the current revolutionary process "has drawn much of its power by re-creating the past symbolically so as to transform the present—making history not only in the sense of influencing the course of events, but also producing the meaning of events."[37] This process of remembering and reanimating of the past makes Bolivia's plurinational revolution distinct, in that it openly and purposefully looks to the past to incite visions of a different future. This idea of radical transformation is neatly summed up in the Aymara adage *quip nayr uñasis sartañani* (to walk ahead while looking back). This idiom carries with it a sense of salvaging the past instead of forgetting or overcoming it to create a more just future.[38]

To think through the ways in which the past, present, and future can be reconceptualized as nonlinear, it is useful to return to the work of René Zavaleta Mercado. As noted in chapter 1, Zavaleta is best known for his conceptualization of Bolivia as a *formación abigarrada*, or a motley, disjointed social formation. This idea expresses the fact that within Bolivia "there are overlapping economic stages (those of common taxonomic usage) without their combining, as if feudalism belongs to one culture and capitalism belongs to another and yet they nevertheless occur in the same space, as if there was one country in feudalism and another in capitalism, overlapping but not combining."[39] With this Zavaleta highlights the ways in which different economic, political, and cultural forms exist within the same national geographic territory without becoming integrated and unified under one dominant mode. James Dunkerley has usefully compared Zavaleta's *formación abigarrada* to Ernst Bloch's "non-simultaneity of the simultaneous." As Bloch argues, "not all people exist in the same Now. They do externally, by virtue of the fact that they are living at the same time with others. Rather, they carry earlier things with them, things which are intricately involved. One has one's times according to where one stands corporeally, above all in terms of classes. Times older than the present continue to effect older strata."[40] While for Zavaleta the parallel existence of distinct temporalities makes societies like Bolivia markedly more complex than those of the North Atlantic already leveled and homogenized by capitalist modernity, this social form also impedes processes of socialist revolutionary change.

However, we can think with Zavaleta's categories to open up new emancipatory possibilities and alternative trajectories of modernity. For example, thinking through the relation between formal subsumption and asynchronous temporalities, Massimiliano Tomba argues that "there is a future that is still encapsulated in the past and can be freed from the contemporaneity of the archaic in constellation with other temporalities. Wherever and whenever existing forms come into contact and conflict with capitalist modernity, the result is a proliferation of temporalities and conflicting asynchronism. In this clash of temporalities the archaic is no longer such, but rather it releases possibilities of emancipation and reorientation of the trajectories of modern civilization."[41] The reactivation of ostensibly archaic, traditional cultures that nevertheless remain vital in community life forces a conflict between temporalities, which can obstruct universalist capitalist modernity and redirect its course. Building on Zavaleta, Silvia Rivera Cusicanqui uses the term *ch'ixi* to theorize the coexistence of sociocultural and temporal forms that run in parallel but do not extinguish each other. *Ch'ixi* expresses "the Aymara idea of something that is and is not at the same time, that is to say, the logic of the included third . . . *ch'ixi* combines the Indian world with its opposite, without mixing the one with the other."[42] This is not simply a rejection of dominant frameworks or a replacing of them with previously subaltern ones, but rather a recalibration between dominant and subordinate. A dichotomy of the indigenous world and its other is constructed but is not total; it is contingent and always open to reformulation. Bolivia's motley society therefore eludes the fusing of various discrete elements into unilinear historical time, operating in an ongoing, nonsyncretic dialectical manner.

Revolutions are struggles over social, political, and economic power and also between cultural and temporal forms. The contrast between temporalities provides an opportunity to rethink the teleological and stagist vision of revolutionary transformation and to reinterpret previous "archaic" modes of organization and accumulation as instigators oriented toward new potential futures. These modes are archaic and traditional not in the sense of a return to a pristine, precapitalist indigenous past, but rather in their acknowledgment and acceptance of the ongoing asynchronies that have always accompanied the implantation of the capitalist mode of accumulation in Bolivia. This is what plurinationality offers on a theoretical and epistemological level for rethinking revolution on a temporal plane.

(NATION-)STATES AND (PLURINATIONAL) REVOLUTIONS

Just as the French Revolution was so important for reframing our understanding of revolution's relation to time, it also laid the basis for the nation-state as the central mechanism over which revolutionary struggles are fought, and through which revolutionary transformations are carried out. The state has come to be viewed as the expression of the unity and general will of the nation, and thus, to truly transform a society, revolutions must unfold beyond the parochial and the particular, with an eye toward the universal as the true locus of emancipation and transformation. In the movement away from particularism and toward universalism, control over the nation-state has become the central emancipatory horizon of many revolutionary theorists and practitioners.[43]

Theda Skocpol, for instance, describes revolutions as "rapid, basic transformations of a society's state and class structures; and they are accompanied and in part carried through by class-based revolts from below."[44] For Charles Tilly, "revolutions do not develop sui generis, subject to laws that separate them entirely from more routine forms of political change." Rather, "revolutions spring from features of states that underlie the operation of states outside of revolutions." A revolution is the culmination of a multistage process that ultimately ends with "a forcible transfer of power over a state."[45] Similarly, Forrest Colburn defines revolution as the "sudden, violent, and drastic substitution of one group governing a territorial political entity for another group formerly excluded from the government, and an ensuing assault on state and society for the purpose of radically transforming society."[46] Farideh Farhi claims that "the idea of revolution, broadly conceived, is a relatively abrupt and popularly inspired change in a country's rulers."[47] For all their differences, each of these definitions retains an underlying focus on state power as a key indicator of revolutionary success and as the central mechanism for implementing revolutionary change. Indeed, for a revolution to even be possible, there first must be a unitary state in place, so that all political, social, and other forms of protest can be focused on a single set of institutions. "It should be self-evident," according to Martin Malia, "that there can be *no* revolution without a state to capture or to overthrow."[48] The state therefore is assumed in much of the social science literature on revolution, in the sense that it is the always already given locus and mechanism of struggle. As such, the essence of revolution is the forceful substitution of one set of rulers for another. And yet, though the state is no doubt important, much of the conventional discussion has a reified understanding of it, which leads to a number of issues for our consideration. Centering attention on the alteration of state power tends to obscure the fact that it is actually social relations that are undergoing transformation. This literature also fails to capture the essential cultural and symbolic transformations and the utopian visions that so often give revolutions their fundamentally revolutionary character.

The Marxist tradition has been more attuned to the importance of social relations in which the state is established. State power does not simply exist in the ether; it is an outcome of a particular correlation of social forces. Nevertheless, many Marxists remain enchanted by state power when theorizing revolutionary transformations. Marx himself understands revolutions as periods of intense political and social change embedded in deeper economic and technological transformations, which, in turn, correspond to shifting ideological interpretations and representations of the world. Despite the broader outline of revolution, Marx saw that all previous revolutions have only perfected the state machine instead of smashing it.[49] The state, for Marx, is the product of irreconcilable class contradictions, and it arises as a mechanism to mediate those contradictions through the construction of a legal order that maintains a particular correlation of class forces. It is, in essence, an apparatus of domination, and previous revolutions have only produced more efficient forms of class domination through the modality of the state.

For Vladimir Lenin, this historical lesson leads to the necessary interregnum of the proletarian dictatorship, before the ultimate withering away of the state. "The proletariat needs state power, the centralized organization of force, the organization of violence both to crush the resistance of the exploiters and to lead the enormous mass of the population— the peasantry, the petty bourgeoisie, the semi-proletarians—in the work of establishing a socialist economy."[50] Yet, this isn't simply the substitution of one group of leaders for another in charge of an abstract governing apparatus. Rather, the old state machine needs to be abolished and replaced with a new governing machine. "Revolution consists not in the new class commanding and governing with the aid of the *old* state machine but in its smashing this machine and commanding and governing with the aid of a *new* machine."[51] Just as the old machine was a dictatorship of the bourgeoisie, this new machine, while it lasts, must command and govern in the interest of the proletariat. During processes of revolutionary change, "the state in this period unavoidably has to be a state that is democratic *in a new way* (for the proletarians and the propertyless in general), and dictatorial *in a new way* (against the bourgeoisie). . . . The transition from capitalism to communism, of course, cannot help but produce a vast abundance and variety of political forms, but the essence will inevitably be the same: *the dictatorship of the proletariat*."[52] Only after the period of proletarian dictatorship has abolished all class divisions and molded society with egalitarian customs will the state as such wither away.

In his analysis of Gramsci's enduring influence for contemporary processes of social change, Stuart Hall too highlights the theoretical and practical importance of the state.[53] Hall notes that one of Gramsci's key contributions was providing us with a profoundly expanded conception of what politics is and, therefore, of how power and authority work. Gramsci demonstrated that social struggles and antagonisms proliferate as societies complexify, and therefore a regime of rule (that is, hegemony) must be constructed, contested, and won on many different planes. Nevertheless, despite this process of diversification, the state remains decisive for social transformation. Hall argues, "the state is clearly absolutely central in articulating the different areas of contestation, the different points of antagonism, into a regime of rule. The moment when you can get sufficient power in the state to organize a central political project is decisive, for then you can use the state to plan, urge, incite, solicit and punish, to conform the different sites of power and consent into a single regime."[54] The state here is both the confluence of various theoretical currents within society and the moment of concrete political power conforming those currents into a single mode of organization and rule.

García Linera, too, remains captivated by state power, albeit in a particular way. Drawing on the work of Gramsci and Lenin, he offers in *¿Que es una revolución?* (What is a revolution?) a complex and compelling understanding of revolutionary processes as more than just the conquering of the state; they are the construction of a new political order. "A revolution is, ultimately, a fierce struggle for the durable monopoly of ideological-political power in society, for a new long-term hegemony. In this sense, every revolution is also a means of nationalizing society."[55] Revolutions are long-term processes composed of various moments, what García Linera described to me as a theoretical dialectic between Gramsci and Lenin.[56] He labels the period of sociocultural struggle over ideas the "Gramscian moment," akin to Gramsci's own war of position. A revolution is impossible without this moment, the period when insurgent sectors organize, agitate, and challenge dominant cultural ideas with their own alternatives. It is the moment of what Gramsci labels trench warfare, as more and more sociocultural territory is discursively and ideologically contested and challenged, gradually building up the political power of insurgent forces. The Gramscian moment gives way to the moment of force, the "Leninist moment," or what García Linera elsewhere calls the "point of bifurcation."[57] The Leninist moment is a "naked battle of forces . . . that settles the question of state power for an unlimited period of time."[58] Without this Leninist moment, according to García Linera, a revolution has not fully succeeded, and, sooner or later, it will fail due to internal conflicts or through counterrevolution. "Consequently, every revolution with a *Gramscian moment* but without a *Leninist moment* will be a truncated, failed revolution. There is no true revolution without a *Gramscian moment* of political, cultural, and moral triumph prior to the taking of state power. But, neither is there control of state power or the dissolution of the old ruling classes as subjects with a defined political project, without the decisive *Leninist moment*."[59] For García Linera, the state is central to the revolution not simply as an indicator of success or as the central terrain of struggle, what has actually already been fought before the moment of political power. The state is crucial because it holds the power to appropriate the appropriators; it provides the ability to seize the material base of the previous elites, causing these elites to lose the power to influence society and make decisions (that is, to lose political power). State power is "a measure to suffocate the power of the governing bourgeoise and open a space for the insurrectionary classes to consolidate their power and historical initiatives."[60]

But it is not simply against the old ruling classes that the state is a key apparatus of power for directing the revolution, it is also effective for controlling those revolutionary subjects themselves that embody, enact, and give life to the revolution. In short, García Linera argues, the protection of the revolution against the previous ruling elite requires the revolutionary state to temporarily assume "a national articulation, a general unification to oversee the relations [*conjunto de movimiento*] between different social sectors; to ensure the ability to work, the circulation of material goods, and, with that, the protection and defense of the revolution against all its detractors, but, fundamentally, against the past that continues to live in the minds of those revolutionaries who 'remember' a better life before [the revolution]."[61] The idea of conquering state power to change society rests on the assumption that the state is sovereign. With this, the state is reified into an autonomous agent above society and the balance of social forces. More than a coercive mechanism under the direction of a certain social class, it becomes an overseer of a unified social totality, the protagonist of historical movement, and the determining agent of the national revolutionary path.

From a related historical tradition but with an opposite view of state power, others have outlined how the conquering of the state actually impedes the prospect of a real revolutionary rupture. John Holloway, drawing inspiration from the Zapatistas, questions the assumption that the state is, or should be, the vantage point from which society can be changed. Not only, argues Holloway, has this route failed historically to "create a self-determining society or promote the reign of freedom which has always been central to the communist aspiration," but it also fetishizes the state and "abstracts it from the web of power relations in which it is embedded."[62] Similar to the manner in which capital alienates producer from product, the state actively negates (becomes a fetishization of) social relations. For Holloway, a revolution is only truly revolutionary if and when it acts against both capital and the state, when it courses an alternative path toward what he terms social self-determination, a society based on mutual recognition of dignity and absolved of power relations. Holloway's reformulation of revolutionary change gets at the central problematic of the state's ontological priority in much of the social scientific and Marxist literature. He argues that this prioritizing of state power leads to a revolutionary strategy of building organizations of counterpower that are anathema to social self-determination and merely strive to replace one dominant and leading group with another. The belief that social self-determination culminates with taking state power is the "terrible, explosive lie at the heart of Leninism," according to Holloway, because the state form itself is the negation of social self-determination. "The state is a specific form of relations developed historically for the purpose of administering on behalf of, that is, excluding."[63] For Holloway, "the apparent impossibility of revolution at the beginning of the twenty-first century reflects in reality the historical failure of a particular concept of revolution, the concept that identified revolution with control of the state."[64]

Building on the work of Holloway, Raquel Gutiérrez Aguilar argues that "taking power is neither a necessary nor a sufficient condition to change the world."[65] According to Gutiérrez Aguilar, indigenous and popular sectors in the 2000–2005 Bolivian insurrections were not simply seeking a more inclusive and democratic state or the capturing of state power. Rather, they desired and demanded an antistatist alternative of self-determination and self-unification, that is, social emancipation. For Gutiérrez Aguilar, the state is an illusory social synthesis that provides stability by organizing everyday life and containing, not resolving, internal conflict. Only when this illusory social synthesis comes to be rejected can "a social rupture of great magnitude" open up to transform the social relations of the ostensible synthesis. "Both the relations of domination and exploitation, in their form and content, and the essential beliefs in a hierarchical categorization of the different segments of the social structure are drastically altered during moments of historical rupture. If this is not the case, this demonstrates that the preceding moment was not a social rupture of great magnitude."[66] This is an understanding of revolutionary transformation clearly distinct from one focused on state power. It is in fact the exact opposite, as Gutiérrez Aguilar argues that the taking of state power through revolutionary means actually impedes the transformative and liberating potential of rebellion. She states, "collective emancipatory action and its deep transformation of social, economic, and political relations *need to be considered from a separate and distinct channel* from the political struggle for the control of the government and the state."[67] It is not that these discrete operations are unrelated, but rather that for Guitérrez Aguilar the conquest of state power is ineffective, if not detrimental, for the advance of revolutionary social emancipation.

This view of revolution against the state is expressed in Guitérrez Aguilar's notion of the community popular, as opposed to Gramsci and Zavaleta's national popular. Whereas the national popular perspective seeks to promote equality through social democratization of a heterogenous social formation in the nation-state, the community popular proposes "the reformulation of the relation between the government and society, reconfiguring and renegotiating the scope of autonomy and the decentralization of power."[68] A key point here involves the issue of sovereignty. For the national popular perspective, sovereignty is located in the nation-state, and therefore the desire to create national popular hegemony channels the struggle toward the conquest of state power. For Gutiérrez Aguilar, this conceptualization confuses the real struggle for self-determination with the illusion of nation-state sovereignty. Yet, a central shortcoming of the opposing perspective, that of the community popular, according to Gutiérrez Aguilar, is its inability to articulate an alternative theoretical mechanism to the social totality of the nation-state that captures the idea of political equality through difference. In this book I have tried to show that the theory of plurinationality does exactly this: it expresses a new type of social contract based on the ideas of dignity, autonomy, respect, and cooperation between independent yet articulated social entities on both a theoretical and a practical level.

This discussion has drawn attention to the centrality of the state in the literature on revolution, even within opposing approaches. Regardless of the perspective, the state is largely presented as a generalized and coherent thing, an instrumental entity to be either conquered or elided, either taken or rejected in the process of revolutionary transformation. The conventional social scientific, Marxist, and anarchist-inspired literatures outlined above thus mistake the nation-state form for "the state" in general. There are certainly debates in all these fields about the state form, but they all take more or less as a given the socioterritorial organization of space in terms of the nation-state and its historical conditions of emergence. In this way, the idea of the nation-state persists as what Tapia calls an "epistemological obstacle," which obscures even thinking through other possible state forms.[69] As I argued in chapter 5, what is called "the state" is nothing more than a social relation that expresses the condensation of social forces at a given time and place. While "the state" does not have a universal, transhistorical form, the fact that it is the ossification of a particular social relation in space and time hinders attempts to think beyond a social formation organized around it. Even Gutiérrez Aguilar's community popular perspective, for all of its opposition to the national popular nation-state, still expresses a state form, albeit in a radically decentralized and horizontal pattern.

Proponents of plurinationality envision an alternative state, a horizon that is beyond the nation-state form but not against the state in general.[70] The plurinational state is conceived as an articulation of diverse but not integrated social groups, similar to what Juan Manuel Arbona and colleagues describe as a "fabric" of interlaced segments that are autonomous yet remain complementary parts of the political body.[71] Rather than overturning the old order to reproduce a more democratic and equitable social totality, the theory of plurinationality outlines a tendency and a capacity to maintain social heterogeneity through a segmented political structure not all that different from the system of *ayllus* discussed in chapter 4. Cherstich, Holbraad, and Tassi are only half right when they claim that revolution implies not "the turning toward a 'new' luminous political horizon embodied by the conquest of the state but rather the turning 'back' toward the segmentary forms of Andean polities activating, potentiating, and expanding them not in order to integrate them into the state but to place them in a horizontal relation of force with it."[72] It is not so much that these articulated segments are in a horizontal relation with the state, but that the horizontal relations and articulations of the segments are in fact the state itself.

This is the way the state has always tended to operate in Bolivia, and as such, the potential of a plurinational revolution in Bolivia is partially about the efflorescence of something that, although marginalized, is already present. But, under the ideological inheritance of the nation-state form as a social totality, the motley composition of Bolivia and its "archaic" modes of organization have typically been viewed as a lingering historical abnormality standing in the way of a more equitable and liberal democratic future. The policies and practices used to overcome this historical abnormality have changed over time, but the underlying goal of a liberal nation-state composed of juridically equal individuals leveled through capitalist modernization has remained more or less constant. Politically, then, the revolutionary upheavals that carried Morales and the MAS to power and continue to reverberate are important because they brought about a change in control of state power, but to an even greater extent because they have offered to cultivate a marginalized but extant form of political organization based on the articulation of diverse and autonomous segments of Bolivian society. The irradiation of polyphonic social and political forms in Bolivia is in fact the plurinational state in material form. Although the plurinational state has more and more been enveloped and appropriated by the hegemonic project of the MAS, its efflorescence in the early twenty-first century has been an important theoretical and practical reminder of alternative state forms and of the idea that revolutionary desires need not express themselves in terms of totalities. The plurinational state volunteers a desire, a conceptual outline of a complex tapestry of peoples, classes, values, worldviews, logics of social and cultural life, economic systems, and forms of political organization interweaving in sometimes productive, oftentimes ambivalent, and occasionally contradictory ways. It is an attempt to institutionalize the multiple modes of being, seeing, doing, and inventing the world in such a way that offers them the dignity, respect, and capability to reproduce themselves (or not), based on their own determination.

The issue of state power is thus still important when theorizing revolution from a plurinational perspective. Yet, the state is understood as more than just a group of political leaders in control of an ahistorical and autonomous mechanism of power. State power cannot just be found lying in the street, as it were, waiting to be taken up and put to use. If the state is the correlation of social forces at any given time, then the transformation of the state is really the transformation of society's social relations. Given that, the change in the institutional apparatus of "the state" is not the defining characteristic of revolution but rather a reflection of the changing balance of social forces. The institutional changes we see in the political system are not the driving causes or consequences of any given revolution. Changes in political institutional form are representations; they symbolize and gauge the ways in which the relations between social forces have been altered. In this sense, Jeffery M. Paige helps us rethink the state-centrism of much revolutionary analysis and offers a better conception of what a plurinational revolution entails. Paige describes revolutions as "a rapid and fundamental transformation in the categories of social life and consciousness, the metaphysical assumptions on which these categories are based, and the power relations in which they are expressed as a result of widespread popular acceptance of a utopian alternative to the current social order."[73] The politics of state power remain significant but are enveloped and can only be fully expressed within the much more thoroughgoing transformations of desires, practices, perceptions, and evaluations of everyday life that make revolutions actually revolutionary. A plurinational revolution no doubt entails political transformation, but it is as much about the social, cultural, and symbolic ruptures of the revolutionary process.

CONTRASTING VISIONS OF TRANSFORMATION IN BOLIVIA'S *PROCESO DE CAMBIO*

The contrasting theories of hegemony and plurinationality by which I have organized this book and through which I have interpreted events in Bolivia offer conflicting logics and visions of society, politics, and revolutionary change. They are conceptual schemes for understanding what societies are and how struggles over value are expressed through a society's politics. Innovative concepts such as plurinationality make new thoughts possible and open our eyes to emerging and ongoing social practices. In that sense, I am interested in the ways that ideas affect people's actions and allow us to interpret reality in different ways. Yet, this focus on ideas is not simply idealist. New conceptual schemes are always linked to the material reality in which they arise. Plurinationality allows us to interpret and understand society in certain ways while also pointing toward particular political practices to bring a new reality into being, but the concept is only thinkable, at least in Bolivia, because of the material history of exclusion, subordination, and exploitation of the country's indigenous peoples. It is in this way that the ideological and the material, theory and practice, converge and become indistinguishable from each other.

I do not mean to argue that hegemony and plurinationality are always in conflict. Indeed, both perspectives aligned during the 2000–2005 insurrectionary period that ultimately brought Evo Morales and the MAS to power, overthrowing the decaying, delegitimized neoliberal order in a sudden and authoritative way. During this period the two approaches overlapped and merged together against a crumbling system of party politics (*partidocracia*), waves of military and police violence, and the pillage of resources by transnational capital while Bolivians faced increased austerity. The point at which these positions diverged is open to interpretation. While they were always in tension with each other, fractures began to clearly appear during the Constituent Assembly, grew larger after Morales's reelection in 2009, when the MAS also took full control of the legislature, and became chasms in 2011 with the TIPNIS conflict. Despite the correspondences and contradictions between these two theoretical perspectives, they both offer an alternative potential future to the recent Bolivian past.

However, as I have argued, for a number of reasons both material and ideological, the MAS government was unable to fully incorporate the radical potentiality of plurinationalism into its official governing project. Despite the MAS's rhetorical inclusion and symbolic uses of plurinationality, the composition of the Bolivian state under the MAS has remained largely within the confines of the traditional nation-state form, and the MAS's design and techniques for radical social change continue to be rooted in the theory of hegemony. It is through an understanding of plurinationality and hegemony as two contrasting theoretical visions of social revolutionary change that we can usefully interpret and understand many of the tensions and contradictions of the period of MAS rule.

This book may be read as a critique of Morales and the MAS and their time in power, as it should. However, I hope that it is read not just as critique but also as an interpretive lens through which to see and understand the Morales era in Bolivia, both its successes and its limitations. If certain ideas presented here can be taken beyond the bounds of Bolivia to interpret processes of social change more broadly, that would be better still. By focusing on the theory of hegemony I hope to have demonstrated that Morales and the MAS understand the world through a particular logic, through which they effected a number of important social, political, economic, and cultural transformations in Bolivia, perhaps more than any previous government in the country's nearly two-hundred-year history. At the same time, the logic of hegemony creates certain limits to what is both thinkable and possible in revolutionary times. Morales and the MAS were compelled by a vision of the nation, the state, the economy, and intersubjectivity that both explains their political strategies and tactics and also draws attention to the various resistances to that project. The central issue with the theory of hegemony, as developed by Lenin and Gramsci in the early twentieth century and later situated in the context of Bolivia by Zavaleta Mercado and García Linera, is the assumption of the nation-state form and its attendant totality of the social. The political terrain is bounded by the territoriality of the nation-state, while the social formation is envisaged as a generalized, homogenous totality. This makes sense in a world order constructed of the nation-state form, yet this assumption opens up certain possibilities for revolutionary transformation while at the same time foreclosing other imaginaries. Plurinationality, as its name implies, envisions different forms of nation, state, economy, and intersubjectivity that compel us to rethink our conceptualizations of revolutionary change. Now, it may in fact be the case that, given current conditions, a real form of plurinationality is unattainable, that it is a radical utopia too easily co-opted discursively from various political positions for contrasting purposes, as well as impossible on a concrete, practical level in a world dominated by the nation-state form and global capitalism. If that is the case, then perhaps the revolutionary politics of hegemony is the politics of what is possible. Nevertheless, this is not what many Bolivians have accepted, and in struggling for plurinationality they have struggled to bring new worlds into being. In the process they have advanced new visions of transformation while also exposing the imperatives and constraints of the old ones.

NOTES

Introduction

1. For a good overview of neoliberalism in Bolivia, see Kohl and Farthing, *Impasse in Bolivia*.
2. See Gill, *Teetering on the Rim*.
3. García Linera, "La muerte de la condición obrera del siglo XX," in *La potencia plebeya*, 162–92.
4. P. Thomas, *The Gramscian Moment*, 145.
5. Dunkerley, "Evo Morales, the 'Two Bolivias,'" 162.
6. In the years between the country's return to democracy in 1982 and the rise of the MAS, three main parties contested for power: the Movimiento Nacionalista Revolucionario (MNR), the Movimiento de Izquierda Revolucionaria (MIR), and the Acción Democrática Nacionalista (ADN).
7. Yashar, *Contesting Citizenship in Latin America*, esp. ch. 5.
8. Assies, "Bolivia: A Gasified Democracy," 31.
9. Tapia, *Una reflexión sobre la idea de un estado plurinacional*, 15.
10. Guha, *Dominance Without Hegemony*.
11. Zavaleta Mercado, *Lo nacional-popular en Bolivia*, 348, 351, 342. The term *rosca* was commonly used to describe the governments of the early twentieth century that operated primarily in the interests of the leading tin baron families.
12. For the 1899 Federal War, see Hylton, "Now Is Not Your Time." On Jesús de Machaca, see Choque Canqui and Ticona Alejo, *Sublevacion y Masacre de 1921*. On Chayanta, see Platt, "The Andean Experience of Bolivian Liberalism." Dunkerley's 1984 *Rebellion in the Veins* remains the preeminent English-

language analysis of the 1952 National Revolution. For the rise of Katarismo, see Hurtado, *El Katarismo*.

13. The literature is by now extensive, but on the so-called Left Turn, see Cameron and Hershberg, *Latin America's Left Turns*; Ellner, *Latin America's Radical Left*; Levitsky and Roberts, *The Resurgence of the Latin American Left*; Webber and Carr, *The New Latin American Left*; Gaudichaud, Modonesi, and Webber, *The Impasse of the Latin American Left*.

14. See, e.g., Crabtree and Chaplin, *Bolivia: Processes of Change*; Escobar, "Latin America at a Crossroads"; Farthing and Kohl, *Evo's Bolivia*; Gutiérrez Aguilar, *Los ritmos del Pachakuti*; Santos, *Refundación del Estado en América Latina*; Webber, *From Rebellion to Reform in Bolivia*; McNelly, *Now We Are In Power*.

15. Hylton and Thomson, *Revolutionary Horizons*, 24. See also Bjork-James, *The Sovereign Street*; Paige, *Indigenous Revolution in Ecuador and Bolivia*; Gilly, "Bolivia: A 21st-Century Revolution."

16. See Webber, *From Rebellion to Reform in Bolivia*; Rivera Cusicanqui, *Mito y desarrollo en Bolivia*.

17. Mamani Ramirez, *El estado neocolonial*, 155.

18. Mamani Ramirez, 223.

19. Gustafson, *Bolivia in the Age of Gas*. See also Anthias, *Limits to Decolonization*.

20. Gustafson, *Bolivia in the Age of Gas*, 20.

21. Gustafson, 244.

22. Gustafson, 222.

23. Luis Tapia, *La idea de estado como obstáculo epistemológico*.

24. Goodale, *A Revolution in Fragments*, 29.

25. Goodale, 241.

26. Postero, "Morales's MAS Government."

27. Postero, *The Indigenous State*. For a similar argument regarding the concept of indigeneity, see Burman, "Black Hole Indigeneity."

28. Postero, *The Indigenous State*, 19.

29. Wagner, *The Invention of Culture*, 41–44.

30. Wagner, 116.

31. Wagner, 116.

32. Wagner, *The Invention of Culture*.

33. The original, unwieldy version of that chapter tried to cover all three communities' attempts to construct Indigenous autonomy. It now focuses solely on Charagua, although it is informed by my time in the other two communities.

34. On the field of comparative political theory, see Gordy, *Living Ideology in Cuba*; M. Thomas, "Orientalism and Comparative Political Theory."

35. Cited in Clifford, "Anthropology and/as Travel," 5.

36. I was told this by Luis Tapia, perhaps the most well-known interpreter of Zavaleta today. Author interview, La Paz, 2016.

37. Rabinow and Sullivan, "The Interpretive Turn," 6.

38.   The discussions of ethnography's place in political science have grown exponentially since roughly 2010. See, e.g., Schatz, *Political Ethnography*; Wedeen, "Reflections on Ethnographic Work in Political Science"; Schwartz-Shea and Majic, "Ethnography and Participant Observation"; Pachirat, *Among Wolves*; Simmons, *Meaningful Resistance*.

Chapter 1

1.   Day, *Gramsci Is Dead*, 13.
2.   Tapia, *La idea de estado como obstáculo epistemológico*, 53.
3.   Wagner, *The Invention of Culture*, 123.
4.   See Buci-Glucksmann, *Gramsci and the State*, 174–75; P. Anderson, "The Antinomies of Antonio Gramsci," 16–17. Perry Anderson's foundational essay has been expanded on in his book *The H-Word* (2017).
5.   Hall, "Gramsci's Relevance for the Study of Race and Ethnicity," 6.
6.   For analyses of Gramsci's theoretical influence in Latin America, see Mignolo, "Mariátegui and Gramsci in 'Latin' America"; Burgos, "The Ups and Downs of an Uncomfortable Legacy." For an in-depth investigation of how the concept of hegemony has been taken up and utilized in Argentina specifically, see Cavooris, "Intellectuals and Political Strategy."
7.   P. Thomas, *The Gramscian Moment*, 42.
8.   Hall, "Gramsci's Relevance for the Study of Race and Ethnicity," 6–7.
9.   Gramsci, *The Modern Prince and Other Writings*, 30.
10.   Gramsci, *Selections from the Prison Notebooks*, 169–70.
11.   Gramsci, 57. In a different, earlier iteration Gramsci uses the term *class* instead of the more general notion of *social group*. According to Derek Boothman, this shows that Gramsci is aware of the prison censors, but also that he has expanded and fully developed his conceptualization of hegemony. See Boothman, "A Note on the Evolution—and Translation—of Some Key Gramscian Terms," 126–27.
12.   P. Thomas, *The Gramscian Moment*, 161.
13.   Gramsci, *Selections from the Prison Notebooks*, 182.
14.   Gramsci, 181–82.
15.   Gwyn Williams, "The Concept of 'Egemonia,'" 587.
16.   Scott, *Weapons of the Weak*, 335, 315. For an earlier iteration of the same argument, see Scott, "Hegemony and the Peasantry."
17.   See Femia, "Hegemony and Consciousness," 35–37.
18.   Gramsci, *Selections from the Prison Notebooks*, 161.
19.   According to Gramsci, "the State is the entire complex of practical and theoretical activities with which the ruling class not only justifies and maintains its domination, but manages to win the active consent of those over whom it rules." Gramsci, *Selections from the Prison Notebooks*, 244. For an extended

discussion of the integral state, see Buci-Glucksmann, *Gramsci and the State*, 91–110, 282–94.

20. See, e.g., Wood, *The Origin of Capitalism*; Tilly, *Coercion, Capital, and European States*; Moore, *Social Origins of Dictatorship and Democracy*.
21. Gramsci, *Selections from the Prison Notebooks*, 238.
22. P. Thomas, *The Gramscian Moment*, 194.
23. Gramsci, *Selections from the Prison Notebooks*, 260.
24. Gramsci, 106.
25. Buci-Glucksmann, "Hegemony and Consent," 116–17.
26. Gramsci, *Selections from the Prison Notebooks*, 57–58.
27. Gramsci, 168.
28. For the concept of *national popular*, see Gramsci, 421n65.
29. Gramsci, 129, 132–33.
30. Gramsci, 130–33.
31. Gramsci, *The Modern Prince and Other Writings*, 169.
32. Gramsci, *Selections from the Prison Notebooks*, 181–82.
33. P. Anderson, "The Heirs of Gramsci."
34. Laclau and Mouffe's reworking of hegemony in *Hegemony and Socialist Strategy* was questioned by many who argued that the term was emptied of its material foundations and its strategic utility. In *The Retreat from Class*, for example, Ellen Meiksins Wood critiques Laclau and Mouffe for their "autonomization of ideology and politics," arguing that their discursive conceptualization of hegemony disassociates working-class interests from the struggle for socialism and implies "that there are no 'fixed' social interests or identities, that all social identities are discursively constructed and 'politically negotiable.' In fact, this is the proposition on which their case ultimately rests; and it entails not only the dissolution of social reality into discourse, but a denial of *history* and the logic of historical process" (61–62). Moreover, "not only is the working class no privileged agent of socialism, there are no historical conditions and no social interests conducive to the development of socialism. This means that no *other* 'social agents' exist whose collective identity, interests, and capacities might replace those of the working class as the basic materials of socialist struggle. In fact, there is no social basis for *any* kind of politics. Discourse is all" (74). In the final instance, according to Wood, Laclau and Mouffe's reformulation of hegemony on discursive grounds "is not an analysis of contemporary society and the conditions of its transformation; it is little more than a verbal conjuring trick" (69). For a reply to some of their critics, see Laclau and Mouffe, "Post-Marxism Without Apologies."
35. See, e.g., Aricó, *La cola del diablo*; Portantiero, *Los usos de Gramsci*; Munck, *Rethinking Latin America*.
36. For a fascinating and lively analysis of Zavaleta's thought and intellectual style, see Dunkerley, "Bolivia en ese entonces," esp. 193–201.

37. Zavaleta Mercado, "Las masas en noviembre" (1983), in *Obra Completa*, 2:102–3, 2:106. See also Antezana, "Dos conceptos en la obra de René Zavaleta Mercado," 122.
38. Zavaleta Mercado, "Las masas en noviembre," in *Obra Completa*, 2:105.
39. Antezana, "Dos conceptos en la obra de René Zavaleta Mercado," 131.
40. See Hardt and Negri, *Empire*, 393–413; Negri et al., *Imperio, multitud y sociedad abigarrada*.
41. For a similar argument using a Zavaletan analysis, see Tapia, *La hegemonía imposible*. While Tapia has analyzed the work of Zavaleta more than most—he wrote his dissertation and a book on the thought of Zavaleta (see Tapia, *La producción del conocimiento local*)—it is unclear in *La hegemonía imposible* why, in fact, it has been impossible to form a hegemony in Bolivia. Tapia does not clarify whether the failure to construct a hegemonic bloc with the power to lead is due to an objective, structural barrier with a basis in Bolivia's social formation, the subjective inability of a particular social group to incorporate dominated social groups into its universal project, or simply the outright impossibility of creating a truly hegemonic state in general terms.
42. Zavaleta Mercado, *Clases sociales y conocimiento*, 159–63; Zavaleta Mercado, *Lo nacional-popular en Bolivia*, 14; Zavaleta Mercado, "Las masas en noviembre," in *Obra Completa*, 2:132.
43. Zavaleta Mercado, "Las masas en noviembre," in *Obra Completa*, 2:124.
44. Zavaleta Mercado, *Lo nacional-popular en Bolivia*, 9. According to Tapia, social democratization in this sense "refers to the processes of growing socioeconomic equality and integration that are generating the modernization of the reorganized economy following the criteria of formal rationality and capitalism." See Tapia, *La producción del conocimiento local*, 193.
45. Zavaleta Mercado, "El poder dual en América Latina" (1973), in *Obra Completa*, 1:377. It should be noted here that this idea of the state comes from one of Zavaleta's most purely Marxist works. Zavaleta's thought is typically segmented into three defined periods. The first, which stretches from the late 1950s to the late 1960s, is where Zavaleta was primarily "nationalist" and is most clearly articulated in *Bolivia: El desarrollo de la conciencia nacional* (1967). The second period, where his work has been analyzed as "orthodox Marxism," culminates with the publication of *El poder dual en América Latina* in 1973/74. The final decade of Zavaleta's life is characterized as a period of "critical Marxism" and is seen in *Las masas en noviembre* (1983) and the posthumously published *Lo nacional-popular en Bolivia* (1986). See Antezana, "Dos conceptos en la obra de René Zavaleta Mercado." However, Zavaleta's theory of the state as a class unity of power over subordinate groups remained fairly stable, despite the fact that his ideas and analyses changed over the years, with him increasingly incorporating ideological and cultural aspects into his ideas on the relationship between state and society.

46. Marx, "The German Ideology," 172–73; Zavaleta Mercado, *Lo nacional-popular en Bolivia*, 149.

47. Zavaleta's notion of *el estado nacional* is similar to Gramsci's concept of an integral or extended state, discussed earlier in this chapter.

48. See Zavaleta Mercado, *Lo nacional-popular en Bolivia*; Zavaleta Mercado, "Cuatro conceptos de democracia" (1981), in *Obra Completa*, 2:513–29.

49. Tapia, *La producción del conocimiento local*, 196; Zavaleta Mercado, *Lo nacional-popular en Bolivia*, 48.

50. Zavaleta Mercado, "Notas sobre la cuestión nacional en América Latina" (1981), in *Obra Completa*, 2:539.

51. Zavaleta Mercado, 2:538–39; see also B. Anderson, *Imagined Communities*.

52. Zavaleta Mercado, "Las masas en noviembre," in *Obra Completa*, 2:105–6. For specific methodological reasons for why crisis is essential for understanding *sociedades abigarradas*, see Laserna, "Bolivia: Crisis de Estado," 550–51.

53. Zavaleta Mercado, "Las masas en noviembre," in *Obra Completa*, 2:106–7. The Battle of Nanawa took place during the Chaco War (1932–35) between Bolivia and Paraguay. According to Zavaleta, the Chaco War as a constitutive moment of crisis was "where Bolivia was to ask itself what it was made of," and was also "the point of departure for modern Bolivia." Zavaleta Mercado, *Lo nacional-popular en Bolivia*, 181.

54. Laserna, "Bolivia: Crisis de Estado," 554. Although Zavaleta used the term *clase obrera* (working class), his usage was often ambivalent. Luis Antezana notes that Zavaleta "felt uncomfortable with the traditional concept of class to characterize the mining proletariat as a 'working class' . . . finally replacing it with the concept of 'the masses.'" Cited in Dunkerley, "Bolivia en ese entonces," 205. In an interview, Zavaleta stated that "it is obvious that when referring to the working class we refer to it as the leader [*caudillo*] of civil society, of the other classes." Laserna, "Bolivia: crisis de Estado," 554. Perhaps it is useful to think about Zavaleta's employment of *clase obrera* as similar to Marx's use of *proletariat*, as Étienne Balibar explains: "In reality, the concept of the proletariat is not so much that of a particular 'class,' isolated from the whole of society, as of a *non-class*, the formation of which immediately precedes the dissolution of all classes and primes the revolutionary process. For this reason, when speaking of it, Marx employs, for preference, the term *'Masse'* ('mass' or 'masses'), which he turns round against the contemptuous use made of it by bourgeois intellectuals in his day." Balibar, *The Philosophy of Marx*, 54.

55. Gramsci, *Selections from the Prison Notebooks*, 238.

56. Zavaleta Mercado, *Lo nacional-popular en Bolivia*, 50.

57. Zavaleta Mercado, "El poder dual en América Latina," in *Obra Completa*, 1:410.

58. Zavaleta Mercado, 1:379.

59. Zavaleta Mercado, 1:410; Tapia, *La producción del conocimiento local*, 308–9.

60. Tapia, *La producción del conocimiento local*, 310.

61. Zavaleta Mercado, "Bolivia—Military Nationalism and the Popular Assembly," 70.

62. Zavaleta Mercado, "Las masas en noviembre," in *Obra Completa*, 2:109, 2:133.

63. For example, he stated that hegemony is nothing more than "the atmosphere that is between men [*sic*] in the midst of production," and that "the measure of hegemony, that is its optimum, consists of the ability of contradictions to be absorbed by it." Zavaleta Mercado, "Las formaciones aparentes en Marx" (1978), in *Obra Completa*, 2:435; Zavaleta Mercado, *Lo nacional-popular en Bolivia*, 195.

64. Zavaleta Mercado, "Bolivia—Military Nationalism and the Popular Assembly," 67.

65. Elias, "Power and Civilization."

66. García Linera, "Autonomías indígenas y Estado multinacional," in *La potencia plebeya*, 230. A number of chapters from *La potencia plebeya* have been reproduced in English under the title *Plebian Power*.

67. García Linera, "Autonomías indígenas y Estado multinacional," 233–34.

68. García Linera, 236.

69. An overview of the different stages of García Linera's thought can be found in Stefanoni, prefacio; and Bosteels, "¿Puede pensarse hoy la actualidad del comunismo?"

70. *Qhanachiri* is Aymara for "the one who knows/clarifies things."

71. Gutiérrez Aguilar and García Linera, "A manera de introduction," 18–19.

72. García Linera, *De demonios escondidos y momentos de revolución*, 255, quoted in Bosteels, "¿Puede pensarse hoy la actualidad del comunismo?," 323.

73. García Linera, quoted in Stefanoni, prefacio, 20–21.

74. This type of critique has certainly been leveled at García Linera. Yet, as Bruno Bosteels points out, many critiques of this nature show little knowledge or understanding of the breadth and sophistication of García Linera's work. Bosteels, "¿Puede pensarse hoy la actualidad del comunismo?," 318n31. And, as James Dunkerley notes, this type of criticism "is a complete boon for commentators. Intellectuals who occupy public office are unusual prey to charges of hypocrisy as they scale speedily down from the heights where theory and sheer high-mindedness inevitably locate them, but apart from the tell-tale loquaciousness of the guild, they bequeath plenty of evidence of 'where they come from.'" Dunkerley, "Evo Morales, the 'Two Bolivias,'" 145. However, it should also be noted that there are a number of polemics between García Linera and some of his former comrades in Grupo Comuna that are more historically informed, but are nevertheless sometimes overlaid with personal animosity.

75. García Linera, "Indianismo y marxismo," in *La potencia plebeya*, 392.

76. García Linera, "El *Manifiesto comunista* y nuestro tiempo," in *La potencia plebeya*, 95. This work was originally published in García Linera et al., *El fantasma insomne*. All citations here are from the version reproduced in *La potencia plebeya*.

77. García Linera, "El *Manifiesto comunista* y nuestro tiempo," 94.
78. García Linera, 90.
79. See Dove, "The *Desencuentros* of History." Perhaps the most explicit and well known example of this critical *indigenismo* is Fausto Reinaga's *La revolución india*. For more contemporary arguments along similar lines, see F. Quispe, *Túpak Katari*; A. Quispe, *Indianismo-Katarismo*.
80. García Linera, "El *Manifiesto comunista* y nuestro tiempo," in *La potencia plebeya*, 98.
81. García Linera, "El movimiento de los movimientos," 38.
82. See García Linera, "La muerte de la condición obrera del siglo XX," in *La potencia plebeya*, 162–92.
83. García Linera, "Sindicato, multitud y comunidad," in *La potencia plebeya*, 294n369.
84. García Linera, "Multitud y sociedad abigarrada," 60–61.
85. Although García Linera does not cite Ernesto Laclau in this context, García Linera's conceptualization of the multitude is similar to Laclau's formulation of the diversity within new social movements. See Laclau, "New Social Movements."
86. García Linera, "Sindicato, multitud y comunidad," in *La potencia plebeya*, 305.
87. On the distinction between hegemony of difference and hegemony over difference, see Gareth Williams, "Social Disjointedness and the State-Form in Álvaro García Linera."
88. García Linera, "El *Manifiesto comunista* y nuestro tiempo," in *La potencia plebeya*, 102–3.
89. García Linera, 120–21.
90. García Linera, author interview, La Paz, 2015.
91. García Linera, "The State in Transition," 34. Similar versions of this article were published in García Linera, *La potencia plebeya*, 392–412; and García Linera et al., *El Estado*. All citations here are to the English translation.
92. For a discussion of these various theories of the state, see Zavaleta Mercado, "El estado en América Latina" (1983), in *Obra Completa*, 2:611–36; Poulantzas, *State, Power, Socialism*; Mitchell, "The Limits of the State."
93. García Linera, "The State in Transition," 35.
94. García Linera, 36–37.
95. Gramsci, *Selections from the Prison Notebooks*, 222.
96. García Linera, "The State in Transition," 47.
97. García Linera, author interview, La Paz, 2015.
98. García Linera, *Las tensiones creativas de la revolución*, 18.
99. García Linera, author interview, La Paz, 2015.
100. García Linera.
101. Gramsci, *Selections from the Prison Notebooks*, 59.
102. García Linera, author interview, La Paz, 2015.
103. For perhaps the most often cited and critiqued example of this position, see García Linera, "El 'capitalismo andino-amazónico.'"

104. This point is highlighted through work on posthegemony theory. See, e.g., Arditi, "Post-Hegemony"; Beasley-Murray, "On Posthegemony"; Beasley-Murray, *Posthegemony*.
105. Howson and Smith, "Hegemony and the Operation of Consensus and Coercion," 10.
106. Beasley-Murray, *Posthegemony*, xv.
107. Beverley, "Multiculturalism and Hegemony," 225.
108. Beasley-Murray, *Posthegemony*, 22.
109. Corrigan and Sayer, *The Great Arch*, 4.
110. Beasley-Murray, *Posthegemony*, ix.

Chapter 2

1. See, e.g., McNelly, *Now We Are in Power*; Modonesi, "Revoluciones pasivas en América Latina"; Hesketh and Morton, "Spaces of Uneven Development and Class Struggle in Bolivia"; Andreucci, "Resources, Regulation and the State."
2. Sassoon, "Passive Revolution and the Politics of Reform," 129.
3. Webber, *The Last Day of Oppression*, 165.
4. Mamani Ramírez, *El estado neocolonial*; Rivera Cusicanqui, *Mito y desarrollo en Bolivia*.
5. García Linera, *Las tensiones creativas de la revolución*.
6. Mayorga, "Balance y escenarios del Estado Plurinacional," 57. See also Mayorga, *Incertidumbres tácticas*.
7. See Keating, *Plurinational Democracy*; Requejo and Caminal, *Political Liberalism and Plurinational Democracies*; Requejo, "Revealing the Dark Side of Traditional Democracies in Plurinational Societies."
8. Keating, *Plurinational Democracy*, 26–27.
9. Keating, 160.
10. Miquel Caminal, "Democracy, Federalism, and Plurinational States."
11. Caminal, 233.
12. John Emerich Edward Dalberg, Lord Acton (1908), quoted in Caminal, 233–34.
13. Caminal, 237–38.
14. Caminal, 240.
15. Loughlin, "The Transformation of the Democratic State in Western Europe"; Tierney, "Reframing Sovereignty?" In certain respects, this line of argument aligns with Michael Hardt and Antonio Negri's claims surrounding the rise of a deterritorialized empire; see Hardt and Negri, *Empire*.
16. Caminal, "Democracy, Federalism, and Plurinational States," 243.
17. Geertz argues that people of the newly established states were animated by two powerful yet distinct and often opposed motives: "the desire to be recognized as responsible agents whose wishes, acts, hopes, and opinions 'matter,' and the desire to build an efficient, dynamic, modern state. The one aim is to be noticed: it is a search for an identity and a demand that the identity be publicly acknowl-

edged as having import, a social assertion of the self as 'being somebody in the world.' The other aim is practical: it is a demand for progress, for a rising standard of living, more effective political order, greater social justice." Geertz, *The Interpretation of Cultures*, 258. It should be noted that Geertz provides a solution to this quandary. He argues: "what the new states—or their leaders—must somehow contrive to do as far as primordial attachments are concerned is not, as they have so often tried to do, wish them out of existence by belittling them or even denying their reality, but domesticate them. They must reconcile them with the unfolding civil order by divesting them of their legitimizing force with respect to governmental authority, by neutralizing the apparatus of the state in relationship to them, and by channeling discontent arising out of their dislocation into properly political rather than parapolitical forms of expression" (277). Despite Geertz's analytic acumen, his political prescriptions are thoroughly imbued with a desire for nation and state correspondence and cohesion, as associated with the modern nation-state. As he later notes, "a simple, coherent, broadly defined ethnic structure, such as is found in most industrial societies, is not an undissolved residue of traditionalism, but an earmark of modernity" (308).

18. For a critical overview of the process of nation-state formation along these lines, see Balibar and Wallerstein, *Race, Nation, Class*; Hall, *The Fateful Triangle*.

19. Sanjinés C., *Mestizaje Upside-Down*. Although this is perhaps the most common contemporary view of *mestizaje*, many question this view, recognizing that *mestizaje* has multiple meanings between sameness and difference, inclusion and exclusion. Some scholars have reappropriated or indigenized the term to highlight its more radical potential for understanding alterity and otherness. See, e.g., Anzaldúa, *Borderlands/La Frontera*; Wade, "Rethinking *Mestizaje*."

20. Ortiz, *Cuban Counterpoint*.

21. Malinowski, introduction, lviii.

22. García Canclini, *Hybrid Cultures*, xxv.

23. Jameson, "The Indigenous Movement in Ecuador."

24. Walsh, "The Plurinational and Intercultural State," 67.

25. Walsh, 69, 68.

26. Walsh, 70–71.

27. CONAIE, *Propuesta de la CONAIE frente a la Asamblea Constituyente*, 9, 7.

28. CONAIE, 6.

29. CONAIE, 10.

30. Cruz Rodríguez, "Estado plurinacional, interculturalidad y autonomía indígena," 57–58.

31. CONAIE, *Propuesta de la CONAIE frente a la Asamblea Constituyente*, 11.

32. Jameson, "The Indigenous Movement in Ecuador," 70.

33. CONAIE, *Propuesta de la CONAIE frente a la Asamblea Constituyente*, 22, 28.

34. Copa Cayo, "Movimiento Indio Tupak Katari—MITKA."

35. Samanamud, "Hacia una 'arquitectónica' del proceso constituyente," 81. See also Ticona Alejo, Rojas, and Albó, *Votos y wiphalas*, 215.
36. Cancio Rojas, CONAMAQ leader, author interview, La Paz, 2015.
37. Sánchez, "Autonomía y pluralismo," 283.
38. Pacto de Unidad, "Propuesta de las Organizaciones," 167.
39. Garcés, *Los indígenas y su Estado (pluri)nacional*, 39.
40. Tapia, *El horizonte plurinacional*, 8.
41. Tapia, 69.
42. Tapia, 69.
43. Mamani Ramírez, "Estado plurinacional," 38, 39.
44. Tapia, *El horizonte plurinacional*, 55.
45. Tapia, 43.
46. See Quijano, "Coloniality of Power, Eurocentrism, and Latin America."
47. Quijano, 564.
48. Tapia, *El horizonte plurinacional*, 43.
49. Tapia, 41. If typically the idea of a nation is linked to a corresponding state, the concept of *communitarian nation* refers to those peoples and nations that have maintained or reconstituted their ancestral social structures, forms of (re)production, language, and worldviews throughout the periods of colonialism and liberal modernity.
50. Tapia, 42.
51. Tapia, 43.
52. Pacto de Unidad, "Propuesta de las Organizaciones," 167. The Pacto de Unidad formed in 2004 and provided crucial support for the MAS and Evo Morales during the 2005 election. It was an umbrella organization of the most important indigenous and peasant movement organizations in the country, including the national peasant union organization CSUTCB (Confederación Sindical Única de Trabajadores Campesinos de Bolivia), the women's peasant movement organization Las Bartolinas (Confederación Nacional de Mujeres Campesinas Indígenas Originarias de Bolivia "Bartolina Sisa"), the lowland indigenous organization CIDOB (Confederación de Pueblos Indígenas de Bolivia), the highland indigenous organization CONAMAQ (Consejo Nacional de Ayllus y Markas del Qullasuyu), and the intercultural organization CSCIB (Confederación Sindical de Comunidades Interculturales de Bolivia, formerly known as the Colonizadores).
53. Pacto de Unidad, "Propuesta de las Organizaciones," 168.
54. Pacto de Unidad, 167.
55. Pacto de Unidad, 169.
56. Pacto de Unidad, 181.
57. Pacto de Unidad, 180.
58. Tapia, *El horizonte plurinacional*, 137.
59. Pacto de Unidad, "Propuesta de las Organizaciones," 178.

60. Pacto de Unidad, 175.
61. Pacto de Unidad, 173.
62. Mamani Ramírez, "Estado plurinacional," 47.
63. Gutiérrez Aguilar, *Los ritmos del Pachakuti*, published in English as *Rhythms of the Pachakuti*.
64. Gutiérrez Aguilar, *Los ritmos del Pachakuti*, 345–46.
65. Gutiérrez Aguilar, "Competing Political Visions and Bolivia's Unfinished Revolution," 276.
66. The term *pachakuti* has sometimes been loosely connected to the concept of revolution, as will be discussed further in the conclusion. In metaphysical terms, it is typically described as a turning upside down or revolution of space and time and is thought about in a long-term, cyclical fashion. According to James Dunkerley, the term conjoins words that variously signify time/earth/place/moment (*pacha*) and change/shift/cycle/alternation (*kuti*). See Dunkerley, "Pachakuti in Bolivia, 2008–2010," 189. For Gutiérrez, the Andean concept is understood to mean "the ambition, the longing, the search for a fundamental inversion of the order of things. Basically, as an inversion of the political order whereby what was inside and below, like the innermost logic of the communities, now becomes visible, valid, legitimate, that which is 'outside' and 'above': it is, then, a general upheaval of the mode of living together, not just a modification of those exercising governmental power." Gutiérrez Aguilar, *Los ritmos del Pachakuti*, 153.
67. Gutiérrez Aguilar, *Los ritmos del Pachakuti*, 346.
68. Gutiérrez Aguilar, *Horizonte comunitario-popular*, 20–21.
69. Gutiérrez Aguilar, "The Rhythms of the *Pachakuti*," 56.
70. Gutiérrez Aguilar, *Horizonte comunitario-popular*, 21.
71. Gutiérrez Aguilar, *Los ritmos del Pachakuti*, 358.
72. Gutiérrez Aguilar, "The Rhythms of the *Pachakuti*," 60.
73. Gutiérrez Aguilar, *Horizonte comunitario-popular*, 32.
74. Viaña, "Estado plurinacional y nueva fase del proceso boliviano," 387.
75. See Fernández, "Municipio, sistema de cargo y autonomía indígena en Bolivia"; Rivera Cusicanqui, "Liberal Democracy and *Ayllu* Democracy in Bolivia."
76. See Goldstein, *The Spectacular City*; Anthias, *Limits to Decolonization*.
77. Prada Alcoreza, "Estado plurinacional comunitario autonómico y pluralismo jurídico," 407. This "pluralist transition" also implies "the disappearance of the figure of the vanguard intellectual . . . and also the disappearance of the figure of the revolutionary party, as an entity outside of or above the social movements" (422).
78. Prada Alcoreza, 408.
79. Prada Alcoreza, 422.
80. Mamani Ramírez, "Estado plurinacional," 38.
81. Mamani Ramírez, author interview, El Alto, 2015. The *wiphala* is a multicolored flag that represents indigenous peoples throughout the Andes. In Bolivia's 2009

constitution, in addition to the traditional red, yellow, and green flag of the republic, the *wiphala* is recognized as a national emblem of the plurinational state.

82. Prada Alcoreza, "Articulaciones de la complejidad," 245.

83. Prada Alcoreza, 210.

84. Prada Alcoreza, 210–11.

85. Mamani Ramírez, "Estado plurinacional," 35.

86. Gutiérrez Aguilar, *Los ritmos del Pachakuti*, 349.

87. Choque Mamani, *Estado plurinacional aparente*.

88. See, e.g., Patzi Paco, *Sistema comunal*, 137–58.

89. Mayorga, author interview, Cochabamba, 2013. See also Mayorga, *Incertidumbres tácticas*, 41–43, 51–52.

90. See Fontana, "The 'Indigenous Native Peasant' Trinity"; Fontana, "Indigenous Peoples vs. Peasant Unions."

91. Tapia, *El horizonte plurinacional*, 96.

92. On the symbolism of plurinationality, see Tórrez and Arce C., Construcción simbólica del estado plurinacional de Bolivia.

93. Mamani Ramírez, "Estado plurinacional," 55.

94. See, e.g., Scott, *Weapons of the Weak*, 304–50; Beasley-Murray, *Posthegemony*; Day, *Gramsci Is Dead*.

Chapter 3

1. The constitutional capital of the country is actually Sucre, but the executive and legislative branches of government are located in La Paz, which is recognized as the de facto capital of Bolivia.

2. Fabricant, *Mobilizing Bolivia's Displaced*, 136.

3. Yubánure and Vargas, quoted in Fundación Tierra, *Marcha indígena por el TIPNIS*, 119–28.

4. Mayorga, *Mandato y contingencia*, 161.

5. Decree quoted in Fundación Tierra, *Marcha indígena por el TIPNIS*, 14.

6. According to the 1993 First Indigenous Census, of the 4,563 inhabitants of the TIPNIS, 68 percent were Mojeño, 26 percent Yuracaré, and 4 percent Chimán, with the remaining 2 percent of other ethnic origin. See García Linera, *Geopolítica de la Amazonía*, 39.

7. Paz, "El conflicto del territorio indígena Parque Nacional Isiboro-Sécure," 57–60; Muñoz, "El conflicto en torno al Territorio Indígena Parque Nacional Isiboro Sécure," 108–9.

8. Yashar, *Contesting Citizenship in Latin America*, 206.

9. Yashar, 194; Fundación Tierra, *Marcha indígena por el TIPNIS*, 14.

10. Valdivia, "Agrarian Capitalism and Struggles over Hegemony."

11. Bottazzi and Rist, "Changing Land Rights Means Changing Society," 535.

12. Bottazzi and Rist, 535.

13. Yashar, *Contesting Citizenship in Latin America*, 206.
14. On the relation between roads and modernity, see Harvey and Knox, *Roads*; Moran, *On Roads*; Khan, "Flaws in the Flow"; Masquelier, "Road Mythographies."
15. Harvey and Knox, "The Enchantments of Infrastructure," 523.
16. Mayorga, *Mandato y contingencia*, 152.
17. See García Linera, *Geopolítica de la Amazonía*, 53–58.
18. García Linera, 59–60.
19. García Linera, 60.
20. Rivera Cusicanqui, *Mito y desarrollo en Bolivia*, 32. As argued in chapter 1, García Linera's own position on the role of the state in Bolivian society in general, and on its relation to the country's indigenous peoples in particular, has fundamentally shifted from his earlier writings and those produced during his time as vice president in the MAS government. See also Bosteels, "¿Puede pensarse hoy la actualidad del comunismo?"
21. Cited in Yashar, *Contesting Citizenship in Latin America*, 194.
22. Coraite, quoted in *La Prensa*, "Roberto Coraite de la CSUTCB afirmó que desea que la Carretera."
23. Rivera Cusicanqui, *Mito y desarrollo en Bolivia*, 50.
24. Gudynas, "El nuevo extractivismo progresista en America del Sur."
25. Gudynas, 85.
26. Farthing and Kohl, *Evo's Bolivia*, 144–45.
27. Webber, *The Last Day of Oppression*, 107–9.
28. Acosta, "Extractivism and Neoextractivism," 62.
29. Svampa, "Resource Extractivism and Alternatives," 118–19.
30. In Bolivia specifically, see Hindrey, *From Enron to Evo*; Laing, "Resource Sovereignties in Bolivia"; López Bárcenas, "Acumulación por desposesión y autonomía indígena"; Perreault, "Extracting Justice."
31. Webber, "Revolution Against 'Progress.'"
32. For a discussion of the IIRSA in relation to Brazilian imperialism in Bolivia, see Gómez Nadal, "La soberanía en juego o el proyecto subimperial de Brasil."
33. Chávez and Chávez, "TIPNIS: el reposicionamiento de las luchas sociales en Bolivia."
34. Muñoz, "El conflicto en torno al Territorio Indígena Parque Nacional Isiboro Sécure"; López Bárcenas, "Acumulación por desposesión y autonomía indígena"; Rivera Cusicanqui, *Mito y desarrollo en Bolivia*, 52.
35. Cited in Springerová and Vališková, "Territoriality in the Development Policy of Evo Morales' Government," 150.
36. PIEB, *Viabilidad económica e institucional para el desarrollo de iniciativas*, 59.
37. Marx, *Capital*, 873.
38. In a famous passage, Marx states that "the discovery of gold and silver in America, the extirpation, enslavement and entombment in mines of the indigenous population of that continent, the beginnings of the conquest and plunder of

India, and the conversion of Africa into a preserve for the commercial hunting of black skins, are all things which characterize the dawn of the era of capitalist production. These idyllic proceedings are the chief moments of primitive accumulation." Marx, *Capital*, 915.

39. Marx, *Capital*, 874–75.
40. Harvey, "The 'New' Imperialism," 73–74.
41. Harvey, *A Brief History of Neoliberalism*, 159.
42. López Bárcenas, "Acumulación por desposesión y autonomía indígena."
43. García Linera, *Geopolítica de la Amazonía*, 73–74.
44. García Linera, 98.
45. García Linera, 100–101.
46. See Robinson, *Latin America and Global Capitalism*.
47. Kaup, "A Neoliberal Nationalization?" See also Kaup, *Market Justice*.
48. Acosta, "Extractivism and Neoextractivism," 69.
49. García Linera, *Geopolítica de la Amazonía*, 107.
50. García Linera, "El 'capitalismo andino-amazónico.'"
51. García Linera, *Geopolítica de la Amazonía*, 108.
52. García Linera, 108.
53. Prada Alcoreza, *Miseria de la geopolítica*, 16.
54. Gudynas, quoted in Acosta, "Extractivism and Neoextractivism," 73.
55. In Bolivia the term is *vivir bien*, whereas in other places such as Ecuador and Peru the term is *buen vivir*. As scholars have pointed out, the translation of *vivir bien/buen vivir* as an umbrella term in Spanish for words from various indigenous languages (e.g., the Aymara *suma qamaña*, the Quechua *sumak kawsay*, and the Guaraní *ñandereco*) is problematic due to the plural ontological worldviews from which the concept comes. The idea has also been translated as *vida plena* (a full life), *vida en armonía* (to live in harmony), and *convivir bien* (to live well together) in order to grasp the various aspects of the original indigenous conceptualizations, where "men and women, together with nature, are part of the Mother Earth and there is a communion and dialogue between them mediated by rituals in which Nature is understood as a sacred being." See Prada Alcoreza, "Buen Vivir as a Model for State and Economy," 145.
56. Acosta, *El Buen Vivir*, 50–51.
57. For an in-depth genealogy of the concept, see Schavelzon, *Plurinacionalidad y Vivir Bien/Buen Vivir*.
58. See Thompson, *Customs in Common*, 85–258; Scott, *The Moral Economy of the Peasant*; Polanyi, *The Great Transformation*.
59. Prada Alcoreza, "Buen Vivir as a Model for State and Economy," 147.
60. Thompson, *Customs in Common*, 188.
61. Scott, *The Moral Economy of the Peasant*, p. 188.
62. Davalos, quoted in Schavelzon, *Plurinacionalidad y Vivir Bien/Buen Vivir*, 185.

63. Prada Alcoreza, "Buen Vivir as a Model for State and Economy," 149.
64. Thompson, *Customs in Common*, 252–53.
65. Acosta, "Extractivism and Neoextractivism," 80.
66. Escobar, "Degrowth, Postdevelopment, and Transitions." For a critique, see Katz, "Considerations on Postdevelopmentalism in Latin America."
67. Article 15.2 of ILO Convention 169 states that "governments shall establish or maintain procedures through which they shall consult these peoples, with a view to ascertaining whether and to what degree their interests would be prejudiced, before undertaking or permitting any programs for the exploration or exploitation of such resources pertaining to their lands." The UNDRIP, in contrast, takes a stronger approach to indigenous peoples' rights in relation to extractive projects and explicitly argues for free, prior, and informed *consent*. Article 32.2 maintains: "States shall consult and cooperate in good faith with the indigenous peoples concerned through their own representative institutions in order to obtain their free and informed consent prior to the approval of any project affecting their lands or territories and other resources, particularly in connection with the development, utilization or exploitation of mineral, water or other resources."
68. Fontana and Grugel, "The Politics of Indigenous Participation Through 'Free Prior Informed Consent,'" 250; Schilling-Vacaflor, "Rethinking the Link Between Consultation and Conflict," 503.
69. Schilling-Vacaflor, "Who Controls the Territory and the Resources?," 1061.
70. Quoted in Fontana and Grugel, "The Politics of Indigenous Participation Through 'Free Prior Informed Consent,'" 253.
71. Constitución Política del Estado (2009), art. 30, 290, 304, 352, and 403. For an overview of the 2006–8 Constituent Assembly, see Schavelzon, *El nacimiento del estado plurinacional de Bolivia*.
72. Humphreys Bebbington, "Consultation, Compensation and Conflict," 59.
73. Humphreys Bebbington; Pellegrini and Ribera Arismendi, "Consultation, Compensation and Extraction in Bolivia After the 'Left Turn'"; Schilling-Vacaflor, "Rethinking the Link Between Consultation and Conflict."
74. Falleti and Riofrancos, "Participatory Democracy in Latin America," 32.
75. Farthing and Kohl, *Evo's Bolivia*, 53; Muñoz, "El conflicto en torno al Territorio Indígena Parque Nacional Isiboro Sécure," 116–17.
76. Morales, quoted in *La Razon*, "Evo Morales dice que ya hay la autorización indígena."
77. Morales, quoted in Canessa, "Conflict, Claim and Contradiction," 164.
78. Farthing and Kohl, *Evo's Bolivia*, 53; Achtenberg, "Bolivia: End of the Road for the TIPNIS Consulta."
79. Achtenberg, "Battle of Reports Sustains Bolivia's TIPNIS Conflict"; FIDH, *Bolivia*.
80. Fontana and Grugel, "The Politics of Indigenous Participation Through 'Free Prior Informed Consent,'" 261.

81. Prada Alcoreza, "Estado plurinacional comunitario autonómico y pluralismo jurídico," 416.
82. Prada Alcoreza, quoted in Tockman and Cameron, "Indigenous Autonomy and the Contradictions of Plurinationalism in Bolivia," 61.
83. For a comprehensive and evenhanded overview, see Farthing and Kohl, *Evo's Bolivia*.
84. See Escobar, "*Sentipensar* con la Tierra."
85. Wagner, *The Invention of Culture*, 140.
86. Gramsci, *Selections from the Prison Notebooks*, 263.
87. Morales, quoted in Schilling-Vacaflor, "Who Controls the Territory and the Resources?," 1065.
88. Gutiérrez Aguilar, "Competing Political Visions and Bolivia's Unfinished Revolution," 276.
89. E. Weber, *Peasants into Frenchmen*, 208.
90. Weber, 218.
91. Weber, 217.
92. Gutiérrez Aguilar, "The Rhythms of the *Pachakuti*," 57.
93. Marx, "The British Rule in India," 217–18.
94. For a similar argument, which also assumes an ethnocentric, linear, and teleological vision of social and economic development based on the experience of the industrially advanced European nations of the time, see Marx and Engels, *The Communist Manifesto*, 84. There, Marx and Friedrich Engels state: "The bourgeoisie, by the rapid improvement of all instruments of production, by the immensely facilitated means of communication, draws all, even the most barbarian, nations into civilization. The cheap prices of its commodities are the heavy artillery with which it batters down all Chinese walls, with which it forces the barbarians' intensely obstinate hatred of foreigners to capitulate. It compels all nations, on pain of extinction, to adopt the bourgeois mode of production; it compels them to introduce what it calls civilization into their midst, i.e., to become bourgeois themselves. In one word, it creates a world after its own image."

    For an excellent discussion of Marx's views on British colonialism in India and his changing analysis of the "progressive" impacts of capitalism and colonialism, see K. Anderson, *Marx at the Margins*, 11–24. Later in life, Marx changed his interpretation of the historical trajectory of development and gave more attention to the specifics of "traditional," non-Western societies. See Marx, *The Ethnological Notebooks*; Marx, *Pre-Capitalist Economic Formations*, esp. 142–45 (the 1881 correspondence between Marx and Vera Zasulich).
95. Morales, quoted in *La Razon*, "Mesa considera que la nueva ley del TIPNIS hipoteca el futuro."
96. García Linera, *Geopolítica de la Amazonía*, 24–26.
97. Larkin, "The Politics and Poetics of Infrastructure," 333.
98. García Linera, "El 'capitalismo andino-amazónico.'"

Chapter 4

1.   Rojas, author interview, La Paz, 2015.
2.   Spivak, *In Other Worlds*, 205. Bolivian scholar Silvia Rivera Cusicanqui problematizes the notion of strategic essentialism through what she labels *strategic ethnicity*. For Rivera Cusicanqui, the employment of an essential ethnic identity runs up against its limits when it is co-opted and used toward the extension of state power. See Rivera Cusicanqui, *Mito y desarrollo en Bolivia*, 49–54.
3.   The term *reconstitution* was chosen quite explicitly. Activists considered the phrase *to return to the ayllu* as a way to describe the project, but discarded it as they felt it signified too much a return to the past. It was decided that the term *reconstitution* was more appropriate. See Dangl, *The Five Hundred Year Rebellion*, 149.
4.   Murra notes that each *ayllu* owned small, dispersed parcels of land to deal with the environmental threats of high-altitude agriculture, such as frosts that occur 250 or more nights per year. In fact, *ayllu* societies used frosts in a productive way. For instance, by exposing meats and vegetables to frost and sunshine in rapid succession, they would freeze-dry the food, allowing it to be stored for long periods of time without rotting. Thus, by cultivating crops in various ecological zones and domesticating cold weather by freeze-drying potatoes (*chuño*) and llama meat (*charki*), Andean *ayllu* communities alleviated the effects of frosts, drought, and other natural threats. See Murra, "Andean Societies."
5.   Choque and Mamani, "Reconstitución del ayllu y derechos de los pueblos indígenas."
6.   Rojas, author interview, La Paz, 2015.
7.   Burman, "El ayllu y el indianismo," 104.
8.   García Linera, Chávez León, and Costas Monje, *Sociología de los movimientos sociales en Bolivia*, 337.
9.   For an overview of this process, see Rivera Cusicanqui, *Oppressed but Not Defeated*; Hurtado, *El Katarismo*.
10.   Albó, "And from Kataristas to MNRistas?," 57.
11.   Mamdani, *Neither Settler nor Native*.
12.   Rivera Cusicanqui, "Liberal Democracy and *Ayllu* Democracy in Bolivia."
13.   Choque and Mamani, "Reconstitución del ayllu y derechos de los pueblos indígenas," 155.
14.   Choque and Mamani, 167; Lucero, "Representing 'Real Indians,'" 44.
15.   Huanca Salles, "Reconstitución del Ayllu," 31.
16.   Gregorio Choque, author interview, La Paz, 2015.
17.   On the role of NGOs in the formation of CONAMAQ, see Andolina, "Between Local Authenticity and Global Accountability." For an analysis of the 1990s reforms, see Kohl and Farthing, *Impasse in Bolivia*.
18.   Lucero, "Representing 'Real Indians,'" 46.
19.   See Stefanoni, "¿A quién representa el Conamaq?"

20. García Linera, Chávez León, and Costas Monje, *Sociología de los movimientos sociales en Bolivia*, 329, 331–32.

21. For an excellent overview of the 2000–2005 insurrectionary cycle, see Hylton and Thomson, "The Chequered Rainbow."

22. For an in-depth account of the Constituent Assembly, see Schavelzon, *El nacimiento del estado plurinacional de Bolivia*.

23. Mayorga, author interview, Cochabamba, 2013.

24. CONAMAQ member, author interview, August 15, 2013.

25. Rojas, author interview, La Paz, 2015.

26. Activists and analysts in Bolivia have labeled the MAS-supported wing that took over CONAMAQ's organizational headquarters "CONAMAS," while referring to the faction headed by the popularly elected leadership in 2012 as "CONAMAQ *orgánico*." The CONAMAS label is used in derogatory fashion to highlight that faction's lack of independence and autonomy from the government, while the term *orgánico* is meant to signify a more authentic and organic link between leadership and base within the opposition faction. "CONAMAS" members, for their part, simply refer to themselves as "CONAMAQ" and describe the opposition faction as ex-members of the organization. These labels are obviously imbued with symbolic meanings meant to scorn one camp while exalting the other. While I do not necessarily agree with all the implications behind these labels, I use them nonetheless throughout this chapter as a commonly understood shorthand for distinguishing between the parallel organizational camps.

27. For descriptions of the confrontation, see Saavedra, "Crónica de un toma gubernamental"; Saavedra, "Segunda parte."

28. Cancio Rojas, author interview, La Paz, 2015; see also Achtenberg, "Rival Factions in Bolivia's CONAMAQ."

29. CONAMAQ member, author interview, 2015.

30. Springerová and Vališková, "Co-optation Without Representation," 63.

31. Laclau, *Politics and Ideology in Marxist Theory*, 143.

32. See, e.g., Germani, *Authoritarianism, Fascism, and National Populism*; Di Tella, "Populism and Reform in Latin America"; Niekerk, *Populism and Political Development in Latin America*; Conniff, *Latin American Populism in Comparative Perspective*; Cardoso and Faletto, *Dependency and Development in Latin America*; O'Donnell, *Modernization and Bureaucratic-Authoritarianism*.

33. See Weyland, "Neoliberal Populism in Latin America and Eastern Europe"; Weyland, "Clarifying a Contested Concept"; Roberts, "Parties and Populism in Latin America."

34. Roberts, "Populism, Political Mobilization, and the Crises of Political Representation," 146–50.

35. See Arditi, *Politics on the Edges of Liberalism*; Panizza, introduction; Peruzzotti, "Populism in Democratic Times"; de la Torre, *Populist Seduction in Latin America*.

36. Weyland, "The Threat from the Populist Left," 18, 20.
37. Edwards, *Left Behind*, 169–75.
38. Weyland, "Populism and Social Policy in Latin America," 117–18.
39. Worsley, quoted in Arditi, *Politics on the Edges of Liberalism*, 43.
40. Peruzzotti, "Populism in Democratic Times," 65.
41. Laclau, *On Populist Reason*; Jansen, "Populist Mobilization."
42. Laclau, "Populism: What's in a Name?," 34.
43. Laclau, 36.
44. Laclau, 36–37.
45. Laclau, *On Populist Reason*, 72–73.
46. Panizza, introduction, 3.
47. Laclau, *On Populist Reason*, 182.
48. Laclau, "Populism: What's in a Name?," 47–48.
49. See Perreault and Green, "Reworking the Spaces of Indigeneity"; Van Cott, *From Movements to Parties in Latin America*, 49–98; Albro, "The Indigenous in the Plural in Bolivian Oppositional Politics"; J.-A. McNeish, "Extraction, Protest and Indigeneity in Bolivia"; Canessa, "Conflict, Claim and Contradiction"; García Linera, *Identidad Boliviana*.
50. Burman, "El ayllu y el indianismo," 112.
51. See, e.g., J.-A. McNeish, "Extraction, Protest and Indigeneity in Bolivia."
52. Rivera Cusicanqui, *Mito y desarrollo en Bolivia*, 51.
53. Lucero, *Struggles of Voice*, 32.
54. Canessa, "Conflict, Claim and Contradiction," 168.
55. Albó, "From MNRistas to Kataristas to Katari," 408–9.
56. Burman, "Now We Are Indígenas."
57. Burman, 260.
58. Hale, "Rethinking Indigenous Politics in the Era of the 'Indio Permitido.'"
59. Fabricant and Postero, "Performing Indigeneity in Bolivia," 252.
60. Burman, "Now We Are Indígenas," 260.
61. CONAMAQ member, author interview, La Paz, 2015.
62. Postero, *The Indigenous State*, 4–5.
63. CONAMAQ member, author interview, La Paz, 2015.
64. This was the position of the CSUTCB and its leadership during my fieldwork. Like with any other movement organization, however, its ideological position has fluctuated over time, and its vision of ethnic indigenous identity, specifically in relation to the social class category of *campesino* (peasant), has also changed in relation to the specific historical conjuncture.
65. Choque, author interview, La Paz, 2015.
66. Pitkin, cited in Arditi, "Populism as an Internal Periphery of Democratic Politics," 80–81.
67. Lucero, *Struggles of Voice*, p. 44.
68. Marx argues that "the small peasants form a vast mass, the members of which live in similar conditions, but without entering into manifold relations with one

another. . . . In so far as millions of families live under economic conditions of existence that divide their mode of life, their interests and their culture from those of other classes, and put them in hostile contrast to the latter, they form a class. In so far as there is merely a local interconnection among these small peasants, and the identity of their interests begets no unity, no national union and no political organization, they do not form a class. They are consequently incapable of enforcing their class interests in their own name, whether through a parliament or through a convention. They cannot represent themselves, they must be represented." In Marx, "The Eighteenth Brumaire of Louis Bonaparte," 608.

69. Arditi, "Populism as an Internal Periphery of Democratic Politics," 83–84.
70. Springerová and Vališková, "Co-optation Without Representation," 60.
71. Laclau, "Populism: What's in a Name?," 47–48.
72. Laclau, *New Reflections on the Revolution of Our Times*, 212.
73. Weyland, "How Populism Corrodes Latin American Parties"; Houle and Kenny, "The Political and Economic Consequences of Populist Rule in Latin America"; Roberts, "Populism, Political Mobilization, and the Crises of Political Representation"; Edwards, *Left Behind*.
74. See Panizza, *Populism and the Mirror of Democracy*.
75. See Virno, *A Grammar of the Multitude*; Hardt and Negri, *Empire*.
76. Virno, *A Grammar of the Multitude*, 21, 25.
77. Burman, "El ayllu y el indianismo," 119.

Chapter 5

1. Exeni Rodríguez, "Autogobierno indígena y alternativas al desarrollo," 15.
2. Hale, "*Resistencia para que?*," 189.
3. Scott, *Seeing Like a State*.
4. Miller and Rose, *Governing the Present*.
5. Dombrowski, quoted in Canessa, "Conflict, Claim and Contradiction," 164.
6. Abrams, "Notes on the Difficulty of Studying the State," 61, 63.
7. Miliband, *The State in Capitalist Society*, 49.
8. Evans, Rueschemeyer, and Skocpol, *Bringing the State Back In*.
9. See, e.g., Cleary, "Subordinated Autonomy and the Political Inclusion of Women"; Cooke, "Uses of Autonomy"; Garcés, "The Domestication of Indigenous Autonomies in Bolivia"; Hale, "*Resistencia para que?*"
10. See, e.g., Adamovsky et al., *Pensar las autonomías*; Dinerstein, *The Politics of Autonomy in Latin America*; Esteva, "The Hour of Autonomy"; Gutiérrez Aguilar, *Horizonte comunitario-popular*; Zibechi, *Territories in Resistance*.
11. Postero, *The Indigenous State*, 175.
12. Postero, 14–16.
13. Poulantzas, *State, Power, Socialism*, 128–29.
14. See García Linera, "The State in Transition."

15. Fallaw and Nugent, preface, xx.
16. Hansen and Stepputat, introduction, 1.
17. See, e.g., Nugent, "Before History and Prior to Politics."
18. Mitchell, "The Limits of the State," 88.
19. Mitchell, 93.
20. See, e.g., Clastres, *Society Against the State*.
21. Garcés, "The Domestication of Indigenous Autonomies in Bolivia," 53.
22. Garcés, 63.
23. Choque Canqui, *El indigenismo y los movimientos indígenas en Bolivia*; Garcés, *Los indígenas y su Estado (pluri)nacional*.
24. Albó, "From MNRistas to Kataristas to Katari," 408–9.
25. Kohl and Farthing, *Impasse in Bolivia*, 130–31.
26. Tockman and Cameron, "Indigenous Autonomy and the Contradictions of Plurinationalism in Bolivia," 49.
27. Regalsky, "Political Processes and the Reconfiguration of the State in Bolivia," 41–42.
28. Articles 2 and 290 specifically recognize indigenous rights to territory and autonomy as essential elements of plurinationality.
29. For an extended analysis of each municipality, see Augsburger and Haber, "Visions in Conflict."
30. Morell i Torra, "La (difícil) construcción de autonomías indígenas."
31. Bazoberry Chali, *Participación, poder popular y desarollo*, 62–63.
32. Albó, *El Chaco Guaraní camino a la autonomía originaria*, 92.
33. Though they chose not to participate in the autonomy process, the Mennonite population will certainly affect the operation of the AIOC, particularly if some of the proposed reforms regarding Mennonite land use and tenure practices are seriously considered in the future. For details of Mennonite land use and some critique, see Pifarré, *Historia de un pueblo*. For more on the Mennonite population in Bolivia, see Kopp, *Las colonias menonitas en Bolivia*. For analysis of Mennonite colonies throughout Latin America more generally, see le Polain de Waroux et al., "Pious Pioneers."
34. Saignes, *Historia del pueblo Chiriguano*; Pifarré, *Historia de un pueblo*.
35. The initial rebellion, under the leadership of Apiaguaiki Tumpa, is one of the clearest documented examples of a lowland indigenous uprising against the republican order to which the Guaraní were subordinated. According to Isabelle Combès, the massacre marked the end point of a long era of indigenous resistance and rebellion in the area. "Kuruyuki was the final real battle, the last armed struggle against the *karai*." See Combès, "Las batallas de Kuruyuki," 224. For Oscar Bazoberry, the massacre at Kuruyuki marked the point in time when the Guaraní and their territory in the Chaco were completely opened up under the auspices of liberal modernization, leading to a prolonged period of indigenous quiescence. See Bazoberry Chali, *Participación, poder popular y desarollo*, 63n31.

36. Bazoberry Chali, *Participación, poder popular y desarollo*, 64.

37. For an overview of the creation of the APG, see Mendoza Fernández, *Asamblea del Pueblo Guaraní*; Anzaldo García and Gutiérrez Galean, "Avances y desafíos de la Autonomía Guaraní Charagua Iyambae," 91.

38. Quoted in Albó, *El Chaco Guaraní camino a la autonomía originaria*, 66.

39. Ortiz, author interview, Charagua, 2017.

40. Díez Astete and Murillo, *Pueblos indígenas de tierras bajas*, 100.

41. With the 2009 Constitution, TCOs were to be converted into *territorios indígena originario campesinas* (TIOCs, indigenous, original peoples, peasant territories). The 1996 INRA legislation involved a struggle over the naming of the TCOs as either indigenous territories or indigenous lands. Whereas indigenous groups put forward the name of *territorios indígenas*, the government of Gonzalo Sánchez de Lozada argued that the idea of indigenous territory put the Bolivian nation's territorial integrity at risk; it instead introduced the TCO name. In relation to AIOC, Alcides Vadillo Pinto and Patricia Costas Monje argue that TCOs and TIOCs as indivisible, communally held property provide the material resources for indigenous community reproduction, while AIOC expands this power to include political control and administration. See Vadillo Pinto and Costas Monje, "La autonomía indígena tiene su propio sello en Charagua," 278.

42. Tockman, "Decentralisation, Socio-Territoriality and the Exercise of Indigenous Self-Governance in Bolivia," 160.

43. Plata, "Charagua: El autogobierno Guaraní Iyambae," 216.

44. Albó, *El Chaco Guaraní camino a la autonomía originaria*, 60.

45. Alberto, author interview, Charagua, 2017.

46. Quisbert Q., "Hacia autonomías indígenas y sus riesgos latentes," 133; Tockman and Cameron, "Indigenous Autonomy and the Contradictions of Plurinationalism in Bolivia," 56.

47. MAS-affiliated lawyer, author interview, 2015.

48. Tockman and Cameron, "Indigenous Autonomy and the Contradictions of Plurinationalism in Bolivia."

49. Plata, author interview, La Paz, 2015.

50. APG member, author interview, Charagua, 2015.

51. See Plata, "Charagua: El autogobierno Guaraní Iyambae."

52. Albó, *El Chaco Guaraní camino a la autonomía originaria*, 126.

53. Gómez, author interview, Charagua, 2015.

54. Plata, "Charagua: El autogobierno Guaraní Iyambae," 212.

55. Plata, 210.

56. International Save the Children employee, author interview, Charagua, 2015.

57. Choquindi, author interview, Charagua, 2017.

58. Gutiérrez, author interview, Charagua, 2017.

59. Gutiérrez.

60. González, "Indigenous Territorial Autonomy in Latin America," 19.

61. Tockman, Cameron, and Plata, "New Institutions of Indigenous Self-Governance in Bolivia." For a vision of the AIOC process as projected from the position of the state, see *Ruta para la construcción de la autonomía indígena originario campesina.* An interesting document, it breaks the process down into seven distinct steps, each with anywhere from three to five substeps, and presents AIOC as a relatively standardized, quick, and hassle-free proceeding, quite distinct from the years-long, bureaucratic labyrinth it has been thus far.

62. Garcés, "The Domestication of Indigenous Autonomies in Bolivia," 164.

63. On the expansion of union structures, see Albó, "From MNRistas to Kataristas to Katari"; Dunkerley, *Rebellion in the Veins*; Hurtado, *El Katarismo*; Rivera Cusicanqui, *Oppressed but Not Defeated.*

64. Rivera Cusicanqui, "Liberal Democracy and *Ayllu* Democracy in Bolivia"; Platt, *Estado boliviano y ayllu andino.*

65. Gotkowitz, *A Revolution for Our Rights*, 274–75.

66. Urioste and Kay, *Latifundios, avasallamientos y autonomías.*

67. Valdivia, "Agrarian Capitalism and Struggles over Hegemony."

68. Rivera Cusicanqui, "Liberal Democracy and *Ayllu* Democracy in Bolivia," 105, 111.

69. Soliz, *Fields of Revolution.*

70. Mouffe, "Critique as Counter-Hegemonic Intervention."

71. Ávila, author interview, Charagua, 2022. For similar claims across Latin America, see le Polain de Waroux et al., "Pious Pioneers."

72. García, quoted in Navia Gabriel, "El puente 'clandestino' de los menonitas lleva la deforestación."

73. Berril, author interview, Charagua, 2022.

74. Quoted in "El Gobierno Autonómo Guaraní de Charagua asegura que el puente clandestino," *Revista Nómadas.*

75. Cuellar, author interview, Charagua, 2022.

76. Justiniano, author interview, Charagua, 2022.

77. The other two autonomous municipalities, Uru Chipaya and Salinas de Garci Mendoza, are both small municipalities located in the department of Oruro. They gained formal AIOC status in January 2018 and May 2019, respectively, after more than a decade of effort.

78. Hale, "*Resistencia para que?*," 189.

Conclusion

1. Marx, *Grundrisse*, 278.

2. A number of journalists and scholars offered their analyses as the crisis unfolded, although much of this discussion revolved around issues of potential electoral fraud and the question of whether a coup had in fact taken place. Several publications analyzing the crisis in more depth were released a few years

later. See, e.g., Mamani Ramírez (ed.), *Wiphalas, luchas, y la nueva nación*; Farthing and Becker, *Coup*; Claros and Díaz Cuéllar, *Crisis política en Bolivia*.

3. On the foundation of the MAS, see Zuazo, *¿Como nació el MAS?*
4. On the internal democracy of the MAS, see Anria, *When Movements Become Parties*. For the increasing symbolic importance of Morales, see Mayorga, *Mandato y contingencia*.
5. Cavooris, "Origins of the Crisis."
6. Solón, author interview, La Paz, 2017.
7. García Linera, quoted in Farthing and Becker, *Coup*, 124.
8. See, e.g., Choque Mamani, *Estado plurinacional aparente*; Mayorga, *Incertidumbres tácticas*; Mayorga, *Mandato y contingencia*; Tapia, *El horizonte plurinacional*.
9. Postero, *The Indigenous State*, 42–43.
10. Tapia, *Una reflexión sobre la idea de un estado plurinacional*, 78.
11. Regalsky, "Political Processes and the Reconfiguration of the State in Bolivia," 45.
12. Farthing, "An Opportunity Squandered?"
13. Miliband, "The Coup in Chile," 472.
14. McNelly, *Now We Are in Power*.
15. Mayorga, "Balance y escenarios del Estado Plurinacional," 53–54.
16. Farthing, "An Opportunity Squandered?," 212–29; Wolff, "Business Power and the Politics of Postneoliberalism."
17. García Linera, author interview, La Paz, 2015.
18. Salazar Lohman, "Las condiciones para la crisis política de 2019 en Bolivia," 125–29.
19. For Latin America more generally, see Svampa, *Neo-Extractivism in Latin America*.
20. Wanderley, "Bolivian Cooperative and Community Enterprises."
21. McKay, "Agrarian Extractivism in Bolivia"; Radhuber, Chávez León, and Andreucci, "Expansión extractivista, resistencia comunitaria y 'despojo política' en Bolivia."
22. Marston and Kennemore, "Extraction, Revolution, Plurinationalism." See also Anthias, *Limits to Decolonization*.
23. Díaz Cuéllar, "Un giro de casi 360 grados," 441–49.
24. Gilly, "Bolivia: A 21st-Century Revolution."
25. Cherstich, Holbraad, and Tassi, *Anthropologies of Revolution*, 131.
26. Koselleck, *Futures Past*, 41.
27. R. Williams, *Keywords*, 271.
28. O'Kane, "Revolution and Social Science," xvii.
29. Malia, *History's Locomotives*, 193.
30. Koselleck, *Futures Past*, 48, 51.
31. Hunt, "Revolutionary Time and Regeneration," 66, 68.

32. Marx, "The Eighteenth Brumaire of Louis Bonaparte," 597. For further analysis of this idea in Marx, see Neocleous, "Let the Dead Bury Their Dead."
33. See Gutiérrez Aguilar, *Los ritmos del Pachakuti*; Hylton and Thomson, *Revolutionary Horizons*; Paige, *Indigenous Revolution in Ecuador and Bolivia*.
34. Swinehart, "Decolonial Time in Bolivia's *Pachakuti*," 99.
35. Cherstich, Holbraad, and Tassi, *Anthropologies of Revolution*, 150.
36. Cherstich, Holbraad, and Tassi, 153.
37. Hylton and Thomson, *Revolutionary Horizons*, 29–30.
38. Hylton and Thomson, 149.
39. Zavaleta Mercado, "Las masas en noviembre" (1983), in *Obra Completa*, 2:105.
40. Dunkerley, "Bolivia en ese entonces," 210–11; Bloch, "Nonsynchronism and the Obligation to Its Dialectics," 22.
41. Tomba, "On the Capitalist and Emancipatory Use of Asynchronies in Formal Subsumption," 303. For an expanded analysis of asynchronous temporalities and modernity, see Tomba, *Insurgent Universality*.
42. Rivera Cusicanqui, *Ch'ixinakax utxiwa*, 69–70.
43. See Geertz, *The Interpretation of Cultures*, 234–310.
44. Skocpol, *States and Social Revolutions*, 4. For an afterthought on the role of ideology in revolutions, see Skocpol, *Social Revolutions in the Modern World*.
45. Tilly, *European Revolutions*, 7–8.
46. Colburn, *The Vogue of Revolution in Poor Countries*, 6.
47. Farhi, "The Democratic Turn," 31.
48. Malia, *History's Locomotives*, 310.
49. Marx, "The Eighteenth Brumaire of Louis Bonaparte," 607.
50. Lenin, *The State and Revolution*, 24–25.
51. Lenin, 104.
52. Lenin, 32.
53. Hall, "Gramsci and Us."
54. Hall, 20.
55. García Linera, *¿Que es una revolución?*, 177.
56. García Linera, author interview, La Paz, 2015.
57. García Linera, "The State in Transition."
58. García Linera, *¿Que es una revolución?*, 191.
59. García Linera, 191.
60. García Linera, 213.
61. García Linera, 197.
62. Holloway, *Change the World Without Taking Power*, 12, 14.
63. Holloway, 232, 234.
64. Holloway, 12.
65. Gutiérrez Aguilar, *Los ritmos del Pachakuti*, 50.
66. Gutiérrez Aguilar, 32.
67. Gutiérrez Aguilar, 54.
68. Gutiérrez Aguilar, 345.

69.   Tapia, *La idea de estado como obstáculo epistemológico.*

70.   Garcés, *Los indígenas y su Estado (pluri)nacional*, 10–11.

71.   Arbona et al., *El proceso de cambio popular.*

72.   Cherstich, Holbraad, and Tassi, *Anthropologies of Revolution*, 64.

73.   Paige, *Indigenous Revolution in Ecuador and Bolivia*, 29. See also Paige, "Finding the Revolutionary in the Revolution."

BIBLIOGRAPHY

Abrams, Philip. "Notes on the Difficulty of Studying the State." 1977. *Journal of Historical Sociology* 1, no. 1 (1988): 58–89.

Achtenberg, Emily. "Battle of Reports Sustains Bolivia's TIPNIS Conflict." *Rebel Currents* (blog), *NACLA*, January 18, 2013. https://nacla.org/column/7334.

Achtenberg, Emily. "Bolivia: End of the Road for TIPNIS Consulta." *Rebel Currents* (blog), *NACLA*, December 13, 2012. https://nacla.org/column/7334.

Achtenberg, Emily. "Contested Development: The Geopolitics of Bolivia's TIPNIS Conflict." *NACLA Report on the Americas* 46, no. 2 (2013): 6–11.

Achtenberg, Emily. "Rival Factions in Bolivia's CONAMAQ: Internal Conflict or Government Manipulation?" *Rebel Currents* (blog), *NACLA*, February 2, 2014. https://nacla.org/column/7334.

Achtenberg, Emily. "Road Rage and Resistance: Bolivia's TIPNIS Conflict." *NACLA Report on the Americas* 44, no. 6 (2011): 3–4.

Acosta, Alberto. *El Buen Vivir: Sumak Kawsay, una oportunidad para imaginar otros mundos*. Barcelona: Icaria Editorial, 2013.

Acosta, Alberto. "Extractivism and Neoextractivism: Two Sides of the Same Curse." In Lang and Mokrani, *Beyond Development*, 61–86.

Adamovsky, Ezequiel, Claudio Albertani, Benjamin Arditi, Ana Esther Ceceña, Raquel Gutiérrez, John Holloway, Francisco López Bárcenas et al. *Pensar las autonomías: Alternativas de emancipación al capital y el Estado*. Mexico City: Bajo Tierra Ediciones, 2011.

Albó, Xavier. "And from Kataristas to MNRistas? The Surprising and Bold Alliance Between Aymaras and Neoliberals in Bolivia." In *Indigenous Peoples and Democracy in Latin America*, edited by Donna Lee Van Cott, 55–82. New York: St. Martin's Press, 1994.

Albó, Xavier. *El Chaco Guaraní camino a la autonomía originaria: Charagua, Gutiérrez y proyección regional*. La Paz: CIPCA, 2012.

Albó, Xavier. "From MNRistas to Kataristas to Katari." In Stern, *Resistance, Rebellion, and Consciousness in the Andean Peasant World*, 379–419.

Albó, Xavier. *Movimientos y poder indígena en Bolivia, Ecuador y Perú*. La Paz: CIPCA, 2008.

Albó, Xavier. *Tres municipios andinos camino a la autonomía indígena: Jesús de Machaca, Chayanta, and Tarabuco*. La Paz: CIPCA, 2012.

Albro, Robert. "The Indigenous in the Plural in Bolivian Oppositional Politics." *Bulletin of Latin American Research* 24, no. 4 (2005): 433–53.

Anderson, Benedict. *Imagined Communities: Reflections on the Origin and Spread of Nationalism*. New York: Verso Books, 1983.

Anderson, Kevin B. *Marx at the Margins: On Nationalism, Ethnicity, and Non-Western Societies*. Chicago: University of Chicago Press, 2016.

Anderson, Perry. "The Antinomies of Antonio Gramsci." *New Left Review* 1, no. 100 (1976): 5–78.

Anderson, Perry. "The Heirs of Gramsci." *New Left Review* 100 (2016): 71–97.

Anderson, Perry. *The H-Word: The Peripeteia of Hegemony*. New York: Verso Books, 2017.

Andolina, Robert. "Between Local Authenticity and Global Accountability: The Ayllu Movement in Contemporary Bolivia." In *Beyond the Lost Decade: Indigenous Movements, Development, and Democracy in Latin America*, edited by José Antonio Lucero, 87–108. Princeton, N.J.: Princeton University Press, 2003.

Andreucci, Diego. "Resources, Regulation and the State: Struggles over Gas Extraction and Passive Revolution in Evo Morales's Bolivia." *Political Geography* 61 (November 2017): 170–80.

Anria, Santiago. *When Movements Become Parties: The Bolivian MAS in Comparative Perspective*. New York: Cambridge University Press, 2018.

Antezana, Luis H. "Dos conceptos en la obra de René Zavaleta Mercado: Formación abigarrada y democracia como autodeterminación." In *Pluralismo epistemológico*, by León Olivé, Boaventura de Sousa Santos, Cecilia Salazar de la Torre, Luis H. Antezana, Wálter Navia Romero, Luis Tapia, Guadalupe Valencia García et al., 117–42. La Paz: Muela del Diablo Editores, 2009.

Anthias, Penelope. *Limits to Decolonization: Indigeneity, Territory, and Hydrocarbon Politics in the Bolivian Chaco*. Ithaca, N.Y.: Cornell University Press, 2018.

Anzaldo García, Alejandra, and Magaly Gutiérrez Galean. "Avances y desafíos de la Autonomía Guaraní Charagua Iyambae." *T'inkazos* 17, no. 36 (2014): 81–91.

Anzaldúa, Gloria. *Borderlands/La Frontera: The New Mestiza*. San Francisco: Aunt Lute Books, 1987.

Anzaldúa, Gloria. "(Un)natural Bridges, (Un)safe Spaces." In *This Bridge We Call Home: Radical Visions for Transformation*, edited by Gloria E. Anzaldúa and AnaLouise Keating, 540–78. New York: Routledge, 2002.

Arbona, Juan Manuel, María Elena Canedo, Carmen Medeiros, and Nico Tassi. *El proceso de cambio popular: Un tejido político con anclaje en el país*. La Paz: Centro de Investigaciones Sociales, 2016.

Arditi, Benjamin. *Politics on the Edges of Liberalism: Difference, Populism, Revolution, Agitation*. Edinburgh: Edinburgh University Press, 2007.

Arditi, Benjamin. "Populism as an Internal Periphery of Democratic Politics." In Panizza, *Populism and the Mirror of Democracy*, 72–98.

Arditi, Benjamin. "Post-Hegemony: Politics Outside the Usual Post-Marxist Paradigm." *Contemporary Politics* 13, no. 3 (2007): 205–26.

Argirakis Jordán, Helena. "El campo politico reconfigurado como 'estructura disipadora': Cuando la lucha inter hegemónica antagonista deviene en lucha intra hegemónica agonista." *Revista Boliviana de Investigación* 10, no. 1 (2013): 263–92.

Aricó, José María. *La cola del diablo: Itinerario de Gramsci en América Latina*. Buenos Aires: Puntosur Editores, 1988.

Assies, Willem. "Bolivia: A Gasified Democracy." *European Review of Latin American and Caribbean Studies*, no. 76 (2004): 25–43.

Assies, Willem. "David Versus Goliath in Cochabamba: Water Rights, Neoliberalism, and the Revival of Social Protest in Bolivia." *Latin American Perspectives* 30, no. 3 (2003): 14–36.

Assies, Willem. "Land Tenure Legislation in a Pluri-Cultural and Multi-Ethnic Society: The Case of Bolivia." *Journal of Peasant Studies* 33, no. 4 (2006): 569–611.

Assies, Willem, Gemma van der Haar, and André J. Hoekema, eds. *The Challenge of Diversity: Indigenous Peoples and Reform of the State in Latin America*. Amsterdam: Thela Thesis, 2000.

Augsburger, Aaron, and Paul Haber. "Constructing Indigenous Autonomy in Plurinational Bolivia: Possibilities and Ambiguities." *Latin American Perspectives* 45, no. 6 (2018): 53–67.

Augsburger, Aaron, and Paul Haber. "Visions in Conflict: State Hegemony Versus Plurinationality in the Construction of Indigenous Autonomy in Bolivia." *Latin American and Caribbean Ethnic Studies* 13, no. 2 (2018): 135–56.

Balibar, Étienne. *The Philosophy of Marx*. New York: Verso Books, 2017.

Balibar, Étienne, and Immanuel M. Wallerstein. *Race, Nation, Class: Ambiguous Identities*. New York: Verso Books, 1991.

Bautista, Rafael, Marxa Chávez, Patricia Chávez, Sarela Paz, Raúl Prada, and Luis Tapia. *La victoria indígena del TIPNIS*. La Paz: Autodeterminación, 2012.

Bazoberry Chali, Oscar. *Participación, poder popular y desarollo: Charagua y Moxos*. La Paz: CIPCA, 2008.

Beasley-Murray, Jon. "On Posthegemony." *Bulletin of Latin American Research* 22, no. 1 (2003): 117–25.

Beasley-Murray, Jon. *Posthegemony: Political Theory and Latin America*. Minneapolis: University of Minnesota Press, 2010.

Beverley, John. "Multiculturalism and Hegemony." In *Critical Latin American and Latino Studies*, edited by Juan Poblete, 223–37. Minneapolis: University of Minnesota Press, 2003.

Bjork-James, Carwil. *The Sovereign Street: Making Revolution in Urban Bolivia*. Tucson: University of Arizona Press, 2020.

Blaser, Mario. "Bolivia: Los desafíos interpretativos de la coincidencia de una doble crisis hegemónica." In *Reinventando la nación en Bolivia: Movimientos sociales, Estado y poscolonialidad*, edited by Karin Monasterios, Pablo Stefanoni, and Hervé Do Alto, 11–21. La Paz: Plural Editores, 2007.

Bloch, Ernst. "Nonsynchronism and the Obligation to Its Dialectics." *New German Critique*, no. 11 (Spring 1977): 22–38.

Boothman, Derek. "A Note on the Evolution—and Translation—of Some Key Gramscian Terms." *Socialism and Democracy* 14, no. 2 (2007): 115–30.

Boothman, Derek. "The Sources for Gramsci's Concept of Hegemony." *Rethinking Marxism* 20 no. 2 (2008): 201–15.

Bosteels, Bruno. "¿Puede pensarse hoy la actualidad del comunismo? Reflexiones en torno al pensamineto teórico de Álvaro García Linera." *Revista Boliviana de Investigación* 10, no. 1 (2013): 293–323.

Bottazzi, Patrick, and Stephan Rist. "Changing Land Rights Means Changing Society: The Sociopolitical Effects of Agrarian Reforms Under the Government of Evo Morales." *Journal of Agrarian Change* 12, no. 4 (2012): 528–51.

Buci-Glucksmann, Christine. *Gramsci and the State.* London: Lawrence and Wishart, 1980.

Buci-Glucksmann, Christine. "Hegemony and Consent: A Political Strategy." In Sassoon, *Approaches to Gramsci*, 116–26.

Burgos, Raúl. "The Ups and Downs of an Uncomfortable Legacy: The Complicated Dialogue Between Gramsci and the Latin American Left." Translated by Victoria J. Furio. *Latin American Perspectives* 42, no. 5 (2015): 169–85.

Burman, Anders. "Black Hole Indigeneity: The Explosion and Implosion of Radical Difference as Resistance and Power in Andean Bolivia." *Journal of Political Power* 13, no. 2 (2020): 179–200.

Burman, Anders. "El ayllu y el indianismo: Autenticidad, representatividad y territorio en el quehacer político del CONAMAQ, Bolivia." In *Los nuevos caminos de los movimientos sociales en Latinoamérica*, edited by Anne Marie Ejdesgaard Jeppsen, Helene Balslev Clausen, and Mario Alberto Velázquez García, 100–122. Monterrey: Tilde Editores, 2015.

Burman, Anders. "'Now We Are Indígenas': Hegemony and Indigeneity in the Bolivian Andes." *Latin American and Caribbean Ethnic Studies* 9, no. 3 (2014): 247–71.

Calderón, Fernando, and Jorge Dandler, eds. *Bolivia: La fuerza histórica del campesinado: Movimientos campesinos y etnicidad.* La Paz: Centro de Estudios de la Realidad Económica y Social.

Calderón, Fernando, and Jorge Dandler. "Movimientos Campesinos y Estado en Bolivia." In Calderón and Dandler, *Bolivia*, 15–50.

Calla, Ricardo. "Indigenous Peoples, the Law of Popular Participation and Changes in Government: Bolivia, 1994–1998." In Assies, Haar, and Hoekema, *The Challenge of Diversity*, 77–96.

Cameron, John. "Bolivia's Contentious Politics of 'Normas y Procedimientos Propios.'" *Latin American and Caribbean Ethnic Studies* 8, no. 2 (2013): 179–201.

Cameron, John, and Gonzalo Colque. "The Difficult Marriage of Liberal and Indigenous Democracy in Jesús de Machaca, Bolivia." In *Struggles for Local Democracy in the Andes*, by John Cameron, 139–86. Boulder, Colo.: Lynne Rienner, 2009.

Cameron, Maxwell, and Eric Hershberg, eds. *Latin America's Left Turns: Politics, Policies, and Trajectories of Change*. Boulder, Colo.: Lynne Rienner, 2010.

Caminal, Miquel. "Democracy, Federalism, and Plurinational States." In Requejo and Caminal, *Political Liberalism and Plurinational Democracies*, 226–51.

Canessa, Andrew. "Conflict, Claim and Contradiction in the New 'Indigenous' State of Bolivia." *Critique of Anthropology* 34, no. 2 (2014): 153–73.

Cardoso, Fernando Henrique, and Enzo Faletto. *Dependency and Development in Latin America*. Translated by Marjory Mattingly Urquidi. Berkeley: University of California Press, 1979.

Cavooris, Robert. "Intellectuals and Political Strategy: Hegemony, Posthegemony, and Post-Marxist Theory in Latin America." *Contemporary Politics* 23, no. 2 (2017): 231–49.

Cavooris, Robert. "Origins of the Crisis: On the Coup in Bolivia." *Viewpoint Magazine*, November 18, 2019. https://viewpointmag.com/2019/11/18/origins.

Chávez, Patricia, and Marxa Chávez. "TIPNIS: el reposicionamiento de las luchas sociales en Bolivia." In Bautista et al., *La victoria indígena del TIPNIS*, 69–94.

Chávez León, Marxa Nadia. "Autonomías indígenas y Estado Plurinacional: Proyectos políticos de los movimientos indígenas y campesinos en Bolivia." *Observatorio Social de América Latina* 9, no. 24 (2008): 51–71.

Cherstich, Igor, Martin Holbraad, and Nico Tassi. *Anthropologies of Revolution: Forging Time, People, and Worlds*. Oakland: University of California Press, 2019.

Choque, María Eugenia. "El ayllu: Una alternativa de descolonización." In *Conocimiento indígena y globalización*, edited by Ethel (Wara) Alderete, 59–70. Quito: Abya-Yala, 2005.

Choque, María Eugenia, and Carlos Mamani. "Reconstitución del ayllu y derechos de los pueblos indígenas: El movimiento indio en los Andes de Bolivia." In Ticona Alejo, *Los Andes desde los Andes*, 147–70.

Choque Canqui, Roberto. *Cinco siglos de historia*. Vol. 1 of *Jesús de Machaqa: La marka rebelde*. La Paz: CIPCA, 2003.

Choque Canqui, Roberto. *El indigenismo y los movimientos indígenas en Bolivia*. La Paz: Instituto Internacional de Integración del Convenio Andrés Bello, 2014.

Choque Canqui, Roberto. "La historia aimara." In Ticona Alejo, *Los Andes desde los Andes*, 15–38.

Choque Canqui, Roberto, and Esteban Ticona Alejo. *Sublevación y massacre de 1921*. Vol. 2 of *Jesús de Machaqa: La marka rebelde*. La Paz: CIPCA, 1996.

Choque Mamani, Teófilo. *Estado plurinacional aparente*. La Paz: Autodeterminación, 2014.

Claros, Luis, and Vladimir Díaz Cuéllar, eds. *Crisis política en Bolivia, 2019–2020*. La Paz: Rosa Luxemburg Stiftung, 2022.

Clastres, Pierre. *Society Against the State: Essays in Political Anthropology*. New York: Zone Books, 1987.

Cleary, Matthew R. "Subordinated Autonomy and the Political Inclusion of Women in Indigenous Mexico." *Latin American Politics and Society* 62, no. 3 (2020): 44–64.

Clifford, James. "Anthropology and/as Travel." *Etnofoor* 9, no. 2 (1996): 5–15.

Clifford, James. "Indigenous Articulations." *Contemporary Pacific* 13, no. 2 (2001): 468–90.

Clifford, James. *The Predicament of Culture: Twentieth-Century Ethnography, Literature, and Art*. Cambridge, Mass.: Harvard University Press, 1988.

Clifford, James, and George E. Marcus. *Writing Culture: The Poetics and Politics of Ethnography*. Berkeley: University of California Press, 1986.

Colburn, Forrest. *The Vogue of Revolution in Poor Countries*. Princeton, N.J.: Princeton University Press, 1994.

Colque, Gonzalo. "Gobierno local comunitario en Jesús de Machaca: Apuntes para convertir el Gobierno Municipal en Gobierno de Ayllus y Comunidades." In *Municipio indígena: Análisis del proceso y perspectivas viables*, by Mario Galindo Soza, 83–98. La Paz: CEBEM, 2008.

Colque, Gonzalo, Efrain Tinta, and Esteban Sanjinés. *Segunda reforma agraria: Una historia que incomoda*. La Paz: Fundación Tierra, 2016.

Combès, Isabelle. "Las batallas de Kuruyuki: Variaciones sobre una derrota chiriguana." *Bulletin de L'Institut Français d'Études Andines* 34, no. 2 (2005): 221–33.

CONAIE (Confederación de Nacionalidades y Pueblos Indígenas del Ecuador). *Propuesta de la CONAIE frente a la Asamblea Constituyente*. Quito: CONAIE, 2007.

Conniff, Michael L. *Latin American Populism in Comparative Perspective*. Albuquerque: University of New Mexico Press, 1982.

Cooke, Erik. "Uses of Autonomy: The Evolution of Multicultural Discourse in Bolivian Politics." In *Latin America's Multicultural Movements: The Struggle Between Communitarianism, Autonomy, and Human Rights*, edited by Todd Eisenstadt, Michael S. Danielson, Moises Jaime Bailon Corres, and Carlos Sorroza Polo, 67–87. New York: Oxford University Press, 2013.

Copa Cayo, Isidro. "Movimiento Indio Tupak Katari—MITKA." *Presencia*, May 23, 1978.

Corrigan, Philip, and Derek Sayer. *The Great Arch: English State Formation as Cultural Revolution*. New York: Blackwell, 1985.

Crabtree, John, and Ann Chaplin. *Bolivia: Processes of Change*. New York: Zed Books, 2013.

Cruz Rodríguez, Edwin. "Estado plurinacional, interculturalidad y autonomía indígena: Una reflexión sobre los casos de Bolivia y Ecuador." *Revista VIA IURIS*, no. 14 (January–June 2013): 55–71.

Dangl, Benjamin. *The Five Hundred Year Rebellion: Indigenous Movements and the Decolonization of History in Bolivia*. Chico, Calif.: AK Press, 2019.

Dargatz, Anja, and Moira Zuazo, eds. *Democracia en transformación: ¿Qué hay de nuevo en los nuevos Estados andinos?* La Paz: Friedrich Ebert Stiftung, 2012.

Davidson, Alastair. "The Uses and Abuses of Gramsci." *Thesis Eleven* 95, no. 1 (2008): 68–94.

Day, Richard J. F. *Gramsci Is Dead: Anarchist Currents in the Newest Social Movements*. London: Pluto Press, 2005.

de la Torre, Carlos. *Populist Seduction in Latin America*. Columbus: Ohio University Press, 2010.

de la Torre, Carlos, ed. *The Promise and Perils of Populism: Global Perspectives*. Lexington: University Press of Kentucky, 2015.

de la Torre, Carlos, and Cynthia J. Arnson, eds. *Latin American Populism in the Twenty-First Century*. Baltimore: Johns Hopkins University Press, 2013.

Delgado-P., Guillermo, and John Brown Childs, eds. *Indigeneity: Collected Essays*. Santa Cruz, Calif.: New Pacific Press, 2012.

Díaz Cuéllar, Vladimir. "Un giro de casi 360 grados: El régimen de noviembre y el retorno del MAS." In Claros and Díaz Cuéllar, *Crisis política en Bolivia, 2019–2020*, 441–77.

Díez Astete, Alvaro, and David Murillo. *Pueblos indígenas de tierras bajas: Características principales*. La Paz: Ministerio de Desarrollo Sostenible, 1998.

Dinerstein, Ana Cecilia. *The Politics of Autonomy in Latin America: The Art of Organizing Hope*. New York: Palgrave Macmillan, 2015.

Di Tella, Torcuato S. "Populism and Reform in Latin America." In *Obstacles to Change in Latin America*, edited by Claudio Veliz, 47–74. Cambridge: Cambridge University Press, 1965.

Dove, Patrick. "The *Desencuentros* of History: Class and Ethnicity in Bolivia." *Culture, Theory and Critique* 56, no. 3 (2015): 313–32.

Dunkerley, James. "Bolivia en ese entonces: *Bolivia, hoy* revisitado 30 años después." *Revista Boliviana de Investigación* 10, no. 1 (2013): 191–212.

Dunkerley, James. "The Bolivian Revolution at 60: Politics and Historiography." *Journal of Latin American Studies* 45, no. 2 (2013): 325–50.

Dunkerley, James. "Evo Morales, the 'Two Bolivias' and the Third Bolivian Revolution." *Journal of Latin American Studies* 39, no. 1 (2007): 133–66.

Dunkerley, James. "Pachakuti in Bolivia, 2008–10: A Personal Diary." In Pearce, *Evo Morales and the Movimiento al Socialismo in Bolivia*, 175–212.

Dunkerley, James. *Rebellion in the Veins: Political Struggle in Bolivia, 1952–1982*. New York: Verso Books, 1984.

Edwards, Sebastian. *Left Behind: Latin America and the False Promise of Populism*. Chicago: University of Chicago Press, 2010.

Elias, Norbert. "Power and Civilization." *Journal of Power* 1, no. 2 (2008): 135–42.

Ellner, Steve, ed. *Latin America's Radical Left: Challenges and Complexities of Political Power in the Twenty-First Century*. New York: Rowman and Littlefield, 2014.

Escobar, Arturo. "Degrowth, Postdevelopment, and Transitions: A Preliminary Conversation." *Sustainability Science* 10, no. 3 (2015): 451–62.

Escobar, Arturo. "Latin America at a Crossroads: Alternative Modernizations, Post-Liberalism, or Post-Development?" *Cultural Studies* 24, no. 1 (2010): 1–65.

Escobar, Arturo. "Post-extractivismo y pluriverso." *América Latina en movimiento,* no. 473 (March 2012): 14–17.

Escobar, Arturo. "*Sentipensar* con la Tierra: Las luchas territoriales y la dimensión ontológica de las epistemologías del sur." *Revista de Antropología Iberoamaericana* 11, no. 1 (2016): 11–32.

Espasandín López, Jesús, and Pablo Iglesias Turrión, eds. *Bolivia en movimiento: Acción colectiva y poder político.* Barcelona: El Viejo Topo, 2007.

Esteva, Gustavo. "The Hour of Autonomy." *Latin American and Caribbean Ethnic Studies* 10, no. 1 (2015): 134–45.

Evans, Peter B., Dietrich Rueschemeyer, Theda Skocpol, eds. *Bringing the State Back In.* New York: Cambridge University Press, 1985.

Exeni Rodríguez, José Luis. "Autogobierno indígena y alternativas al desarrollo." In Exeni Rodríguez, *La larga marcha,* 13–71.

Exeni Rodríguez, José Luis, ed. *La larga marcha: El proceso de autonomías indígenas en Bolivia.* La Paz: Fundación Rosa Luxemburg, 2015.

Fabricant, Nicole. *Mobilizing Bolivia's Displaced: Indigenous Politics and the Struggle over Land.* Chapel Hill: University of North Carolina Press, 2012.

Fabricant, Nicole, and Nancy Postero. "Performing Indigeneity in Bolivia: The Struggle over the TIPNIS." In *Indigenous Life Projects and Extractivism: Ethnographies from South America,* edited by Cecilie Vindal Ødegaard and Juan Javier Rivera Andía, 245–76. New York: Palgrave Macmillan, 2019.

Fallaw, Ben, and David Nugent. Preface to *State Formation in the Liberal Era: Capitalisms and Claims of Citizenship in Mexico and Peru,* edited by Ben Fallaw and David Nugent, ix–xxiii. Tucson: University of Arizona Press, 2020.

Falleti, Tulia G., and Thea Riofrancos. "Participatory Democracy in Latin America: The Collective Right to Prior Consultation in Ecuador and Bolivia." Paper presented at the LASA (Latin American Studies Association) Congress, Chicago, May 21–24, 2014.

Farhi, Farideh. "The Democratic Turn: New Ways of Understanding Revolution." In Foran, *The Future of Revolutions,* 30–41.

Farthing, Linda. "An Opportunity Squandered? Elites, Social Movements, and the Government of Evo Morales." *Latin American Perspectives* 46, no. 1 (2019): 212–29.

Farthing, Linda, and Thomas Becker. *Coup: A Story of Violence and Resistance in Bolivia.* Chicago: Haymarket Books, 2021.

Farthing, Linda, and Benjamin Kohl. *Evo's Bolivia: Continuity and Change.* Austin: University of Texas Press, 2015.

Femia, Joseph. "Hegemony and Consciousness in the Thought of Antonio Gramsci." *Political Studies* 23, no. 1 (1975): 29–48.

Fernández, Francisca. "Municipio, sistema de cargo y autonomía indígena en Bolivia: El caso de Jesús de Machaca, departamento de La Paz." *Journal of Latin American and Caribbean Anthropology* 23, no. 3 (2018): 579–92.

FIDH (Federación Internacional de Derechos Humanos). *Bolivia: Informe de verificación de la consulta realizada en el territorio indígena Parque Nacional Isiboro-Sécure.* Paris: FIDH, 2013.

Finnegan, William. "Leasing the Rain." *New Yorker*, April 8, 2002.

Fontana, Benedetto. "Hegemony and Power in Gramsci." In Howson and Smith, *Hegemony*, 80–106.

Fontana, Lorenza B. "The 'Indigenous Native Peasant' Trinity: Imagining a Plurinational Community in Evo Morales' Bolivia." *Environmental Planning D: Society and Space* 32, no. 3 (2014): 518–34.

Fontana, Lorenza B. "Indigenous Peoples vs. Peasant Unions: Land Conflicts and Rural Movements in Plurinational Bolivia." *Journal of Peasant Studies* 41, no. 3 (2014): 297–319.

Fontana, Lorenza B., and Jean Grugel. "The Politics of Indigenous Participation Through 'Free Prior Informed Consent': Reflections from the Bolivian Case." *World Development* 77 (2016): 249–61.

Foran, John, ed. *The Future of Revolutions: Rethinking Radical Change in the Age of Globalization*. New York: Zed Books, 2003.

Foran, John, ed. *Theorizing Revolutions*. New York: Routledge, 1997.

Fundación Tierra. *Marcha indígena por el TIPNIS: La lucha en defensa de los territorios*. La Paz: Fundación Tierra, 2012.

Garcés, Fernando. "The Domestication of Indigenous Autonomies in Bolivia: From the Pact of Unity to the New Constitution." In *Remapping Bolivia: Resources, Territory, and Indigeneity in a Plurinational State*, edited by Nicole Fabricant and Bret Gustafson, 46–67. Santa Fe, N.Mex.: School for Advanced Research Press, 2011.

Garcés, Fernando. *Los indígenas y su Estado (pluri)nacional: una mirada al proceso constituyente boliviano*. Cochabamba, Bolivia: CLACSO, 2013.

García Canclini, Néstor. *Hybrid Cultures: Strategies for Entering and Leaving Modernity*. Minneapolis: University of Minnesota Press, 1995.

García Linera, Álvaro. *De demonios escondidos y momentos de revolución: Marx y la revolución social en las extremidades del cuerpo capitalista*. La Paz: Ofensiva Roja, 1991.

García Linera, Álvaro. "El 'capitalismo andino-amazónico.'" *Le Monde diplomatique*, Chilean Edition, January 2006. https://www.lemondediplomatique.cl/El-capitalismo-andino-amazonico.html.

García Linera, Álvaro. "El movimiento de los movimientos." In Negri et al., *Imperio, multitud y sociedad abigarrada*, 13–40.

García Linera, Álvaro. "Estado Plurinacional: Una propuesta democrática y pluralista para la extinción de la exclusión de las naciones indígenas." In García Linera, Tapia, and Prada Alcoreza, *La transformación pluralista del Estado*, 19–88.

García Linera, Álvaro. *Geopolítica de la Amazonía: Poder hacendal-patrimonial y acumulación capitalista*. La Paz: Vicepresidente del Estado Plurinacional, 2013.

García Linera, Álvaro. *Identidad Boliviana: Nación, mestizaje, y plurinacionalidad*. La Paz: Vicepresidencia del Estado, 2014.

García Linera, Álvaro. *La potencia plebeya: Acción colectiva e identidades indígenas, obreras y populares en Bolivia*. Buenos Aires: CLACSO, 2008.

García Linera, Álvaro. *Las tensiones creativas de la revolución: La quinta fase del proceso de cambio*. La Paz: Vicepresidencia del Estado Plurinacional, 2010.

García Linera, Álvaro. "Multitud y sociedad abigarrada." In Negri et al., *Imperio, multitud y sociedad abigarrada*, 41–66.

García Linera, Álvaro. *Plebeian Power: Collective Action and Indigenous, Working-Class and Popular Identities in Bolivia*. Chicago: Haymarket Books, 2014.

García Linera, Álvaro. *¿Que es una revolución?* Buenos Aires: CLACSO, 2020.

García Linera, Álvaro. "The State in Transition: Power Bloc and Point of Bifurcation." *Latin American Perspectives* 37, no. 4 (2010): 34–47.

García Linera, Álvaro, Marxa Chávez León, and Patricia Costas Monje. *Sociología de los movimientos sociales en Bolivia: Estructuras de movilización, repertorios culturales y acción política*. La Paz: Plural Editores, 2008.

García Linera, Álvaro, Raquel Gutiérrez, Raúl Prada, and Luis Tapia. *El fantasma insomne: Pensando el presente desde el Manifiesto Comunista*. La Paz: Muela del Diablo, 1999.

García Linera, Álvaro, Raúl Prada, Luis Tapia, and Oscar Vega Camacho. *El Estado: Campo de lucha*. La Paz, CLACSO, 2010.

García Linera, Álvaro, Luis Tapia, and Raúl Prada Alcoreza, eds. *La transformación pluralista del Estado*. La Paz: Muela del Diablo Editores, 2007.

Gaudichaud, Franck, Massimo Modonesi, and Jeffery R. Webber. *The Impasse of the Latin American Left*. Durham, N.C.: Duke University Press, 2022.

Geddes, Mike. "The Old Is Dying but the New Is Struggling to Be Born: Hegemonic Contestation in Bolivia." *Critical Policy Studies* 8, no. 2 (2014): 165–82.

Geertz, Clifford. *The Interpretation of Cultures*. New York: Basic Books, 1973.

Germani, Gino. *Authoritarianism, Fascism, and National Populism*. New Brunswick, N.J.: Transaction Books, 1978.

Gill, Lesley. *Teetering on the Rim: Global Restructuring, Daily Life, and the Armed Retreat of the Bolivian State*. New York: Columbia University Press, 2000.

Gilly, Adolfo. "Bolivia: A 21st-Century Revolution." *Socialism and Democracy* 19, no. 3 (2005): 41–54.

Goldstein, Daniel. *The Spectacular City: Violence and Performance in Urban Bolivia*. Durham, N.C.: Duke University Press, 2004.

Goldstone, Jack A., ed. *Revolutions: Theoretical, Comparative, and Historical Studies*. New York: Harcourt Brace Jovanovich, 1986.

Gómez Nadal, Paco. "La soberanía en juego o el proyecto subimperial de Brasil." In Rivera Cusicanqui et al., *TIPNIS*, 181–91.

González, Miguel. "Indigenous Territorial Autonomy in Latin America: An Overview." *Latin American and Caribbean Ethnic Studies* 10, no. 1 (2015): 10–36.

Goodale, Mark. *A Revolution in Fragments: Traversing Scales of Justice, Ideology, and Practice in Bolivia*. Durham, N.C.: Duke University Press, 2019.

Gordy, Katherine. *Living Ideology in Cuba: Socialism in Principle and Practice*. Ann Arbor: University of Michigan Press, 2015.

Gotkowitz, Laura. *A Revolution for Our Rights: Indigenous Struggles for Land and Justice in Bolivia, 1880–1952*. Durham, N.C.: Duke University Press, 2007.

Goudsmit, Into A. *Deference Revisited: Andean Ritual in the Plurinational State*. Durham, N.C.: Carolina Academic Press, 2016.

Gramsci, Antonio. *The Modern Prince and Other Writings*. New York: International, 2000.

Gramsci, Antonio. *Selections from the Prison Notebooks*. New York: International, 1971.

Grimson, Alejandro, and Karina Bidaseca, eds. *Hegemonía cultural y políticas de la diferencia*. Buenos Aires: CLACSO, 2013.

Gudynas, Eduardo. "El nuevo extractivismo progresista en America del Sur." In *Colonialismos del Siglo XXI: Negocios extractivos y defensa del territorio en América Latina*, by A. Acosta, E. Gudynas, F. Houtart, L. Macas, J. Martínez Alier, H. Ramírez Soler, and E. Siliprandi, 75–92. Barcelona: Icaria Editores, 2011.

Guha, Ranajit. *Dominance Without Hegemony: History and Power in Colonial India*. Cambridge, Mass.: Harvard University Press, 1997.

Gustafson, Bret. *Bolivia in the Age of Gas*. Durham, N.C.: Duke University Press, 2020.

Gutiérrez Aguilar, Raquel. "Competing Political Visions and Bolivia's Unfinished Revolution." *Dialectical Anthropology* 35, no. 3 (2011): 275–77.

Gutiérrez Aguilar, Raquel. *Horizonte comunitario-popular: Antagonismo y producción de lo común en América Latina*. Cochabamba, Bolivia: SOCEE, 2015.

Gutiérrez Aguilar, Raquel. *Los ritmos del Pachakuti: Movilización y levantamiento indígena-popular en Bolivia (2000–2005)*. Mexico: Bajo Tierra Ediciones, 2009.

Gutiérrez Aguilar, Raquel. "The Rhythms of the *Pachakuti*: Brief Reflections Regarding How We Have Come to Know Emancipatory Struggles and the Significance of the Term *Social Emancipation*." *South Atlantic Quarterly* 111, no. 1 (2012): 51–64.

Gutiérrez Aguilar, Raquel. *Rhythms of the Pachakuti: Indigenous Uprising and State Power in Bolivia*. Durham, N.C.: Duke University Press, 2014.

Gutiérrez Aguilar, Raquel, and Álvaro García Linera. "A manera de introduction." In *Forma valor y forma comunidad: Aproximación teórica-abstracta a los fundamentos civilizatorios que preceden al Ayllu Universal*, by Álvaro García Linera, 15–29. La Paz: CLACSO, 2009.

Hale, Charles. "*Resistencia para que*? Territory, Autonomy and Neoliberal Entanglements in the 'Empty Spaces' of Central America." *Economy and Society* 40, no. 2 (2011): 184–210.

Hale, Charles. "Rethinking Indigenous Politics in the Era of the 'Indio Permitido.'" *NACLA Report on the Americas* 38, no. 2 (2004): 16–21.

Hall, Stuart. *The Fateful Triangle: Race, Ethnicity, Nation*. Cambridge, Mass.: Harvard University Press, 2017.

Hall, Stuart. "Gramsci and Us." *Marxism Today*, June 1987, 16–21.

Hall, Stuart. "Gramsci's Relevance for the Study of Race and Ethnicity." *Journal of Communication Inquiry* 10, no. 2 (1986): 5–27.

Hansen, Thomas Blom, and Finn Stepputat. Introduction to Hansen and Stepputat, *States of Imagination*, 1–38.

Hansen, Thomas Blom, and Finn Stepputat, eds. *States of Imagination: Ethnographic Explorations of the Postcolonial State*. Durham, N.C.: Duke University Press, 2001.

Hardt, Michael, and Antonio Negri. *Empire*. Cambridge: Harvard University Press, 2000.

Harten, Sven. *The Rise of Evo Morales and the MAS*. New York: Zed Books, 2011.

Harvey, David. *A Brief History of Neoliberalism*. New York: Oxford University Press, 2007.

Harvey, David. "The 'New' Imperialism: Accumulation by Dispossession." *Socialist Register* 40 (2004): 63–87.

Harvey, Penny, and Hannah Knox. "The Enchantments of Infrastructure." *Mobilities* 7, no. 4 (2012): 521–36.

Harvey, Penny, and Hannah Knox. *Roads: An Ethnography of Infrastructure and Expertise*. Ithaca, N.Y.: Cornell University Press, 2015.

Hesketh, Chris, and Adam David Morton. "Spaces of Uneven Development and Class Struggle in Bolivia: Transformation or *Trasformismo*?" *Antipode* 46, no. 1 (2014): 149–69.

Hindrey, Derrick. *From Enron to Evo: Pipeline Politics, Global Environmentalism, and Indigenous Rights in Bolivia*. Tucson: University of Arizona Press, 2013.

Holloway, John. *Change the World Without Taking Power: The Meaning of Revolution Today*. New York: Pluto Press, 2005.

Houle, Christian, and Paul D. Kenny. "The Political and Economic Consequences of Populist Rule in Latin America." *Government and Opposition* 53, no. 2 (2018): 256–87.

Howson, Richard, and Kylie M. Smith. "Hegemony and the Operation of Consensus and Coercion." In Howson and Smith, *Hegemony*, 1–15.

Howson, Richard, and Kylie M. Smith, eds. *Hegemony: Studies in Consensus and Coercion*. New York: Routledge, 2008.

Huanca Salles, Cristóbal. "Reconstitución del Ayllu: Los desafíos del movimiento indígena en Bolivia bajo el socialism del Siglo XXI." *LASA Forum* 48, no. 3 (2017): 29–36.

Humphreys Bebbington, Denise. "Consultation, Compensation and Conflict: Natural Gas Extraction in Weenhayek Territory, Bolivia." *Journal of Latin American Geography* 11, no. 2 (2012): 49–71.

Hunt, Lynn. "Revolutionary Time and Regeneration." *Diciottesimo Secolo* 1 (2016): 62–76.

Hurtado, Javier. *El Katarismo*. 1986. La Paz: Biblioteca del Bicentenario de Bolivia, 2016.

Hylton, Forrest. "'Now Is Not Your Time; It's Ours': Insurgent Confederation, 'Race War,' and Liberal State Formation in the Bolivian Federal War of 1899." *South Atlantic Quarterly* 110, no. 2 (2011): 487–503.

Hylton, Forrest, Felix Patzi, Sergio Serulnikov, and Sinclair Thomson. *Ya es otro tiempo el presente: Cuatro momentos de insurgencia indígena*. La Paz: Muela del Diablo Editores, 2011.

Hylton, Forrest, and Sinclair Thomson. "The Chequered Rainbow." *New Left Review* 35 (2005): 41–64.

Hylton, Forrest, and Sinclair Thomson. *Revolutionary Horizons: Past and Present in Bolivian Politics*. New York: Verso Books, 2007.

Jameson, Kenneth P. "The Indigenous Movement in Ecuador: The Struggle for a Plurinational State." *Latin American Perspectives* 38, no. 1 (2011): 63–73.

Jansen, Robert S. "Populist Mobilization: A New Theoretical Approach to Populism." In de la Torre, *The Promise and Perils of Populism*, 159–88.

John, S. Sándor. *Bolivia's Radical Tradition: Permanent Revolution in the Andes*. Tucson: University of Arizona Press, 2009.

Joseph, Gilbert M., and Daniel Nugent, eds. *Everyday Forms of State Formation: Revolution and the Negotiation of Rule in Modern Mexico*. Durham, N.C.: Duke University Press, 1994.

Katz, Claudio. "Considerations on Postdevelopmentalism in Latin America." *International Socialist Review*, no. 97 (2015). http://isreview.org/issue/97/considerations -postdevelopmentalism-latin-america.

Kaup, Brent. *Market Justice: Political Economic Struggle in Bolivia*. New York: Cambridge University Press, 2013.

Kaup, Brent. "A Neoliberal Nationalization? The Constraints on Natural Gas-Led Development in Bolivia." *Latin American Perspectives* 37, no. 3 (2010): 123–38.

Keating, Michael. *Plurinational Democracy: Stateless Nations in a Post-Sovereignty Era*. New York: Oxford University Press, 2011.

Khan, Naveeda. "Flaws in the Flow: Roads and Their Modernity in Pakistan." *Social Text* 24, no. 4 (89) (2006): 87–113.

Kohl, Benjamin, and Linda Farthing. *Impasse in Bolivia: Neoliberal Hegemony and Popular Resistance*. New York: Zed Books, 2006.

Kopp, Adalberto. *Las colonias menonitas en Bolivia: Antecedentes, asentamientos y propuestas para un diálogo*. La Paz: Fundación Tierra, 2015.

Koselleck, Reinhart. *Futures Past: On the Semantics of Historical Time*. Cambridge: MIT Press, 1985.

Laclau, Ernesto. *New Reflections on the Revolution of Our Times*. New York: Verso Books, 1990.

Laclau, Ernesto. "New Social Movements and the Plurality of the Social." In *New Social Movements and the State in Latin America*, edited by David Slater, 27–42. Amsterdam: CEDLA, 1985.

Laclau, Ernesto. *On Populist Reason*. New York: Verso Books, 2007.

Laclau, Ernesto. *Politics and Ideology in Marxist Theory*. 1979. New York: Verso Books, 2011.

Laclau, Ernesto. "Populism: What's in a Name?" In Panizza, *Populism and the Mirror of Democracy*, 32–49.

Laclau, Ernesto, and Chantal Mouffe. *Hegemony and Socialist Strategy: Towards a Radical Democratic Politics*. New York: Verso Books, 1985.

Laclau, Ernesto, and Chantal Mouffe. "Post-Marxism Without Apologies." *New Left Review* 166 (1987): 79–106.

Laing, Anna. "Resource Sovereignties in Bolivia: Re-Conceptualizing the Relationship Between Indigenous Identities and the Environment During the TIPNIS Conflict." *Bulletin of Latin American Research* 34, no. 2 (2015): 149–66.

Lang, Miriam, and Dunia Mokrani, eds. *Beyond Development: Alternative Visions from Latin America*. Amsterdam: Transnational Institute, 2013.

La Prensa. "Roberto Coraite de la CSUTCB afirmó que desea que la Carretera evite que los indígenas del TIPNIS vivan como indigentes." June 9, 2011.

La Razon. "Evo Morales dice que ya hay la autorización indígena para construer la carretera por el TIPNIS." October 8, 2012.

La Razon. "Mesa considera que la nueva ley del TIPNIS hipoteca el futuro del agua y el oxígeno en Bolivia." August 14, 2017.

Larkin, Brian. "The Politics and Poetics of Infrastructure." *Annual Review of Anthropology* 42 (2013): 327–43.

Larsen, Neil. *Modernism and Hegemony: A Materialist Critique of Aesthetic Agencies*. Minneapolis: University of Minnesota Press, 1990.

Laserna, Roberto. "Bolivia: Crisis de Estado. Una entrevista inédita con René Zavaleta Mercado." *Estudios Sociológicos* 3, no. 9 (1985): 547–59.

Lenin, Vladimir I. *The State and Revolution*. New York: Penguin Classics, 1992.

le Polain de Waroux, Yann, Janice Neumann, Anna O'Driscoll, and Kerstin Schreiber. "Pious Pioneers: The Expansion of Mennonite Colonies in Latin America." *Journal of Land Use Science* 16, no. 1 (2021): 1–17.

Levitsky, Steven, and Kenneth M. Roberts, eds. *The Resurgence of the Latin American Left*. Baltimore, Md.: Johns Hopkins University Press, 2011.

Lewis, Tom. "The Politics of 'Andean-Amazonian Capitalism.'" *International Socialist Review*, no. 83 (2012). http://isreview.org/issue/83/politics-andean-amazonian-capitalism.

López Bárcenas, Francisco. "Acumulación por desposesión y autonomía indígena." In Rivera Cusicanqui et al., *TIPNIS*, 135–42.

López Bárcenas, Francisco. "Las autonomías indígenas en América Latina." In Adamovsky et al., *Pensar las autonomías*, 67–102.

Loughlin, John. "The Transformation of the Democratic State in Western Europe." In Requejo and Caminal, *Political Liberalism and Plurinational Democracies*, 44–72.

Lucero, José Antonio. "Representing 'Real Indians': The Challenges of Indigenous Authenticity and Strategic Constructivism in Ecuador and Bolivia." *Latin American Research Review* 41, no. 2 (2006): 31–56.

Lucero, José Antonio. *Struggles of Voice: The Politics of Indigenous Representation in the Andes*. Pittsburgh, Pa.: University of Pittsburgh Press, 2008.

Malia, Martin. *History's Locomotives: Revolutions and the Making of the Modern World*. New Haven, Conn.: Yale University Press, 2006.

Malinowski, Bronislaw. Introduction to Ortiz, *Cuban Counterpoint*, lvii–lxiv.

Malloy, James M. "Revolutionary Politics." In *Beyond the Revolution: Bolivia Since 1952*, edited by James M. Malloy and Richard S. Thorn, 111–56. Pittsburgh, Pa.: University of Pittsburgh Press, 1971.

Mamani Ramírez, Pablo. *El estado neocolonial: Una mirada al proceso de la lucha por el poder y sus contradicciones en Bolivia*. La Paz: Rincón Ediciones, 2017.

Mamani Ramírez, Pablo. "Estado plurinacional: Entre el nuevo proyecto y la factualidad colonial." *Willka* 3, no. 3 (2009): 31–67.

Mamani Ramírez, Pablo, ed. *Wiphalas, luchas, y la nueva nación*. La Paz: Editorial Nina Katari, 2021.

Mamdani, Mahmood. *Neither Settler nor Native: The Making and Unmaking of Permanent Minorities*. Cambridge, Mass.: Harvard University Press, 2020.

Marston, Andrea, and Amy Kennemore. "Extraction, Revolution, Plurinationalism: Rethinking Extractivism from Bolivia." *Latin American Perspectives* 46, no. 2 (2019): 141–60.

Marx, Karl. "The British Rule in India." 1853. In *Dispatches for the New York Tribune: Selected Journalism of Karl Marx*, edited by James Ledbetter, 212–18. New York: Penguin, 2007.

Marx, Karl. *Capital*. Vol. 1. New York: Penguin Classics, 1990.

Marx, Karl. "The Eighteenth Brumaire of Louis Bonaparte." In Tucker, *The Marx-Engels Reader*, 594–617.

Marx, Karl. *The Ethnological Notebooks*. Amsterdam: Van Gorcum, 1972.

Marx, Karl. "The German Ideology: Part I." In Tucker, *The Marx-Engels Reader*, 146–200.

Marx, Karl. *Grundrisse: Foundations of the Critique of Political Economy*. New York: Penguin, 1973.

Marx, Karl. *Pre-Capitalist Economic Formations*. New York: International, 1965.

Marx, Karl, and Friedrich Engels. *The Communist Manifesto*. New York: Penguin Books, 1985.

Masquelier, Adeline. "Road Mythographies: Space, Mobility, and the Historical Imagination in Postcolonial Niger." *American Ethnologist* 29, no. 4 (2002): 829–56.

Mayorga, Fernando. *Antinomias: El azaroso camino de la reforma política*. Cochabamba, Bolivia: CESU-UMSS, 2009.

Mayorga, Fernando. "Balance y escenarios del Estado Plurinacional." In *Estado Plurinacional y Democracias*, edited by Boaventura de Sousa Santos and José Luis Exeni Rodríguez, 49–62. La Paz: Friedrich Ebert Stiftung, 2019.

Mayorga, Fernando. *Incertidumbres tácticas: Ensayos sobre democracia, populismo y ciudadanía*. La Paz: Plural Editores, 2014.

Mayorga, Fernando. "La democracia boliviana: Avances y desafíos." In *Democracias en Transformación: ¿Que hay de nuevo en los Estados andinos?*, edited by Anja Dargatz and Moira Zuazo, 23–80. La Paz: Friedrich Ebert Stiftung, 2012.

Mayorga, Fernando. *Mandato y contingencia: Estilo de gobierno de Evo Morales*. Buenos Aires: CLACSO, 2020.

McKay, Ben M. "Agrarian Extractivism in Bolivia." *World Development* 97 (2017): 199–211.

McNeish, John-Andrew. "Extraction, Protest and Indigeneity in Bolivia: The TIPNIS Effect." *Latin American and Caribbean Ethnic Studies* 8, no. 2 (2013): 221–42.

McNelly, Angus. *Now We Are In Power: The Politics of Passive Revolution in Twenty-First Century Bolivia*. Pittsburgh, Pa.: University of Pittsburgh Press, 2023.

Mendoza Fernández, Eduardo. *Asamblea del Pueblo Guaraní: Nueva organización Guaraní-Chiriguano*. La Paz: Universidad Mayor de San Andrés, 1992.

Mignolo, Walter. "Mariátegui and Gramsci in 'Latin' America: Between Revolution and Decoloniality." In *The Postcolonial Gramsci*, edited by Neelam Srivastava and Baidik Bhattacharya, 191–217. New York: Routledge, 2012.

Miliband, Ralph. "The Coup in Chile." *Socialist Register* 10 (1973): 451–74.

Miliband, Ralph. *The State in Capitalist Society*. New York: Basic Books, 1969.

Miller, Peter, and Nikolas Rose. *Governing the Present: Administering Economic, Social and Personal Life*. Cambridge: Polity Press, 2008.

Mitchell, Timothy. "The Limits of the State: Beyond Statist Approaches and Their Critics." *American Political Science Review* 85, no. 1 (1991): 77–96.

Modonesi, Massimo. "Revoluciones pasivas en América Latina: Una aproximación gramsciana a la caracterización de los gobiernos progresistas de inicio del siglo." In Thwaites Rey, *El Estado en América Latina*, 139–66.

Moore, Barrington, Jr. *Social Origins of Dictatorship and Democracy: Lord and Peasant in the Making of the Modern World*. Boston: Beacon Press, 1967.

Moran, Joe. *On Roads: A Hidden History*. London: Profile, 2010.

Morell i Torra, Pere. "La (difícil) construcción de autonomías indígenas en el estado plurinacional de Bolivia: Consideraciones generales y una aproximación al caso de la autonomía Guaraní Charagua Iyambae." *REAF*, no. 22 (2015): 94–135.

Morton, Adam David. *Unraveling Gramsci: Hegemony and Passive Revolution in the Global Political Economy*. London: Pluto Press, 2007.

Mouffe, Chantal. "Critique as Counter-Hegemonic Intervention." *Art of Critique* (journal), *Transversal Texts*, August 2008. http://eipcp.net/transversal/0808/mouffe/en.

Munck, Ronaldo. *Rethinking Latin America: Development, Hegemony, and Social Transformation*. New York: Palgrave Macmillan, 2013.

Muñoz, María José. "El conflicto en torno al Territorio Indígena Parque Nacional Isiboro Sécure: Un conflicto multidimensional." *Cultura y representaciones sociales* 7, no. 14 (2013): 67–141.

Murra, John. "Andean Societies." *Annual Review of Anthropology* 13 (1984): 119–41.

Navia Gabriel, Roberto. "El puente 'clandestino' de los menonitas lleva la deforestación a los Bañados de Isoso y amenaza al Kaa Iya." *Revista Nómadas*, January 26, 2022. https://www.revistanomadas.com/el-puente-clandestino-de-los-menonitas-lleva-la-deforestacion-a-los-banados-de-isoso-y-amenaza-al-kaa-iya/.

Negri, Toni, Michael Hardt, Giuseppe Cocco, Judith Revel, Álvaro García Linera, and Luis Tapia. *Imperio, multitud y sociedad abigarrada*. La Paz: CLACSO, 2008.

Neocleous, Mark. "Let the Dead Bury Their Dead." *Radical Philosophy* 128 (2004): 23–32.

Nicolas, Vincent, and Pablo Quisbert. *Pachakuti: El retorno de la nación*. La Paz: Programa de Investigación Estratégica en Bolivia, 2014.

Niekerk, A. E. van. *Populism and Political Development in Latin America*. Rotterdam: Rotterdam University Press, 1974.

Nugent, David. "Before History and Prior to Politics: Time, Space, and Territory in the Modern Peruvian Nation-State." In Hansen and Stepputat, *States of Imagination*, 257–83.

O'Donnell, Guillermo A. *Modernization and Bureaucratic-Authoritarianism.* Berkeley: Institute of International Studies, University of California, 1979.

O'Kane, Rosemary H. T. "Revolution and Social Science: Movements in Method, Theory and Practice." In *Revolution: Critical Concepts in Political Science*, vol. 1, edited by Rosemary H. T. O'Kane, xvii–xxxix. New York: Routledge, 2000.

Olivera, Oscar, and Tom Lewis. *Cochabamba! Water War in Bolivia.* Cambridge, Mass.: South End Press, 2004.

Ortiz, Fernando. *Cuban Counterpoint: Tobacco and Sugar.* 1940. Durham, N.C.: Duke University Press, 1995.

Pachirat, Timothy. *Among Wolves: Ethnography and the Immersive Study of Power.* New York: Routledge, 2017.

Pachirat, Timothy. "The Political in Political Ethnography: Dispatches from the Kill Floor." In Schatz, *Political Ethnography*, 143–62.

Pacto de Unidad. "Propuesta de las Organizaciones Indígenas, Originarias, Campesinas y de Colonizadores hacia la Asamblea Constituyente." August 5, 2006. *Observatorio Social de América Latina* 8, no. 22 (2007): 165–84.

Paige, Jeffery M. "Finding the Revolutionary in the Revolution: Social Science Concepts and the Future of Revolution." In Foran, *The Future of Revolutions*, 19–29.

Paige, Jeffery M. *Indigenous Revolution in Ecuador and Bolivia, 1990–2005.* Tucson: University of Arizona Press, 2020.

Panizza, Francisco. Introduction to Panizza, *Populism and the Mirror of Democracy*, 1–31.

Panizza, Francisco, ed. *Populism and the Mirror of Democracy.* New York: Verso Books, 2010.

Patzi Paco, Felix. *Insurgencia y sumisión: Movimientos sociales e indígenas.* La Paz: Ediciones Yachaywasi, 2007.

Patzi Paco, Felix. *Sistema comunal: Una propuesta alternativa al sistema liberal.* La Paz: Editorial Vicuña, 2009.

Paz, Sarela. "El conflicto del territorio indígena Parque Nacional Isiboro-Sécure (TIPNIS) y sus consecuencias para el Estado Plurinacional de Bolivia." In Bautista et al., *La victoria indígena del TIPNIS*, 11–68.

Pearce, Adrian, ed. *Evo Morales and the Movimiento al Socialismo in Bolivia: The First Term in Context, 2006–2010.* London: Institute for the Study of the Americas, 2011.

Pellegrini, Lorenzo, and Marco Ribera Arismendi. "Consultation, Compensation and Extraction in Bolivia After the 'Left Turn': The Case of Oil Exploration in the North of La Paz Department." *Journal of Latin American Geography* 11, no. 2 (2012): 103–20.

Perreault, Tom. "Extracting Justice: Natural Gas, Indigenous Mobilization and the Bolivian State." In *The Politics of Resource Extraction: Indigenous Peoples, Multi-*

national Corporations and the State, edited by Suzana Sawyer and Edmund Terence Gomez, 75–102. London: Palgrave, 2012.

Perreault, Tom, and Barbara Green. "Reworking the Spaces of Indigeneity: The Bolivian Ayllu and Lowland Autonomy Movements Compared." *Environment and Planning D: Society and Space* 31, no. 1 (2013): 43–60.

Peruzzotti, Enrique. "Populism in Democratic Times: Populism, Representative Democracy, and the Debate on Democratic Deepening." In de la Torre and Arnson, *Latin American Populism in the Twenty-First Century*, 61–84.

Petras, James, and Henry Veltmeyer. *Social Movements and State Power: Argentina, Brazil, Bolivia, Ecuador.* Ann Arbor, Mich.: Pluto Press, 2005.

PIEB (Programa de Investigación Estratégica en Bolivia). *Viabilidad económica e institucional para el desarrollo de iniciativas que reduzcan la deforestación en el Territorio Indígena Parque Nacional Isiboro Sécure.* La Paz: PIEB, 2011.

Pifarré, Francisco. *Historia de un pueblo: Los Guaraní—Chiriguano.* La Paz: CIPCA, 1989.

Plata, Wilfredo. "Charagua: El autogobierno Guaraní Iyambae." In Exeni Rodríguez, *La larga marcha*, 195–256.

Platt, Tristan. "The Andean Experience of Bolivian Liberalism, 1925–1900: Roots of Rebellion in 19th-Century Chayanta (Potosí)." In Stern, *Resistance, Rebellion, and Consciousness in the Andean Peasant World*, 280–323.

Platt, Tristan. *Estado boliviano y ayllu andino: Tierra y tributo en el norte de Potosí.* 1982. La Paz: Biblioteca del Bicentenario de Bolivia, 2016.

Polanyi, Karl. *The Great Transformation: The Political and Economic Origins of Our Time.* Boston: Beacon Press, 2001.

Portantiero, Juan Carlos. *Los usos de Gramsci.* Buenos Aires: Grijalbo, 1999.

Postero, Nancy. "Andean Utopias in Evo Morales's Bolivia." *Latin American and Caribbean Ethnic Studies* 2, no. 1 (2007): 1–28.

Postero, Nancy. *The Indigenous State: Race, Politics, and Performance in Plurinational Bolivia.* Berkeley: University of California Press, 2017.

Postero, Nancy. "Morales's MAS Government: Building Indigenous Popular Hegemony in Bolivia." *Latin American Perspectives* 37, no. 3 (2010): 18–34.

Postero, Nancy, "The Struggle to Create a Radical Democracy in Bolivia." *Latin American Research Review* 45 (2010): 59–78.

Poulantzas, Nicos. *State, Power, Socialism.* 1978. New York: Verso Books, 2014.

Prada Alcoreza, Raúl. "Articulaciones de la complejidad." In García Linera, Tapia, and Prada Alcoreza, *La transformación pluralista del Estado*, 199–270.

Prada Alcoreza, Raúl. "Buen Vivir as a Model for State and Economy." In Lang and Mokrani, *Beyond Development*, 145–58.

Prada Alcoreza, Raúl. "Estado plurinacional comunitario autonómico y pluralismo jurídico." In *Justicia Indígena, Plurinacionalidad e Interculturalidad en Bolivia*, edited by Boaventura de Sousa Santos and José Luis Exeni Rodríguez, 407–44. La Paz: Fundación Rosa Luxemburg, 2012.

Prada Alcoreza, Raúl. *Horizontes de la asamblea constituyente*. La Paz: Ediciones Yachaywasi, 2006.

Prada Alcoreza, Raúl. *Miseria de la geopolítica: Crítica a la geopolítica extractivista*. La Paz: Bolpress, 2012.

Quijano, Anibal. "Coloniality of Power, Eurocentrism, and Latin America." *Nepantla: Views from South* 1, no. 3 (2000): 533–80.

Quisbert Q., Máximo. "Hacia autonomías indígenas y sus riesgos latentes." *Willka* 3, no. 3 (2009): 93–145.

Quispe, Ayar. *Indianismo-Katarismo*. La Paz: Ediciones Pachakuti, 2014.

Quispe, Felipe. *Túpak Katari: Vuelve y vive . . . carajo*. La Paz: Ofensiva Roja, 1990.

Rabinow, Paul, and William M. Sullivan. "The Interpretive Turn: A Second Look." In *Interpretive Social Science: A Second Look*, edited by Paul Rabinow and William M. Sullivan, 1–30. Berkeley: University of California Press, 1987.

Radhuber, Isabella M., Marxa Chávez León, and Diego Andreucci. "Expansión extractivista, resistencia comunitaria y 'despojo político' en Bolivia." *Journal of Political Ecology* 28, no. 1 (2021): 205–23.

Ranta, Eija. *Vivir Bien as an Alternative to Neoliberal Globalization: Can Indigenous Terminologies Decolonize the State?* New York: Routledge, 2018.

Read, Benjamin L. "More Than an Interview, Less Than Sedaka: Studying Subtle and Hidden Politics with Site-Intensive Methods." In *Contemporary Chinese Politics: New Sources, Methods, and Field Strategies*, edited by Allen Carlson, Mary E. Gallagher, Kenneth Lieberthal, and Melanie Manion, 145–61. New York: Cambridge University Press, 2010.

Regalsky, Pablo. "Political Processes and the Reconfiguration of the State in Bolivia." Translated by Mariana Ortega Breña. *Latin American Perspectives* 37, no. 3 (2010): 35–50.

Reinaga, Fausto. *La revolución india*. La Paz: MINKA, 2010.

Requejo, Ferran. "Revealing the Dark Side of Traditional Democracies in Plurinational Societies: The Case of Catalonia and the Spanish 'Estado de las Autonomías.'" *Nations and Nationalism* 16, no. 1 (2010): 148–68.

Requejo, Ferran, and Miquel Caminal, eds. *Political Liberalism and Plurinational Democracies*. New York: Routledge, 2011.

Revista Nómadas. "El Gobierno Autonómo Guaraní de Charagua asegura que el puente clandestino 'no se hizo para favorecer a las comunidades, sino, para explotar el territorio del otro lado del Parapetí.'" February 9, 2022. https://www.revistanomadas.com/el-gobierno-autonomo-guarani-de-charagua.

Rivera Cusicanqui, Silvia. *Ch'ixinakax utxiwa: Una reflexión sobre prácticas y discursos descolonizadores*. Buenos Aires: Tinta Limón, 2010.

Rivera Cusicanqui, Silvia. "Liberal Democracy and *Ayllu* Democracy in Bolivia: The Case of Northern Potosí." *Journal of Development Studies* 26, no. 4 (1990): 97–121.

Rivera Cusicanqui, Silvia. *Mito y desarrollo en Bolivia: El giro colonial del gobierno del MAS*. La Paz: Plural Editores, 2015.

Rivera Cusicanqui, Silvia. *Oppressed but Not Defeated: Peasant Struggles Among the Aymara and Qhechwa in Bolivia, 1900–1980*. Geneva: UN Research Institute for Social Development, 1987.

Rivera Cusicanqui, Silvia, Gustavo Soto Santiesteban, Raquel Gutiérrez Aguilar, Paloma Tórrez, Patricia Quiñones Guzmán, Marcelo Becerra Matías, and Virginia Ayllón et al. *TIPNIS: Amazonia en resistencia contra el Estado colonial en Bolivia*. Santander, Spain: Editorial Otramérica, 2013.

Roberts, Kenneth M. "Parties and Populism in Latin America." In de la Torre and Arnson, *Latin American Populism in the Twenty-First Century*, 37–60.

Roberts, Kenneth M. "Populism, Political Mobilization, and the Crises of Political Representation." In de la Torre, *The Promise and Perils of Populism*, 140–58.

Robinson, William I. *Latin America and Global Capitalism: A Critical Globalization Perspective*. Baltimore, Md.: Johns Hopkins University Press, 2008.

Ruta para la construcción de la autonomía indígena originario campesina. La Paz: Ministerio de la Presidencia, 2021.

Saavedra, José Luis. "Crónica de un toma gubernamental: El ataque a la sede del CONAMAQ." *Nueva Crónica y Buen Gobierno*, no. 139 (March 2014): 12–13.

Saavedra, José Luis. "Segunda parte: Crónica del ataque a la sede del CONAMAQ." *Nueva Crónica y Buen Gobierno*, no. 140 (March 2014): 14–15.

Saignes, Thierry. *Historia del pueblo Chiriguano*. La Paz: Plural Editores, 2007.

Salazar Lohman, Huáscar. "Las condiciones para la crisis política de 2019 en Bolivia: Una mirada *crítica* más allá de la estéril polarización." In Claros and Díaz Cuéllar, *Crisis política en Bolivia, 2019–2020*, 121–46.

Salazar Lohman, Huáscar. *Se han adueñado del proceso de lucha: Horizontes comunitario-populares en tensión y la reconstitución de la dominación en la Bolivia del MAS*. Cochabamba, Bolivia: SOCEE, 2015.

Samanamud, Jiovanny. "Hacia una 'arquitectónica' del proceso constituyente." *Willka* 3, no. 3 (2009): 69–92.

Sánchez, Consuelo. "Autonomía y pluralismo: Estados plurinacionales y pluriétnicos." In *La autonomía a debate: Autogobierno indígena y estado plurinacional en América Latina*, edited by Miguel González, Araceli Burguete Cal y Mayor, and Pablo Ortiz, 259–88. Quito: FLACSO, 2011.

Sanchez-Lopez, Daniela. "Reshaping Notions of Citizenship: The TIPNIS Indigenous Movement in Bolivia." *Development Studies Research* 2, no. 1 (2015): 20–32.

Sanjinés C., Javier. *Mestizaje Upside-Down: Aesthetic Politics in Modern Bolivia*. Pittsburgh, Pa.: University of Pittsburgh Press, 2004.

Santos, Boaventura de Sousa. *Refundación del Estado en América Latina: Perspectivas desde una epistemología del Sur*. La Paz: Plural Editores, 2010.

Sassoon, Anne Showstack, ed. *Approaches to Gramsci*. London: Writers and Readers, 1982.

Sassoon, Anne Showstack. "Passive Revolution and the Politics of Reform." In Sassoon, *Approaches to Gramsci*, 127–48.

Schaefer, Timo. "Engaging Modernity: The Political Making of Indigenous Movements in Bolivia and Ecuador, 1900–2008." *Third World Quarterly* 30, no. 2 (2009): 397–413.

Schatz, Edward, ed. *Political Ethnography: What Immersion Contributes to the Study of Power*. Chicago: University of Chicago Press, 2009.

Schavelzon, Salvador. *El nacimiento del estado plurinacional de Bolivia: Etnografía de una asamblea constituyente*. La Paz: Plural Editores, 2012.

Schavelzon, Salvador. *Plurinacionalidad y Vivir Bien/Buen Vivir: Dos conceptos leídos desde Bolivia y Ecuador post-constituyentes*. Quito: Abya Yala, 2015.

Schilling-Vacaflor, Almut. "Rethinking the Link Between Consultation and Conflict: Lessons from Bolivia's Gas Sector." *Canadian Journal of Development Studies* 35, no. 4 (2014): 503–21.

Schilling-Vacaflor, Almut. "Who Controls the Territory and the Resources? Free Prior and Informed Consent (FPIC) as a Contested Human Rights Practice in Bolivia." *Third World Quarterly* 38, no. 5 (2017): 1058–74.

Schwartz-Shea, Peregrine, and Samantha Majic, intro. "Ethnography and Participant Observation: Political Science Research in This 'Late Methodological Moment.'" Symposium. *PS: Political Science and Politics* 50, no. 1 (2017): 97–138.

Scott, James C. "Hegemony and the Peasantry." *Politics and Society* 7, no. 3 (1977): 267–96.

Scott, James C. *The Moral Economy of the Peasant: Rebellion and Subsistence in Southeast Asia*. New Haven, Conn.: Yale University Press, 1976.

Scott, James C. *Seeing Like a State: How Certain Schemes to Improve the Human Condition Have Failed*. New Haven, Conn.: Yale University Press, 1998.

Scott, James C. *Weapons of the Weak: Everyday Forms of Peasant Resistance*. New Haven, Conn.: Yale University Press, 1985.

Simmons, Erica S. *Meaningful Resistance: Market Reforms and the Roots of Social Protest in Latin America*. New York: Cambridge University Press, 2016.

Sinani Paz, Rodolfo C. *Pensamiento y conciencia en la revolución plurinacional*. La Paz: Grupo Editorial Kipus, 2011.

Skocpol, Theda. *States and Social Revolutions: A Comparative Analysis of France, Russia, and China*. New York: Cambridge University Press, 1979.

Skocpol, Theda. *Social Revolutions in the Modern World*. New York: Cambridge University Press, 1994.

Soliz, Carmen. *Fields of Revolution: Agrarian Reform and Rural State Formation in Bolivia, 1935–1964*. Pittsburgh, Pa.: University of Pittsburgh Press, 2021.

Spivak, Gayatri Chakravorty. *In Other Worlds: Essays in Cultural Politics*. New York: Methuen, 1987.

Springerová, Pavlína, and Barbora Vališková. "Co-optation Without Representation: The Relationship Between the Bolivian State and the Indigenous Organization CONAMAQ." *Latin American Policy* 14, no. 1 (2023): 46–68.

Springerová, Pavlína, and Barbora Vališková. "Territoriality in the Development Policy of Evo Morales' Government and Its Impacts on the Rights of Indigenous People: The Case of TIPNIS." *Canadian Journal of Latin American and Caribbean Studies* 41, no. 2 (2015): 147–72.

Stefanoni, Pablo. "¿A quién representa el Conamaq?" *Rebelión*, January 31, 2011. https://rebelion.org/a-quien-representa-el-conamaq/.

Stefanoni, Pablo. Prefacio to *La potencia plebeya: Acción colectiva e identidades indígenas, obreras y populares en Bolivia*, by Álvaro García Linera, 9–22. Buenos Aires: CLACSO, 2008.

Stern, Steve J., ed. *Resistance, Rebellion, and Consciousness in the Andean Peasant World: 18th to 20th Centuries*. Madison: University of Wisconsin Press, 1987.

Ströbele-Gregor, Juliana. "Culture and Political Practice of the Aymara and Quechua in Bolivia: Autonomous Forms of Modernity in the Andes." *Latin American Perspectives* 23, no. 2 (1996): 72–90.

Svampa, Maristella. *Neo-Extractivism in Latin America: Socio-Environmental Conflicts, the Territorial Turn, and New Political Narratives*. New York: Cambridge University Press, 2019.

Svampa, Maristella. "Resource Extractivism and Alternatives: Latin American Perspectives on Development." In Lang and Mokrani, *Beyond Development*, 117–43.

Swinehart, Karl. "Decolonial Time in Bolivia's *Pachakuti*." *Signs and Society* 7, no. 1 (2019): 96–114.

Tapia, Luis. *El horizonte plurinacional*. La Paz: Autodeterminación, 2015.

Tapia, Luis. *La hegemonía imposible: Ensayos sobre el estado en Bolivia*. La Paz: Autodeterminación, 2015.

Tapia, Luis. *La idea de estado como obstáculo epistemológico*. La Paz: CIDES-UMSA, Autodeterminación, 2020.

Tapia, Luis. *La producción del conocimiento local: Historia y política en la obra de René Zavaleta*. La Paz: Muela del Diablo Editores, 2002.

Tapia, Luis. *Lo político y lo democrático*. La Paz: Autodeterminación, 2013.

Tapia, Luis. *Una reflexión sobre la idea de un estado plurinacional*. La Paz: Oxfam, 2008.

Thomas, Megan. "Orientalism and Comparative Political Theory." *Review of Politics* 72, no. 4 (2010): 653–77.

Thomas, Peter D. *The Gramscian Moment: Philosophy, Hegemony and Marxism*. Chicago: Haymarket Books, 2011.

Thompson, E. P. *Customs in Common: Studies in Traditional Popular Culture*. New York: New Press, 1993.

Thwaites Rey, Mabel, ed. *El Estado en América Latina: Continuidades y rupturas*. Santiago: CLACSO, 2012.

Ticona Alejo, Esteban, ed. *Los Andes desde Los Andes*. La Paz: Ediciones Yachaywasi, 2003.

Ticona Alejo, Esteban, and Xavier Albó. *La lucha por el poder comunal*. Vol. 3 of *Jesús de Machaqa: La marka rebelde*. La Paz: CIPCA, 1997.

Ticona Alejo, Esteban, Gonzalo Rojas, and Xavier Albó. *Votos y wiphalas: Campesinos y pueblos originarios en democracia*. La Paz: CIPCA, 1995.

Tierney, Stephen. "Reframing Sovereignty? Sub-State National Societies and the Contemporary Challenges to the Nation-State." In Requejo and Caminal, *Political Liberalism and Plurinational Democracies*, 115–38.

Tilly, Charles. *Coercion, Capital, and European States, AD 990–1992*. Cambridge, Mass.: Blackwell, 1992.

Tilly, Charles. *European Revolutions, 1492–1992*. Oxford: Blackwell, 1995.

Tilly, Charles. *From Mobilization to Revolution*. New York: McGraw-Hill, 1978.

Tockman, Jason. "Decentralisation, Socio-Territoriality and the Exercise of Indigenous Self-Governance in Bolivia." *Third World Quarterly* 37, no. 1 (2016): 153–71.

Tockman, Jason, and John Cameron. "Indigenous Autonomy and the Contradictions of Plurinationalism in Bolivia." *Latin American Politics and Society* 56, no. 3 (2014): 46–69.

Tockman, Jason, John Cameron, and Wilfredo Plata. "New Institutions of Indigenous Self-Governance in Bolivia: Between Autonomy and Self-Discipline." *Latin American and Caribbean Ethnic Studies* 10, no. 1 (2015): 37–59.

Tomba, Massimiliano. *Insurgent Universality: An Alternative Legacy of Modernity*. New York: Oxford University Press, 2019.

Tomba, Massimiliano. "On the Capitalist and Emancipatory Use of Asynchronies in Formal Subsumption." *Review (Fernand Braudel Center)* 38, no. 4 (2015): 287–306.

Tórrez, Yuri F., and Claudia Arce C. *Construcción simbólica del estado plurinacional de Bolivia: Imaginarios políticos, discursos, rituales y celebraciones*. La Paz: Programa de Investigación Estratégica en Bolivia, 2014.

Tucker, Robert C., ed. *The Marx-Engels Reader*. 2nd ed. New York: W. W. Norton, 1978.

Urioste, Miguel, and Cristóbal Kay. *Latifundios, avasallamientos y autonomías: La reforma agraria inconclusa en el Oriente*. La Paz: Fundación Tierra, 2005.

Vadillo Pinto, Alcides, and Patricia Costas Monje. "La autonomía indígena tiene su propio sello en Charagua." In *Reconfigurando territorios, reforma agraria, control territorial y gobiernos indígenas en Bolivia*, by Fundación Tierra, 273–87. La Paz: Fundación Tierra, 2010.

Valdivia, Gabriela. "Agrarian Capitalism and Struggles over Hegemony in the Bolivian Lowlands." *Latin American Perspectives* 37, no. 4 (2010): 67–87.

Valentine, Jeremy. "The Hegemony of Hegemony." *History of the Human Sciences* 14, no. 1 (2001): 88–104.

Van Cott, Donna Lee. *From Movements to Parties in Latin America*. Cambridge: Cambridge University Press, 2005.

Van Cott, Donna Lee. *Radical Democracy in the Andes*. Cambridge: Cambridge University Press, 2008.

Varese, Stefano. *Witness to Sovereignty: Essays on the Indian Movement in Latin America*. Copenhagen: IWGIA, 2006.

Varnoux Garay, Marcelo, Marisol Bilbao la Vieja, and Erich Kierig Calvo. *Para vivir bien en democracia con automías*. La Paz: Asociación Boliviana de Ciencia Política, 2013.

Viaña, Jorge. "Estado plurinacional y nueva fase del proceso boliviano." In Thwaites Rey, *El Estado en América Latina*, 375–94.

Viaña, Jorge, Miguel Foronda, and Hernán Pruden. *Configuración y horizontes del estado plurinacional*. La Paz: Vicepresidencia del Estado, 2014.

Villalba, Unai. "Buen Vivir vs Development: A Paradigm Shift in the Andes?" *Third World Quarterly* 34, no. 8 (2013): 1427–42.

Virno, Paolo. *A Grammar of the Multitude*. New York: Semiotext(e), 2004.

Wade, Peter. "Rethinking *Mestizaje*: Ideology and Lived Experience." *Journal of Latin American Studies* 37 (2005): 239–57.

Wagner, Roy. *The Invention of Culture*. Chicago: University of Chicago Press, 1981.

Walsh, Catherine. "The Plurinational and Intercultural State: Decolonization and State Re-Founding in Ecuador." *Kult* 6, Fall 2009, 65–84.

Wanderley, Fernanda. "Bolivian Cooperative and Community Enterprises: Economic and Political Dimensions." In *Social Enterprise in Latin America: Theory, Models, and Practice*, edited by Luiz Inácio Gaiger, Marthe Nyssens, and Fernanda Wanderley, 58–86. New York: Routledge, 2019.

Webber, Jeffery R. "Bolivia's Passive Revolution." *Jacobin*, October 29, 2015. https://www.jacobinmag.com/2015/10/morales-bolivia-chavez-castro-mas/.

Webber, Jeffery R. *From Rebellion to Reform in Bolivia: Class Struggle, Indigenous Liberation, and the Politics of Evo Morales*. Chicago: Haymarket Books, 2011.

Webber, Jeffery R. *The Last Day of Oppression, and the First Day of the Same: The Politics and Economics of the New Latin American Left*. Chicago: Haymarket Books, 2017.

Webber, Jeffery R. "Revolution Against 'Progress': The TIPNIS Struggle and Class Contradictions in Bolivia." *International Socialism*, no. 133 (2012). http://isj.org.uk/the-tipnis-struggle-and-class-contradictions-in-bolivia/.

Webber, Jeffery R., and Barry Carr, eds. *The New Latin American Left: Cracks in the Empire*. New York: Rowman and Littlefield, 2013.

Weber, Eugen. *Peasants into Frenchmen: The Modernization of Rural France, 1870–1914*. Stanford, Calif.: Stanford University Press, 1976.

Weber, Max. *The Vocation Lectures*. Edited by David Owen and Tracy B. Strong. Cambridge, Mass.: Hackett, 2004.

Wedeen, Lisa. "Ethnography as Interpretive Enterprise." In Schatz, *Political Ethnography*, 75–94.

Wedeen, Lisa. "Reflections on Ethnographic Work in Political Science." *Annual Review of Political Science* 13 (2010): 255–72.

Weyland, Kurt. "Clarifying a Contested Concept: Populism in the Study of Latin American Politics." *Comparative Politics* 34, no. 1 (2001): 1–22.

Weyland, Kurt. "How Populism Corrodes Latin American Parties." *Journal of Democracy* 33, no. 4 (2021): 42–55.

Weyland, Kurt. "Neoliberal Populism in Latin America and Eastern Europe." *Comparative Politics* 31, no. 4 (1999): 379–401.

Weyland, Kurt. "Populism and Social Policy in Latin America." In de la Torre and Arnson, *Latin American Populism in the Twenty-First Century*, 117–44.

Weyland, Kurt. "The Threat from the Populist Left." *Journal of Democracy* 24, no. 3 (2013): 18–32.

Wickham-Crowley, Timothy P. *Exploring Revolution: Essays on Latin American Insurgency and Revolutionary Theory*. New York: M. E. Sharpe, 1991.

Williams, Gareth. "Social Disjointedness and State-Form in Álvaro García Linera." *Culture, Theory and Critique* 56, no. 3 (2015): 297–312.

Williams, Gwyn. "The Concept of 'Egemonia' in the Thought of Antonio Gramsci: Some Notes on Interpretation." *Journal of the History of Ideas* 21, no. 4 (1960): 586–99.

Williams, Raymond. *Keywords: A Vocabulary of Culture and Society*. New York: Oxford University Press, 1976.

Williams, Raymond. *Marxism and Literature*. New York: Oxford University Press, 1977.

Wolf, Eric. *Peasant Wars of the Twentieth Century*. Norman: University of Oklahoma Press, 1969.

Wolff, Jonas. "Business Power and the Politics of Postneoliberalism: Relations Between Governments and Economic Elites in Bolivia and Ecuador." *Latin American Politics and Society* 58, no. 2 (2016): 124–47.

Wolff, Jonas. "Towards Post-Liberal Democracy in Latin America? A Conceptual Framework Applied to Bolivia." *Journal of Latin American Studies* 45, no. 1 (2013): 31–59.

Wood, Ellen Meiksins. *The Origin of Capitalism*. New York: Verso Books, 2017.

Wood, Ellen Meiksins. *The Retreat from Class: A New "True" Socialism*. New York: Verso Books, 1998.

Yanow, Dvora, and Peregrine Schwartz-Shea, eds. *Interpretation and Method: Empirical Research Methods and the Interpretive Turn*. Armonk, N.Y.: M. E. Sharpe, 2014.

Yashar, Deborah. *Contesting Citizenship in Latin America: The Rise of Indigenous Movements and the Postliberal Challenge*. New York: Cambridge University Press, 2005.

Zavaleta Mercado, René. "Bolivia—Military Nationalism and the Popular Assembly." *New Left Review* 73 (1972): 63–82.

Zavaleta Mercado, René. "Bolivia Will Be Socialist or It Will Never Be a Modern Country." *NACLA's Latin America and Empire Report* 8, no. 2 (1974): 10–11.

Zavaleta Mercado, René. *Clases sociales y conocimiento*. La Paz: Los Amigos del Libro, 1988.

Zavaleta Mercado, René. *Lo nacional-popular en Bolivia*. 1986. La Paz: Plural Editores, 2008.

Zavaleta Mercado, René. *Obra Completa*. Vols. 1 and 2. La Paz: Plural Editores, 2011–13.

Zibechi, Raúl. *Dispersing Power: Social Movements as Anti-State Forces*. Oakland, Calif.: AK Press, 2010.

Zibechi, Raúl. *Territories in Resistance: A Cartography of Latin American Social Movements*. Oakland, Calif.: AK Press, 2012.

Zuazo, Moira. *¿Cómo nació el MAS? La ruralización de la política en Bolivia*. La Paz: Friedrich Ebert Stiftung, 2009.

Zuazo, Moira. "¿Los movimientos sociales en el poder? El gobeirno del MAS en Bolivia." *Nueva Sociedad*, no. 227 (2010): 120–35.

INDEX

Note: figures and maps are indicated by page numbers followed by *f* and *m* respectively.

Abrams, Philip, 135
accumulation: Bolivia and, 87–88; by dis-
    possession, 90; export-oriented, 168;
    extractivist, 166; MAS party and, 11,
    163, 166–68; primitive, 89–90, 205n38.
    See also extractivism
Acosta, Alberto, 87, 92
AIOC (*autonomía indígena originario
    campesina*): bureaucratic process, 147–
    48, 152, 155; collective decision-making
    in, 150–52; recognition and, 133–35;
    socialization workshops, 132–33, 146–
    47; state and, 76–77, 140, 153, 158–59,
    214n61; state transformation and, 135,
    140; territorial governance, 140. *See
    also* Charagua; indigenous autonomy
Alberto, Marcelo, 146
Albó, Xavier, 110, 124, 139, 145
Alegre, Luís, 145
Amazonian region: agro-industrialism,
    82, 85, 154, 168; *colonos* migration,
    81–82, 83*m*, 83, 123; indigenous peo-
    ples, 73, 78–82, 85–86; infrastructure
    development, 80, 82; participatory
    consultation, 96–97; subsistence-based

production, 40, 81; TIPNIS conflict,
    76, 78–80, 84–85
Anderson, Perry, 193n4
Áñez, Jeanine, 162, 169–70
Antezana, Luis H., 34, 196n54
Arbona, Juan Manuel, 185
Arce, Luis, 170
Asamblea Constituyente para el Estatuto
    AIOC, 148–49
Asamblea del Pueblo Guaraní (APG),
    144–46, 148
Asamblea Permanente de Derechos
    Humanos de Bolivia, 99, 115
Assies, Willem, 7
Ávila, José, 156
ayllus: agriculture and, 110, 208n4; com-
    munal ownership, 110–12, 122–23, 139,
    208n4; CONAMAQ and, 110–12, 115,
    125–26; cultural reproduction and, 131;
    land tenure and, 154; NGOs and, 112,
    208n17; reconstitution of, 110–12, 131,
    208n3; regional organizations, 111–12
Aymara people: AIOCs and, 148–49;
    ayllus and, 112; land and territory,
    123; *machaq mara* (new year), 3–4;

populism: chain of equivalence, 120–22; economic development and, 117–18; hegemonic formation, 121–22; ideological content, 118–19; indigeneity in, 119, 128; as political logic, 119–21, 130–31; representation and, 117–18, 128–31; social demands, 119–22

postcolonialism, 58, 111

Postero, Nancy, 13, 125–26, 136–37, 164

Potosí, 109, 111–12, 153

Poulantzas, Nicos, 48, 137

power: centralization of, 30, 51, 74; class and, 31; coloniality, 11, 64; dual, 38–39, 49; hegemony and, 75; ideological, 29, 36; race and, 10, 60. *See also* state power

Prada, Raúl, 71–72, 93, 99–100

primitive accumulation, 89–90, 205n38

prior consultation: common consensus, 102–3; extractivism and, 67, 80; indigenous peoples and, 22, 96–99, 107; manipulation of, 99; prior consent and, 97; social/political tensions and, 99–100; TIPNIS and, 97–99

proceso de cambio (process of change): indigenous autonomy and, 133; MAS party and, 10–11, 50, 161–62; nation-state hegemony and, 9, 13–15, 161, 169, 171; plurinationalism and, 13–15, 161, 164, 171; revolutionary, 10–14, 23–24; social conflicts and, 14, 18, 73, 169; state governmentality and, 12–13; structural constraints, 11–12; TIPNIS conflict and, 100

proletariat: class alliance and, 26–28, 32; dictatorship, 180; hegemony of, 26–28, 32; Marx concept of, 196n54; mining, 39, 45–46, 196n54; peasantry and, 27–28; state power and, 179–80

Quechua people, 82–83, 112, 123, 142, 148–49

Quijano, Anibal, 64

Quispe, Felipe, 7

Rabinow, Paul, 20

Rancière, Jacques, 13

Regalsky, Pablo, 140, 165

Reinaga, Fausto, 44, 198n79

revolutionary change: colonial reproduction and, 111; creative tensions in, 49–50, 55; dual power and, 39; elites and, 49–50, 182; Gramsci influence on, 21, 181; hegemony and, 25, 27–28, 45, 170, 181; indigenous peoples and, 171–72; Leninist moment, 181; nation-state and, 178–79; *pachakuti*, 175, 202n66; plurinationality and, 71–73, 165–66, 170, 172, 175–78, 186–87, 189; *proceso de cambio* and, 23–24; self-determination and, 182–83; social class and, 178–80; social emancipation and, 172–73; social transformation and, 10–14, 24, 161, 173; state power and, 43, 161, 178–87; temporality, 173–74, 177–78; war of position, 47–48

Riofrancos, Thea, 97

Rivera Cusicanqui, Silvia, 85–86, 109, 123, 177, 208n2

road building: environmental destruction, 89–90; extractivism and, 88–91; land disputes, 151–52; modernity and, 83–84, 204n14; national unification and, 84–85, 103; prior consultation, 97–99; regional interdependence and, 88; TIPNIS and, 22, 76, 78, 80–84, 86–91, 97–99, 101

Rojas, Cancio, 109, 114

Rojas, Nilda, 110

Rosaldo, Renato, 19

Rose, Nikolas, 135

Sanchez, Consuelo, 63

Sánchez de Lozada, Gonzalo, 113, 213n41

Santiago, Francisco Javier, 145

Sayer, Derek, 52

ABOUT THE AUTHOR

Aaron Augsburger is assistant professor in the School of Interdisciplinary Global Studies at the University of South Florida.